The Luftwaffe and the War at Sea 1939–45

As Seen By Officers of the Kriegsmarine and Luftwaffe

Grossadmiral Karl Doenitz, Kontreadmiral Gerhard Wagner, General der Flieger Ulrich O. E. Kessler, Vizeadmiral Eberhard Weichold, Oberst i.G. Walter Gaul, Kapitan zur See Hans-Jurgen Reinecke, Korvetten Kapitan Otto Mejer, Kapitanleutnant Hans-Diedrich Freiherr von Tiesenhausen

Edited by David C Isby

CHATHAM PUBLISHING
LONDON

STACKPOLE BOOKS
PENNSYLVANIA

Copyright © Chatham Publishing 2005

First published in Great Britain in 2005 by Chatham Publishing,
Lionel Leventhal Ltd, Park House, 1 Russell Gardens,
London NW11 9NN

And in North America by Stackpole Books,
5067 Ritter Road, Mechanicsburg, PA 17055-6921

British Library Cataloguing in Publication Data
- The Luftwaffe and the war at sea, 1939–1945: as seen by
Officers of the Kriegsmarine and Luftwaffe
1. Germany. Luftwaffe – History – Sources. 2. Germany
Kriegsmarine 3. World War, 1939–1945 – Aerial operations,
German – Sources 4. World War, 1939–1945 – Naval operations,
German – Sources
I. Isby, David C.
940.5'44'943

ISBN 1 86176 256 9

Designed and typeset by Servis Filmsetting Ltd, Manchester
Printed and bound in Great Britain by CPD (Wales) Ebbw Vale

CONTENTS

IV. The Battle of the Atlantic

V. Conclusion

INTRODUCTION

This book is a collection of accounts written by German military officers – Luftwaffe and Kriegsmarine – about the naval air war in the European theater, concentrating on that in the north Atlantic and around Great Britain.

This collection is published under the same editorial "rules" as *The Luftwaffe Fighter Force: The View From the Cockpit* and *Fighting the Bombers*, the two previous edited volumes from Luftwaffe leadership figures that have appeared by Greenhill Press. These are largely the same format that has been used by Garland Press in its editions of some of the post-war essays by German officers and officials. The contemporary translations are used. Standardization of capitalization, spelling and terminology is left (largely) as in the originals, which leads to variations. Technical terms and abbreviations are introduced without explanation in most of these documents.

This collection is set up to be read as military history, where the Garland editions were for reference. Hence the provision of a glossary, list of contributors and illustrations. The important story is the one the Germans who were doing the flying and fighting are telling, not that told by the editor. Thus, editorial additions and alterations have been minimized and the original 1940s translations – with their own problems and inconsistencies – retained. Some documents here have been divided by the editor into two parts (as noted under sources). This is to help narrative flow for those reading this volume from cover-to-cover. The original documents were all extracted from those held by the US National Archives, Naval Historical Center, and National Defense University library, as specified in the note on sources. While additions such as an index, more and better illustrations, maps and charts done specifically for this volume, appendices, and other editorial apparatus and additions would have been desirable, adding them would push the sale price of this volume towards that normally associated with scholarly volumes rather than those aimed at a larger audience.

Most of the essays were written post-war for the US services by these officers, either held as prisoners of war or working under contract. Some of the chapters are wartime German documents, written for internal use by military staffs, and translated after they fell into Allied hands. The material used in this book, being written by the Germans officers that fought the maritime air war, written either during the war or immediately after, has the value of immediacy. They were done when memories were fresh and, in many cases, by those involved with the actions described. Most of those involved did not revisit this subject matter in print in any language, so this is the sum total of their contribution to the historical record. However, none of this mandates accuracy, truthfulness or completeness. While these accounts still have value today (as demonstrated by their appearance in many bibliographies), they are by no means the last word on their subject matter area. However, as the select bibliography in this volume suggests, many of the better recent works on the subject are in German and have not been translated.

This book is not comprehensive, although the provision of two sections dealing with the origins of German maritime military aviation and wartime operations provides coverage. It has focused on the Luftwaffe operations in the Battle of the Atlantic and its predecessor campaigns of 1939–40 because this is an area where German air operations have not been thoroughly covered in English-language operational accounts. Many maritime air operations are not covered in detail. This includes the multi-year naval-air campaign over the Mediterranean (including the siege of Malta), those over the Baltic and Black Seas, the Luftwaffe's defense against Allied anti-shipping and ASW campaigns (though this was treated in *The Luftwaffe Fighter Force*), the operations against the Russia convoys. These are all mentioned but not discussed in detail. Each one merits a complete book on its own (the select bibliography provides suggestions).

In addition to the subject matter that could not be fitted into the current book, there are gaps in what the authors have been willing to talk about. The German involvement in the Spanish Civil War included a substantial naval air component. Air attacks on surface warships, submarines and merchant ships alike must have had an impact, but largely glossed over in these accounts. Both the guided missile and the magnetic mine – each thought by many to be a "silver bullet" solution against Allied seapower – are also only considered briefly. Other naval air operations, such as those of the Kriegsmarine's catapult ships, receive little mention. Again, those looking for a more comprehensive treatment are referred to the titles in the bibliography.

The history recounted in this book has already had an effect on subsequent decisions. The US Naval Historical Team (Bremerhaven) was organized from the German naval officers that constituted the US Navy's post-war historical studies and analysis staff. They effectively transitioned to thinking about the establishment of the Bundesmarine in the early 1950s (allowing the US Navy to encourage these efforts at a time when the Royal Navy remained hostile to German naval rearmament). A number of the members of this effort – including Kontreadmiral Wagner and Vizeadmiral Weichold, among the authors of these studies – worked closely with the Blank Office that laid the groundwork for the establishment of the armed forces of the Federal Republic of Germany in 1956.

One thing that was clear to the authors of these studies, as they reformed the German military, was that the navy had to have its own air arm, even if it lacked aircraft carriers. This air arm would be manned by naval personnel and have the authority to issue its own requirements and manage its own procurements. There were other factors influencing the emergence of the Marineflieger. Once they were reconciled to German naval re-armament, the British wanted a German customer for their combat aircraft after it became apparent the Luftwaffe would fly US-designed fighters. The Bundesmarine's Marineflieger served throughout the Cold War and today is participating in the global war on terror with its Atlantic maritime patrol aircraft. Its origins can be found in the history of its predecessors as contained in these essays.

DAVID C ISBY
Washington, 2005

GLOSSARY

AA	Anti-aircraft
Abschittsfuehrer	Section leader
a/c	Aircraft
a.D.	ausser Dienst, no longer in active service
air corps	Fliegerkorps (q.v.)
air force	Luftflotte (q.v.)
Ar	Arado
ASR	air sea rescue
B.d.U.	Befehlshaber der U-Boats, Commander U-Boats (Admiral Doenitz at the start of the war)
Bf	Bayerische Flugzeugwerke, later Messerschmitt
Bordflieger	Shipboard aircraft unit, organized in gruppe and staffel sizes (q.v.)
B.S.O.	Befehlshaber der Sicherungs Streitkrafte (Commander, Baltic Approaches)
B.S.W.	Seebefehlshaber West (flottenchef). Naval Commander West (Fleet Commander) (Vice Admiral Luetjens at the start of the war)
BV	Blohm & Voss
BZA	Dive-bombing gunsight package for Ju-88A-1/4/5) including automatically deploying dive brakes. Used mechanical computer to direct automatic pullout. Ju-87s used similar equipment
C	Chef des Stabes, chief of staff of a high level staff, "Der Chef"
CinC GAF	Goering (q.v. Ob. d. L.)
CO	Commanding officer
Coastal Group	Kustenfliegergruppe
Commander, Air	Fliegerfuehrer (q.v.)
Commander in Chief, Air	Ob. d. L (q.v.)

Commander in Chief, Navy	Ob.d.M (q.v.)
Commander, Naval Air	F.d.L (q.v.)
Commander (in Chief), Submarines	B.d.U. (q.v.)
Condor	FW-200 (q.v.)
Dackelbauch	(lit.) 'Dachshund's belly': auxiliary fuel tank on Me-110.
Deckungsschwarm	Cover flight
D/F	Direction finding (DF'd=located via direction finding)
Do	Dornier
E-Boat	Allied designation for Schnell-Boat, German motor torpedo boats
Erganzung	Reserve/replacement unit
Erpobung	Test or evaluation
F5	18-inch aerial torpedo, five meters in length
F.d.L	Fuehrer der Marineluftstreitkraefte, Naval Air Commander (Major General Geisler at the start of the war). Also known as Fuehrer der Luft. Became subject to Luftwaffe tactical command, under indirect Kriegsmarine operational command. Had operational responsibilities over the North Sea and Baltic approaches. Placed under Luftflotte 3 (q.v.) April 1942
Fi	Fieseler
Flak	anti-aircraft artillery
Fleet Command	B.S.W. (q.v.)
Fliegerfuehrer	Air officer commanding a specific operation, usually also a commander of one of the units involved. Fliegerfuehrer Atlantik was organized 1941, absorbed by X Fliegerkorps 1944 but had few organic aircraft, using mainly those temporarily assigned to its operational command. Fliegerfuehrer Nord used assets of Luftflotte 5 against northern convoys
Fliegerdivision	Air division
Fliegerkorps	Air corps. Operational formation composed of an unspecified number of units, but usually multiple geschwaders, several hundred aircraft strong. Could be under a Luftflotte command or independent

Fuhrungsstab	Operations staff of the OKL
FW	Focke Wulf
G.A.F.	German Air Force (US/UK usage)
General Staff Officer	A member of the German General Staff, a small body whose members received extensive training
Generaladmiral	Equivalent to US or RN Admiral
Generalfeldmarshall	Equivalent to US General of the Army or RAF Marshal of the Royal Air Force rank
Generalleutnant	Equivalent to US Major General or RAF Air Vice Marshal
Generalmajor	Equivalent to US Brigadier General or RAF Air Commodore
Generaloberst	Equivalent to US General or RAF Air Chief Marshal
Gen.Kdo	General officer commanding or headquarters, followed by formation
Genst-LW	Generalstabe des Luftwaffe, Luftwaffe General Staff
Gefechtsverbande	Combat formation
Geschwader	Wing, usually composed of three or more gruppe
German Supreme Command	OKW (q.v.)
Geschwader Z.b.V	Wing-sized force of miscellaneous units
Grossadmiral	Grand Admiral, equivalent to US or British Admiral
Gruppe	Unit of 27–80 aircraft. Three or more made up a geschwader. Designated by a roman numeral and the designation of its parent geschwader (e.g, V/KG 40) or by arabic numerals if independent
Gruppenkommandeur	CO of a gruppe
Hauptmann	Equivalent to US Captain or RAF Flight Lieutenant
He	Heinkel
Hptm	Hauptmann (captain)
HQ	headquarters
i.G	im Generalsstabdienst. On General Staff duties
JG	Jagdgeschwader, fighter wing
Ju	Junkers
Kapitan zur See	Equivalent to USN/RN naval captain

Kapitanleutnant	Equivalent to USN/RN lieutenant
Kdre	kommodore (commanding officer)
Kette	three-plane tactical formation, usually flown in a "v"
Kommando	Independent detachment, often named for its commander or base
Kommodore	Commanding officer of a geschwader (LW). As a naval rank, a Kapitan zur See commanding a squadron (similar to RN usage)
Kommandeur	Commanding officer of a gruppe
Kompanie	company or squadron
Kondor	FW-200 four engine combat aircraft, also known as Kurier (from its civil designation).
Konteradmiral	Equivalent to USN/RN rear admiral.
Korvetten Kapitan	Equivalent to USN/RN lieutenant commander
KTB	kriegstagebuch, war diary
Lehr	instructional
L. Fl. K	Luftflotte HQ
LM	Luftmine, aerial mine
LMA	Luftmine A, 500 kg magnetic mine
LMB	Luftmine B, 1,000 kg magnetic mine
Lofte 7D	High altitude computing bombsight fitted to FW-200C-3. On 22 May 1943, used to sink SS *Alpera* from 15,000 feet
LT	Lufttorpedo, aerial torpedo
L/T	Landline telephone
Luftflotte	A formation of fliegerkorps or multiple geschwaders of different types. Roughly equivalent to a USAAF numbered air force
Luftflotte 2	Northeast Germany area command, 1939–40, later in Norwegian campaign, Battle of Britain, other campaigns
Luftflotte 3	Parent organization of Fliegerfuhrer Atlantik 1941–44
Luftflotte 5	Norway and northern front area command 1940–45. Parent organization of Fliegerfuehrer Nord
Luftgau (kommando)	Air zone (headquarters). Used as administrative and support command echelon pre-war
Luftkreis VI – (See)	Air Force Deport VI – Naval
Luftwaffenkommando (See)	Naval Air Command

LW	Luftwaffe, German Air Force
MG 131	13mm machinegun
MG 151	15mm (later 20mm) cannon
Milch	Generalfeldmarschall Erhard Milch. Director General of Equipment for the Luftwaffe from November, 1941 to May, 1944. Sentenced to 15 years for war crimes involving use of slave labor
Nachrichten	Signals (including radar)
Nafu	Signals unit
Naval Command	OKM (q.v.)
Ob. d. L.	Oberbefelshaber der Luftwaffe, Commander in Chief Luftwaffe (Reichmasrchall Goering for most of war)
Ob. d. M.	Oberbefelshaber der Kriegsmarine, Commander in Chief Navy (Grossadmiral Raeder, succeeded by Doenitz)
Oberleutnant	Equivalent to US First Lieutenant or RAF Flying Officer
Oberst	Equivalent to US Colonel or RAF Group Captain
OKL	Oberkommando der Luftwaffe, Air Force High Command. Its 8th Abteilung was responsible for military assessment and history
OKM	Oberkommando der Marine, Navy High Command
OKW	Oberkommando der Wehrmacht, Armed Forces High Command
Ops.	Operations
PC	Panzer cylindrisch, armor piercing bomb
P/W	Prisoner of War
Quartermaster/QM	Quatermeister. In charge of all types of supply, broader than US term "quartermaster"
RAF	Royal Air Force
Reich	Greater Germany, includes both the post-Versailles borders and territory annexed from neighboring countries but not areas only under military occupation
Reichsmarchall	Goering
Rotte	two-plane tactical formation, usually flown in by a leader and wingman
RP	rocket projectile

RM	Reichsmarine, the Weimar Republic's navy
R/T	radio (voice) telephone
RTU	replacement training unit
SC	Spring cylandrisch, high explosive bomb
Schwarm	four-plane tactical formation, usually flown in a "finger-four" formation
SE	single engine
Seekreigsleitung/SKL	Naval War Staff
Squadron (air)	staffel (q.v.)
Stab	staff of a unit
Stab-	prefix of a unit or formation size, indicating the staff of a unit or a subunit of aircraft flown by that staff
Staffel	Unit of about 9–16 aircraft. Three or more usually made up a gruppe
Stuka	A dive bomber, but especially the Ju-87
TE	twin engine
T/O	table of organization
TOE	Table of organization and equipment. A unit's war establishment, indicating the personnel, equipment, and subordinate units it is supposed to have under it
VB	*Volkischer Beobachter*, Nazi propaganda newspaper
V.H/F	Very high frequency
Vizeadmiral	Equivalent to a German Generalmajor, or US Commodore rank, a "one-star"
W/L	Wireless
W/T	Wireless telegraphy (morse)
Wuerzburg	Short range ground radar, used for fire control
"Y" service	Allied designation for monitoring of enemy radio transmissions
z.b.v.	for special duties (zur besonderen verwendung)
Zerstroer	Twin engine day fighter
ZG	Zestoerergeschwader, twin engine day fighter wing
I	Operations division on a German staff (includes both operations and intelligence)
Ia.	Operations officer/section on a German staff
Ic.	Intelligence officer/section on a German staff

CONTRIBUTORS

Abteilung 8, OKL Staff
War Studies/Historical Section, also responsible for operational analyses. For much of the war, its chief was Generalmajor Hans-Detlef Herhuth von Roehden. Hauptmann Dula did much of this organization's naval-air work.

Grossadmiral Karl Doenitz
Served in U-boats in Great War. Captured after eight war patrols, first envisioned "wolfpack" tactics as PoW. Commander/Commander-in-Chief U-boats 1936–45. Commander in Chief of the German Navy January 1943–May 1945. Both sons killed in action in Kriegsmarine service. Went to Hitler's side after 20 July 1944 assassination attempt to assure him of Navy loyalty. Appointed chief of state by Hitler, April 1945. Arrested 20 May 1945. Tried for war crimes, served 10 years.

Oberst i.G. Walter Gaul
A former Reichsmarine officer in the 1920s and 1930s, Gaul spent the entire war from September 1939 to 1945 as chief of the Verbindungsstelle d. O.K.L. beim Ob.d.M. (Luftwaffe liaison office attached to the Commander-in-Chief of the Navy). Appointed as a major and subsequently a lieutenant colonel, his date of rank as Oberst was 4 January 1943. Post-war served as the naval air expert of the Naval Historical Team.

General der Flieger Ulrich O. E. Kessler
A 1914–18 veteran and a former Reichsmarine officer, Kessler joined the Luftwaffe in 1933. He served as Fliegerfuehrer Atlantik at the height of the Battle of the Atlantic (May 1942 – March 1944), at the end of which he was relieved, promoted to General der Flieger and awarded the Knight's Cross. Previously, had served as: commanding officer of KG 1 (1939), Chief of Staff of Luftflotte 1 and X Fliegerkorps 1939–40 (Polish and Norwegian campaigns); and on OKL staff 1940–42. Anti-Nazi and anti-Goering, he was linked to the 20 July 1944 conspirators. To save him from the Gestapo, he was sent to Japan as air attaché (via U-boat). The

17

U-boat surrendered en route after V-E Day. Kessler swaggered into captivity in full uniform.

Korvetten Kapitan Otto Mejer
Responsible for keeping the war diary (Kriegstagebuch) of the Seekreigsleitung, 1941–45. Naval Historical Team member post-war.

Naval Historical Team
US Navy project manned by former German naval and air officers, based at Bremerhaven. It and its predecessors employed Gaul, Mejer, Reinecke, Reichold and Wagner among other authors.

Kapitan zur See Hans-Jurgen Reinecke
Staff Operations officer, Seekreigsleitung 1938–41 (head of naval planning for Operation Sealion, invasion of Britain). Staff operations officer, Battlecruiser force (First Cruiser Squadron), 1941–43. Captain of cruiser *Prinz Eugen*, December 1943 to surrender. Naval Historical Team member post-war.

Kapitanleutnant Hans-Diedrich Freiherr von Tiesenhausen
Started U-boat operational career with three patrols under well-known "ace" Otto Kretschmer on *U-23*. April 1941, given command of *U-331*, entered Mediterranean, sank battleship HMS *Barham* November 1941, awarded Knight's Cross. Surrendered badly-damaged *U-331* to RAF Hudson off Algiers 17 November 1942, but FAA aircraft, unaware of surrender, torpedoed and sunk it before it could be taken in tow. Lived in Canada post-war.

Kontreadmiral Gerhard Wagner
Close associate of Doenitz. Head of the Operations Department (Chef der Operationsabteilung), Naval War Staff 1941–44. Admiral with the Supreme Command, German Naval Forces 1944–45. Post-war, on Naval Historical Team. Worked with the Blank Office to establish the Bundesmarine.

Vizeadmiral Eberhard Weichold
1933–36, director of the Naval Academy, Kiel. 1936–37 Commanded 1st Destroyer Division. 1937–39. Staff Officer (Operations) of the Fleet. January–June 1940, Chief of Staff for Economic Warfare, OKW. July 1940–April 1942, appointed as Konteradmiral, chief German naval liaison in Rome. Promoted Vizeadmiral, April 1942, added Flag officer of German Naval Command Italy to responsibilities. OKM staff May–December 1943. Director of naval academic training, January 1944–May 1945. Naval Historical Team member post-war.

SOURCES

Chapter 1 (German Naval Air) is a 1947 Office of Naval Intelligence type-script report. It is anonymous, but internal evidence suggests that Otto Mejer and Walter Gaul (q.v.) were among the authors. It is available as a stand-alone document in the National Defense University library (UG635 G3.U53 1947), Washington DC. Chapters 2 and 6 (Gaul) are one document, an undated translation, divided in two parts. Entitled *The German Naval Air Force. The Development of the Naval Air Force Up to the Outbreak of the 1939–45 War and its Activity During the First Seven Months of the War* is in the German Naval Archive, Operational Archives Branch, Naval Historical Center, Washington, D.C. Box T66. The chapter by Weichold is an undated translation, German Naval Archive, Operational Archives Branch, Naval Historical Center, Washington, D.C. Box T75. The chapter by Kessler is report B-485 in the Foreign Military Studies holdings, US National Archives, RG 338. Chapter 8 (Gaul) is an undated translation "compiled from German sources" originally entitled *German Air Force Successes in Operations Against Enemy Shipping in the Channel, Off the East Coast of Britain and in the North Sea Between April 1940 and December 1940 (Inclusive)* in the German Naval Archive, Operational Archives Branch, Naval Historical Center, Washington, D.C. Box T66. *German Army and Air Force Influence on the German Navy During World War II* is an excerpt from *German Army and Air Force Influence on the German Navy*, RG 38.4, Office of Naval Intelligence Monograph Files, US National Archives. It is undated but post-1947. *The Operational Use of the Luftwaffe in the War at Sea 1939–43* is from RG 457 (National Security Agency), Box 743, Item 1861, US National Archives. *Principles Covering the Conduct of Operation by Fliegerfuehrer Atlantik and an Appreciation of the Types of Aircraft Available* is from RG 457 (National Security Agency), Box 174, Item 2070A, US National Archives. *The Role of the German Air Force in the Battle of the Atlantic* is from RG 457 (National Security Agency), Box 62, US National Archives. The chapters by Mejer and Reinicke were both enclosures to COMNAVFORGER Intelligence Report 36-S-47, 27 January 1947. German Naval Archive, Operational Archives Branch, Naval Historical

Center, Washington, D.C. Box T69. Baron von Tiesenhausen's and other wartime accounts are from RG 38.4 Office of Naval Intelligence Monograph Files, US National Archives, Box 33 Air-Naval Cooperation Files 1002–220. The concluding chapter includes the VB quote from RG 38.4 Office of Naval Intelligence Monograph Files, US National Archives, Box 33 Air-Naval Cooperation Files. The Interview is from report Ethint 28 in the RG 338 Foreign Military Studies holdings, US National Archives. The 1946 statement is from RG 38.4 Office of Naval Intelligence Monograph Files, US National Archives, Box 26.

SOURCES OF MAPS AND ILLUSTRATIONS

All photographs not listed below are courtesy of Philip Jarrett.

AAHS from Ray Wagner   p63
US National Archives   pp67, 135, 164, 169, 196, 217, 232
Will Bohn via James Crow   p222

Map and Diagram Sources

Korvettenkapitan Assmann, *Aufgaben und
Probleme der Deutsche Seekriegfurhung,*
11/1941, USNARA RG547 Box 52   pp61, 97

E F Ziemke, *The German Northern Theater of
Operations,* US Government Printing Office,
Washington DC, 1959   pp206, 211

US Navy Technical Mission to Europe, Report
on HS Series of German Guided Missiles,
16 October 1945, in US NARA RG 38 ONI
NTM to Europe, Box 31   p263

US NARA RG 38 ONI Monograph files (maps)   p271

Britain McCue, *U-Boats in the Bay of Biscay,*
National Defense University Press,
Washington DC, 1990   pp272, 277

PART I

OVERVIEW AND PRE-WAR DEVELOPMENT

This section consists of two accounts of the origins of German military aviation approaches to the war at sea. These come from a naval (Chapter 1) and from a pro-naval Luftwaffe (Chapter 2) background, showing how the tensions between the Luftwaffe and the Kriegsmarine, linked to the internal politics of the Nazi regime, made the naval air campaign particularly difficult.

The German Navy had used aircraft effectively in the Great War, defending the Flanders coast against a more powerful Allied threat. Despite this success, these accounts show that, starting in 1935 and accelerating in 1938, Hermann Goering was relentless in trying to reduce the naval influence and control over German airpower and to ensure that everything that flew in the Third Reich was under his control.

In part, this reflected that the German Navy did not have a vision of the use of naval airpower more than as providing reconnaissance support for the surface navy. This lead to the emphasis on the largely naval-manned Kuestenflieger stafflen, equipped with seaplanes (and largely short ranged) in 1939. That these were largely disbanded or transferred to the Luftwaffe by 1941 demonstrated not only Goering's political strength, but that the Navy had not used them effectively. Indeed, Germany lagged behind other combatants in developing an effective torpedo bombing capability both because the Luftwaffe saw it (until 1940) as an expensive diversion of resources but also because the Navy – in charge of torpedo development – did not consider it a priority. Indeed, while the Navy tended to see the role of naval airpower to be limited to fleet support, it was the Luftwaffe that looked to integrate air minelaying, attacks on ports, and support for U-boat operations in the attacks on Britain in 1940. It was only when Luftwaffe attention was shifted to other fronts in 1941 did every maritime sortie become begrudgingly allocated.

Chapter 1

GERMAN NAVAL AIR 1933 TO 1945
A REPORT BASED ON GERMAN NAVAL STAFF
DOCUMENTS

U.S. Office of Naval
Intelligence

Washington, D.C.
15 January 1947

1. Introduction

The Treaty of Versailles prohibited all naval or military air activities. The treaty, however, did not keep German naval units from conducting anti-aircraft exercises. These anti-aircraft exercises provided the first small loophole by which planes could be drawn into naval activities. The loophole was somewhat widened by the interpretation of the Paris Agreement of 1926. Article V of this agreement specifically restated the provisions of the Versailles Treaty. The German Government agreed to prohibit all air training of a military or naval character, and to direct all German Armed Forces to refrain from any aeronautic activity whatsoever, with the one exception of measures on the ground in defense against air attacks.

However, not even the broadest interpretation of these agreements could justify naval air activities of any extent. Therefore secret measures were resorted to. German naval files show clearly that the German Naval Command at no time lost sight of the importance of naval air. By 1927, a system had been developed under which naval air officers were "privately" given training at a naval station at Warnemuende operating under the cover-name of "Radio Experimental Command". In addition, the Navy had started to conduct air training through a Coastal Air Section which was made to appear as a private enterprise.

In the summer of 1929 this system of secret naval air activities was reorganized. On 1 September 1929, the Reich Defense Minister informed the Fleet Command: "The Coastal Air Section which had been guided by the

Navy was dissolved the latter part of April for considerations of internal and foreign policy. The Navy has been able to make a contract with a private air company, the 'Luftdienst G.m.b.H.', whereby the Navy will hire airplanes at a fixed hourly rate. The company has rented the (naval air) installations at Holtenau and Norderney . . . The 'Luftdienst G.m.b.H.' personnel are available only for duties which can be considered permissible in terms of the Paris Agreement of 1926 (target flight, towing of targets). For all other duties, that is especially for gunnery observation and for the direction of naval guns, naval personnel is to be assigned to the planes as observers." The communication pointed out that no more than eight planes could be made available at one time. Another Reich Defense Ministry communication (12 August 1929) informed the Fleet Command that the contract provided for a guarantee of 3,000 flying hours annually to be hired by the Navy at a price of RM 453 per hour. Additional hours were available at a price of RM 70.

The annual total of 3,000 flying hours was assigned as follows during 1929, 1930, and 1931: Station Baltic Sea 950 hours; Station North Sea 1550 hours; and Naval Command 500 hours.

On 31 January 1930 the French Ambassador and the 1st Secretary of the British Embassy each handed a note of protest to the German Foreign Office. The notes charged that (a) training of German pilots had not been listed properly according to agreement, the figure of 358 pilots reported in training being an even 100 less than the actual figure of 458; (b) the German Navy had carried out smoke screen exercises with planes. After conference with the Naval Command, the German Minister of Defense on 10 March 1930 informed the German Foreign Office that no German naval aircraft was in existence ("Marineflugzeuge gibt es nicht"), and that there was no foundation to the reports of combined exercises between ships and aircraft, with planes laying smoke screens. It appears that the incident was thereby closed.

By summer 1930 the Navy began to select annually a small number of naval air cadets. By January 1931, the first regulations concerning cooperation between fleet and naval air units were issued. As a security measure planes were referred to as "motor tenders" in these regulations.

When on 31 January 1933, Adolf Hitler assumed power in Germany the groundwork had been laid for a German naval air arm. Actually, only a limited number of properly trained naval air officers were available, and the planes which the Navy "rented" were numerically and technically too inferior to constitute a proper naval air arm. However, the Navy had achieved its goal of familiarizing a select group of officers with naval aviation.

A decided change took place when shortly after assuming power Hitler appointed Hermann Goering as Reich Minister for Air. His official task was to build up German civilian aeronautics. In addition he was to establish secretly a German Air Force as a new and independent branch of the Armed Forces. A conflict between Navy and Air Force now ensued.

The Navy did not deny the need for an independent operational Air Force. However, it held that naval air formed a part of the fleet, just like PT boats or submarines, and that, as such, all naval air should operate under the Fleet Command. The Reich Air Minister, on the other hand, insisted that all air units should be concentrated in the hands of a Commander in Chief, Air (Chapter 2). [note that this refers to the "chapters" of the original 1947 document.]

By 1935, the first cycle of secret air production had been concluded, and Hitler proclaimed the existence of a powerful German Air Force. Planes began to come off the assembly lines in larger numbers. The question of who was to control naval airplane production and operation was no longer a matter of abstract discussion but became the subject of the first intense clash between the Commander in Chief, Navy, Admiral Raeder and the new Commander in Chief, Air, Goering (Chapter 3).

The controversy was brought to a temporary halt in 1937 by an order of the Reich Defense Ministry which set up distinct operation zones for each of the three branches of the Armed Forces, assigning to the Navy responsibility for defense in the coastal area against all attacks from sea or air, and stating that for such defense the Navy would use air force units and equipment which the Commander in Chief, Air was to assign permanently to the Navy (Chapter 4).

This order did not clarify the situation with regard to reconnaissance at sea, nor did it touch upon the matter of participation of air units in naval operations for reconnaissance, mine-laying, or direct attack against hostile merchant or naval units. Therefore differences of opinion continued to characterize all Navy–Air relations. Finally, on 3 February 1939, a "Protocol" was signed by the Commander in Chief, Navy and the Commander in Chief, Air which was to form the basis for operations in peace and war (Chapter 5).

At the outbreak of the war, this Spring Protocol of 1939 formed the basis for Navy–Air relations. It provided that Commander in Chief, Navy was to have tactical command over all air units assigned to duty with the Navy. The Air Force began to circumvent this agreement by cutting allocations to the Navy and by establishing at the same time its own air units ("Flieger Corps X") assigned to air operations at sea (Chapter 6).

The progress of the war showed the weaknesses of the original agreement. The Navy faced the problem of defending an extended coast line. The Air Force was charged with conducting a "blitz" against England. Both branches of the Armed Forces required therefore additional air strength to function properly. However, the organization now enabled the Air Force to withdraw additional units from naval command, weakening thereby seriously the operational readiness of the Navy (Chapter 7).

By summer 1940 a wide range of issues was subject to controversy between Navy and Air Force command. Prominent among these issues were the use of aerial torpedoes, the laying of mines from the air, the construction of air bases on the French Atlantic coast in support of submarine operations, and air strength required for the day to day operations of naval units. The general disagreement resulted in a violent clash concerning the assignment of Coastal Air Group 606 (Chapter 8).

Actions of the Air Force Command voided the Spring Protocol of 1939. Hitler laid down new rules for Navy–Air Force relations in a sequence of three orders. The final order stated that all air units engaged in coastal patrol should operate under the Commander in Chief, Air. With this order the end of an independent naval air arm was initiated (Chapter 9).

On the basis of the new directive, the Air Force drained the resources of the naval air arm until by fall 1941 only one coastal air group was left to Commander, Naval Air, in addition to two depleted squadrons. By November, the Air Force requested that this last group be transferred from Navy to Air Force command; Commander in Chief, Navy agreed (Chapter 10).

As a result of these actions, Commander, Naval Air and his staff were left without operational air units. The Commander in Chief, Navy desired to maintain this staff intact, but agreed in the end to transfer Commander, Naval Air from Navy to Air Force command (Chapter 11).

The naval air arm had thus ceased to exist. Grand Admiral Raeder summed up its development in a letter to Commander, Naval Air. The officer in charge of the Naval Air Section, Naval Staff (IL) also recorded in a memorandum the growth and decline of the German Naval Air (Chapter 12).

The situation changed somewhat when Admiral Doenitz became Commander in Chief, Navy. In response to his urgent requests, Reichsmarschall Goering agreed in the summer, 1943 to assign all available Air Force units against enemy shipping (Chapter 13).

By this time, however, the tides of war had turned. The German Air Force was no longer free to choose its theater of operations. When by September 1944 a final reorganization of the command of air units operating at sea was ordered, naval air operations for all practical purposes had ceased (Chapter 14).

The following pages contain various documents related to the development of German naval air from 1933 to the end of World War II. The documents were contained in the files of the section of the German Naval Staff which dealt with naval air problems. These files are voluminous; additional Naval Staff files contain further material related to the subject. For the present purpose, only a preliminary screening of the material was carried out. A thorough study of all material available related to this subject must be considered a long-range project.

Where the material appears in quote, a literal translation has been given. As a rule, the text has been given in excerpt.

The German term "Fuehrer der Luft" appears in various meanings in the organization of the naval air arm and of Air Force units for duty at sea, and it requires a word of comment. This term appears originally to have been used to describe the Commander, Naval Air, that is the officer in charge of the air units which were under the operational command of Naval Staff. The full title of this officer was "Fuehrer der Seefliegerverbaende"; in abbreviated form he was usually referred to as "F.d.L.". In 1940, there acted under the "F.d.L." a "F.d.L., West", in charge of naval air in France. The Air Force, in gradually assuming tactical command over the naval air units, also made use of the designation "F.d.L.". Up to 1942 "F.d.L." remained the commander of all naval air units proper, but commanders of air force units assigned for duty at sea were also designated as "F.d.L., Nord", "F.d.L., Atlantik", etc. These latter "F.d.L." however, were under the immediate command of the Air Force.

Air Force units frequently appearing in the text are the group and the squadron. As a rule, each group was composed of three squadrons. Squadrons originally were composed of twelve planes. By 1940, the Air Force began to decrease the strength of squadrons to 11, 9, and even less planes.

2. Beginnings of the Conflict

On 30 January 1933, Hitler assumed power in Germany. Subsequently he appointed his deputy, Hermann Goering, head of the new Ministry for Air (Reichsminister der Luftfahrt). Outwardly, this Ministry was to be in charge of civilian aeronautics; actually it also was to have charge of the secret re-establishment of a German air force.

Prior to this move, the German Navy and, as it appears, the Army as well, had secretly established air units. The new Reich Ministry for Air tried to gain control of these units. Controversies developed between the Reich Ministry for Air and the Naval Staff (Marineleitung). On 2 December 1933 a conference of Naval Staff and Air Ministry division chiefs took place. According to a naval document this conference showed the following cleavage:

Air Ministry	*Naval Staff*
1. Has the concept of an "Air Force" as a third branch of the Armed Forces been recognized? Has it been recognized that the naval air units are part of this Air Force?	1. The concept of an "Air Force" in the form of an operational air fleet is recognized. Naval air force units cannot be considered part of this operational air fleet since they are not an auxiliary naval weapon, but part of the fleet to the same extent as torpedo boats, submarines, etc. This principle will not be recognized with regard to the Naval Air units. They form a "tactical unit" with the fleet. Commanding Admiral, Naval Air must therefore act under the Navy command.
2. Central problem: What is the position of the Commanding Admiral, Naval Air (B.d.Luft)? He holds a position similar to Commanding General, Army Air (Kdr. der Heeresflieger). Both are and will remain under the command of the Reich Air Ministry in every regard.	
Air units will be assigned to the disposition of the Army or Navy command only for operational and joint training purposes.	The training of Naval Air units should be in accord with assignments from Naval Staff or Fleet Command. The Reich Air Ministry may have responsibilities with regard to instruction.
Naturally, close cooperation between Air Command and Navy Command will be maintained.	

No agreement was reached during this conference. No subsequent conferences took place. The Air Ministry incorporated its ideas as outlined above into a proposed directive. Naval Staff answered with a memorandum on 22 January 1934 which contained the following proposals for the organization of the secret German Air Force:

"The German air forces consist of:

(a) the operational Air Force,
(b) the Army Air units,
(c) the Naval Air units.

The operational Air Force is under the authority and command of the Reich Air Ministry.

The Naval Air units are under the command of the Commander, Naval Air, (F.d.Luft). They represent an indivisible part of the fleet. Material and personnel are provided by the Reich Minister for Air.

The Commander, Naval Air is a commanding officer designated by the Reich Minister for Air. In taking over his naval command, he and all air forces under his command are transferred to the command of the fleet with regard to all matters of a strategic, tactical or disciplinary nature. He is responsible for the preservation and development of the Naval, aeronautical and technical training of personnel and for the tactical readiness of the units under his command.

"The planes of the Naval Air Force, their equipment and weapons will be supplied by the Reich Ministry for Air. The planes and the personnel provided by the Reich Ministry for Air will be assigned to the Commander, Naval Air. Thereby they will be transferred to the authority of the Fleet Command."

3. Command – Problems

Controversies continued during 1934 and 1935. Efforts to overcome the differences of opinion failed. However, during those two years the main interest of German naval and air officers and commands was directed toward developing the Air Force from its blueprint stage into reality. Under these circumstances, it appears, only minor attention was given to jurisdiction over Air Force squadrons and Air Force personnel which to a large extent were not yet ready for the field. As far as the Navy's request for construction of special naval planes was concerned, the Reich Ministry for Air showed willingness to cooperate.

In 1935, the Fuehrer proclaimed that Germany henceforth was to have an Air Force. The veil of secrecy which had covered all preparations was lifted. Simultaneously the Reich Minister for Air, Goering, took on the added rank of Commander in Chief, Air (Ob.d.L.).

By 1936, the first cycle of production had been concluded. Planes came in larger numbers off the assembly lines; trained airmen were ready to man the planes. Now the Reich Minister for Air tried to cash in on the understanding which he had shown to naval suggestions and requests during the previous two years. This effort took the form of a friendly letter from the Reich Air Ministry to the Commander in Chief, Navy. The letter was signed "Kesselring" (presumably the later Field Marshal), dated 21 December 1936, and stating in part: (marginal notes made on this letter by Naval Staff given in parenthesis):

"The Reich Minister for Air and Commander in Chief, Air has carefully studied the requests of the Commander in Chief, Navy within the frame of the over-all requests received for the new construction program. In general, the Reich Minister for Air and Commander in Chief, Air agrees to the requests by Commander in Chief, Navy. . . The chain of command for fighter squadrons and multi-purpose squadrons to be newly constructed is to be decided upon later by the order of battle (Marginal note: "This is the devil's foot!"). The Commander in Chief, Navy has requested two land-based long-range reconnaissance squadrons and six land-based long-range fighter squadrons. Their planned assignment will be taken over by the operational Air Force (Marginal note: "It is not fit to do this!").

"Commander in Chief, Air is of the opinion that long-distance reconnaissance over the sea and against hostile coasts and harbors is decidedly the task of the Air Force. This includes the often resulting mining operations (Sperrmassnahmen).

"I believe that the Commander in Chief, Navy will freely agree to these counter-proposals, and that he can do this the more so since numerically only a small cut has been made in carrier squadrons,* and since all other changes have been made only (Marginal note: "!!!") with regard to the chain of command.

"In summing up, the Commander in Chief, Air repeats again that he feels himself fully responsible for assigning to the permanent disposition of Navy and Army all necessary equipment in so far as that is possible. Yet the over-all conduct of the war, and special needs which may arise in the course of war, require the concentration of all fighting forces under the command of the Commander in Chief, Air. . ."

This letter caused Commander in Chief, Navy to take steps designed to have the situation clarified once and for all. Naval files show that Admiral Raeder brought the whole controversy to the attention of a superior authority, presumably the Minister of War, General von Blomberg, in a personal conference. Subsequently, the Commander in Chief, Navy received a letter from the Reich Ministry for Air, dated 4 February 1937, and stating:

"The Commander in Chief, Air has learned of the conference of Commander in Chief, Navy and of his disagreement with certain views held by Commander in Chief, Air. The Commander in Chief, Air believes that it is important to clarify the situation as soon as possible by a personal conference. Preparation thereto, Commander in Chief, Air requests a transcript of the conference held by the Commander in Chief, Navy." To this request Naval Staff added the marginal note: "This will not be done". Instead, Admiral Raeder sent a personal letter to Goering addressing him as "Generaloberst" (General) and stating:

"For purpose of clarification. . . I would appreciate an early, personal conference with you, my dear general. The points which I made in the

---

* The Air Force proposal provided for the construction of one carrier fighter squadron, three carrier multi-purpose squadrons, and one carrier Stuka squadron up to 1 October 1938, and of an additional three multi-purpose and one fighter carrier squadrons up to 1942. The Navy had requested two more fighter carrier and one more Stuka carrier squadron.

conference and which do require clarification, are listed in the attached pages as points for our discussion. Heil Hitler. Raeder, General Admiral".

Naval Staff made utmost efforts to prepare this Goering–Raeder conference as well as possible. Almost every section submitted suggestions, and Naval Intelligence provided material concerning the Naval Air organization of foreign powers.

The essence of this material was incorporated into a "Sprechzettel" for the conference which consisted of (a) statements to be made by Raeder, (b) answers to be expected from Goering, and (c) counter arguments then to be brought forth.

Finally, the main points of Raeder's argument were incorporated into a short memorandum which was to be handed to the Commander in Chief, Air. The main points for the conference were:

"1. Ever since the three branches of the Armed Forces exist, there has been friction between the offices. The controversies are concerned with what the Navy thinks it requires, and what the Air Force thinks it can or should grant. These controversies often deal with minor and unimportant problems. A clarification in principle is required which outlines the division of operation, and the respective fields of activity.

2. Conference are hampered by the impression of naval officers that they have to point out to each and every Air Force office what are essential naval requirements. Important offices of the Air Ministry do not appear to understand the importance of naval requests. A feeling of uncertainty exists whether the Air Force will actually hand over to the command of the Navy those units which are to be transferred in case of mobilization, or whether the Air Force views these units as a part of its own strategic reserve.

3. The naval theater of war is one operational entity, it must remain under a single command. All of the coast including the installations necessary for naval warfare and the defensive installations turned toward the sea are part of the Navy's operational system and cannot be separated from it.

4. The Commander in Chief, Navy proposes a mutual agreement based on the statement that Commander in Chief, Navy is the responsible commander for the whole naval theater of war and for the defense of the coast against attacks from the sea or from the air. Details concerning the cooperation between Navy and Air Force should be worked out on this basis."

The material gathered in preparation for this conference filled a heavy file. The protocol of the conference itself, which took place on 11 March 1937, consisted of a few lines only, culminating in the statement "Commander in Chief, Air will study the memorandum."

4. Establishment of Naval and Air Zones of Operation

Following this conference, higher offices intervened in the Navy–Air conflict. By 1937 the Reich War Ministry was the supreme authority for all Armed Forces; the Minister (von Blomberg) exercised over-all jurisdiction as Commander in Chief, Armed Forces (Ob.d.W.). On 31 March "Ob.d.W." issued a directive which provided:

"In the whole theater of war the primary task is combat

(a) of the Army against the enemy ground forces,
(b) of the Navy against the enemy at sea,
(c) of the Air Force against the enemy air force.

"The only exception to this rule is the combat of Army and Navy in defense against enemy air forces attacking troops, ships or fortifications. For this defense, Army and Navy will use their own equipment and those units of the Air Force which have been permanently assigned to them. . . All other exceptions fall within the jurisdiction of the Armed Forces Command and will be ordered by this command.

"The division of the theater of war into a theater of the Army (operational zone) a theater of the Navy (coastal defense district), and a theater of the Air Force (Reich air defense district) as has been directed, must not lead to a strict isolation of the branches from one another."

This division of theaters was outlined for Navy and Air Force as follows:

"The Coastal Defense District of the Navy is that part of the theater of war which borders on the open sea. It includes territorial waters, fortified areas, naval garrisons and bases. In the Coastal Defense District the Commanding Admiral is responsible for defense against attacks from the sea as well as from the air. Borders between the operational area of the Navy and the operational area of the Air Force can be established only according to the actual and changing situation."

This regulation avoided laying down definite limits for the air force operations in naval theaters, and it did not bring to an end the Navy–Air Force controversy. On 10 May 1937, the matter was taken up again at Naval Staff. A memorandum was circulated which pointed out that Commander in Chief, Air had not yet replied to the memorandum handed to him during the personal conference on 11 March 1937, and that so far no agreement in principle had been given by the Air Force to the position taken by the Navy. In fact, a different view had been expressed by the representative of the Commander in Chief, Air, Kesselring, in a renewed Navy–Air Force staff conference on 1 April 1937, during which "Kesselring promised to do everything the Navy is asking for but on the basis that everything is to be directed toward Air Force requirements."

The matter was again made the subject of a Raeder–Goering conference on 11 May 1937. The notes which Admiral Raeder took to this conference pointed out that "it is absolutely essential that the memorandum previously given to the Commander in Chief, Air be accepted. This is vital for a successful conduct of the war at sea; command at sea can be in only one hand, that of the Commander in Chief, Navy. All arms which serve the naval aims in time of war must be united under his command. During peace, Commander in Chief, Navy must therefore have far-reaching influence over the Naval Air Forces."

Results of the conference were noted as follows:

"1. Handed one copy of Navy statement to Commander in Chief, Air.
"2. Commander in Chief, Navy agreed that operations conducted by the Air Force across the sea, that is from our territory against enemy territory, will be wholly under the command of Commander in Chief, Air.
"3. If Commander in Chief, Navy requests operational Air Force units as reinforcement for the Naval Air units for specific naval operations, these units will operate under the command of Commander in Chief, Navy."

From this note it appears that the conference had not brought about agreement in any of the vital issues. This impression is made a certainty by a note in the Naval Staff files, dated 20 May 1937 and headed: "Present situation of the conferences with the Reich Ministry for Air." This note states:

"1. Commander in Chief, Navy has decided that the demand for command by the Navy over all Naval Air units shall not be voiced.
"2. Our basic principle is that responsibility for operations at sea can be in one hand only. So far this has not yet been clearly and positively accepted by the Reich Air Ministry.
"3. The Reich Ministry for Air is now urgently requesting that fighter squadrons and the aircraft reporting service in the coastal area be transferred to its command. This means that Commander in Chief, Air is now attacking the decision by the Commander in Chief, Armed Forces, according to which in the Coastal Defense District the Navy is responsible for defense against attacks from the sea as well as from the air."

5. The Spring Protocol of February 1939

From 1937 to 1939 the Navy–Air Force conflict continued along the pattern established in the previous years. The attitude of the Reich Minister for Air remained vascillating. While he avoided rejecting openly the claims of the Navy, he was by no means willing to support them to any extent. The Air Ministry offices continued to show willingness to cooperate in all those matters in which the Air Force could in the end profit by naval suggestions and research. For the rest, Commander in Chief, Air ordered establishment, transfer or closing down of Naval Air activities at his own discretion and according to his own plans. A great amount of correspondence dealing with these matters is assembled in German naval files. These files show how the position of the Navy became gradually weaker and weaker.

This fact may have been the result of personalities and of personal and political connections. No new over-all directive concerning the matter appears to have been issued by either Blomberg as War Minister or after the dissolution of the War Ministry in 1938 by Adolf Hitler as Commander in Chief, or his Chief of Staff, General Keitel.

Other than strictly military decisions played their role in shifting the balance of power. Within the rearmament speedup, Goering was named by Hitler as Deputy for the Four Year Plan, acquiring thereby direct control over the allocation of equipment and weapons to all branches of the Armed Forces. Under these circumstances, it appears from naval files that no further effort was made by the Commander in Chief, Navy to gain acquiescence to the program of division of responsibilities which had been described as being vital for the fulfillment of the Navy's task during a war.

Nevertheless, naval authorities were continuously confronted by renewed requests from Air Force authorities, and these requests were no longer limited to matters concerning exclusively that theater of war which had been assigned to the Air Force by the 1937 directive.

Early in 1939 the final phase of the controversy was reached. Another conference took place on 27 January 1939 between Commander in Chief, Navy and Commander in Chief, Air. Agreement was reached whereby control over all Naval Air units passed to the Commander in Chief, Air, this control to be exercised by a General of the Air Force assigned to the Office of the Commander in Chief, Navy. At the same time, the Air Force renounced all responsibility for reconnaissance operations in support of naval coastal operations.

The results of this conference were incorporated in a joint statement which was drawn up in the office of the Adjutant of the Commander in Chief, Air, Major Bodenschatz, and later signed by Raeder and Goering.

This document, which is dated 3 February 1939, formed the basis on which the German Air Force and the German Navy commenced operations in World War II. The provision of the agreement, whereby in time of war the General of the Air Force with the Office of the Commander in Chief, Navy was to be transferred from the command of the Commander in Chief, Air to the command of Commander in Chief, Navy was of limited importance only, since the general was designated as an administrative officer. The major parts of the Naval Air construction program which was to be carried out up to 1941, were cancelled with the outbreak of the war.

In its main parts the Goering–Raeder agreement has the following text:

"In the conference between the Commander in Chief, Air and the Commander in Chief, Navy on 27 January the following points were discussed and agreed upon:

I. Operational areas.

1. It is agreed that for the operation of the Air Force the center of gravity is the British Isles and the sea areas which are not open to naval operations. Whenever the Air Force is able to operate in these sea areas and thereby touches upon the operational area of the Navy, agreement with the Navy is required.
2. Reconnaissance. The Commander in Chief, Air does not assume any responsibility for any reconnaissance duties of the Navy. Reconnaissance over the sea for the purpose of naval operation is the special task of the Navy.
3. Current exchange of information shall be assured by close proximity of the Navy and Air Force command posts.
4. Participation in naval engagements. Tactical participation of Naval Air Units in naval engagements (battle between ships) will take place only when requested by the Navy or when generally agreed upon. For a planned participation in naval engagements only such Naval Air units can be considered in the near future which have been trained by the Navy in naval engagements.
5. Every mine-laying operation requires the agreement of the Navy.

II. Size and Equipment of Naval Air Units.

Agreement exists between Commander in Chief, Navy and Commander in Chief, Air concerning the size and activation of Naval Air units. Up to 1941 Commander in Chief, Air will provide for purposes of naval warfare nine long-distance reconnaissance (F) squadrons, eighteen Naval Air (M) squadrons, twelve carrier squadrons and two shipboard squadrons. Commander in Chief, Air agrees to increase the efficiency of naval aircraft according to the requests of Commander in Chief, Navy, and to make sure in any event that the planes fulfill the naval requirements.

III. Organization.

Commander in Chief, Air informed Commander in Chief, Navy that as of 1 February 1939, the post of a General of the Air Force with the Commander in Chief, Navy (General der Luftwaffe beim Ob.d.M.) has been established. Thereby the present office Air Force Command, Sea will be abolished. . . The General of the Air Force with the Commander in Chief, Navy acts during peace time under the command of the Commander in Chief, Air. In time of war he is to act under the tactical command of the Commander in Chief, Navy.

During peace time he is in administrative command of all Naval Air forces. At the same time he is Inspector General of all Naval Air units. In this capacity he acts under the Chief, Training, Reich Air Ministry. So as to give a maximum of consideration to the training requirements requested by the Commander in Chief, Navy, the General of the Air Force with the Commander in Chief, Navy will be directed to work in close cooperation with the Commander in Chief, Navy, and to give due heed to the requests by the Commander in Chief, Navy. Directives concerning the training of Naval Air forces issued by the Chief, Training Air Force will be submitted to the Commander in Chief, Navy, for agreement previous to submittal to Commander in Chief, Air for signature.

The Commander in Chief, Navy requested that besides the General of the Air Force with the Commander in Chief, Navy, a General Staff officer of the Air Force remain with the Naval Staff. This request is granted by the Field Marshal (Goering). Commander in Chief, Air regards the General of the Air Force with the Commander in Chief, Navy as an administrative officer who in time of war is under the tactical command of the Commander in Chief, Navy, but whose main activity is in administration. Therefore, the Commander in Chief, Air recognizes the necessity for having a specialist for operational and tactical problems within the Naval Staff. This officer will act simultaneously as liaison officer between Commander in Chief, Air and Commander in Chief, Navy.

In the event that this organization should show serious disadvantages, a new conference shall be held after six months.

(signed) Goering. Raeder"

6. The German Air Force sets out to develop its own Naval Air Fleet

At the outbreak of World War II the relations of the Navy and the Air Force were characterized by the following division of functions: (a) The

Air Force was responsible for the procurement, training and equipment of all German air units; (b) The Navy was responsible for air operations at sea and in defense of coastal areas; (c) The Air Force was to provide the Navy with sufficient air strength to carry out the objectives under (b).

Air operations at sea were a new field. It was to be expected, that at the outset difficulties and unexpected tactical problems would be encountered. Cooperation between Navy and Air Force as well as a staff organization to cope with the new problems was urgently required. Instead, the tactical difficulties encountered served only to widen the differences between Naval and Air Force Command.

An indication of this situation was given in the conference between Hitler and Commander in Chief, Navy on 23 October 1939*. Commander in Chief, Navy brought to the attention of the Supreme Commander the fact that Ju-88 planes of the Air Force together with He-115s of the Coastal Air Squadron had attacked in coastal waters of southern England with a resulting loss of four naval planes. This loss appears to have been due partially to the fact that the Ju-88 flew ahead and alerted the English defenses. Commander in Chief, Navy urged the Fuehrer that "no organizational measures be taken, as it is being rumored for instance, that combined (Air Force and naval air) operations over the sea are considered."

The Junkers Ju 88, represented here by a Ju 88A4 bomber, was frequently used against ships in all theatres, using dive-bombing, low-level or high-level attacks with a computing bombsight.

* The transcript of this conference is included in the volume "Fuehrer Naval Conferences 1939".

A Heinkel He 115B-1 has a practice torpedo loaded into its weapons bay. Some B-1s could carry a 1,000kg magnetic parachute mine in addition to their 500kg bomb load. The He 115 equipped most of the KuesteFliegerGruppen from 1939 to 1942, when the type's vulnerability to Allied aircraft forced its withdrawal to secondary theatres and missions.

Raeder once more pointed out the absolute necessity to conduct all training and operation of naval air units in closest cooperation with the fleet.

This transcript of the Fuehrer conference reflects in a mild manner only the situation which developed in less than two months of war. Naval air operations were carried out mainly in the West. The Naval Group Command, West thereby was the command to feel first and most strongly the shortcomings of the arrangements previously made between Navy and Air Force command. On 30 October 1939, Naval Group Command, West submitted to Naval Staff a memorandum, entitled "Air units under Commander, Naval Air, West". The memorandum, signed by Admiral Saalwaechter, stated in part:

"The units under Commander, Naval Air, West are insufficient in strength to cover the tasks of the Naval Group Command. Even under favorable flying conditions air activities had to be restricted extensively to avoid a complete lack of planes after a time. It is significant that after any large-scale operation which requires close reconnaissance, our air units are exhausted and cannot be committed effectively for several days. This situation has made it impossible to obtain current up-to-date information on enemy activities in the central and northern North Sea, even though visibility has been exceptionally favorable this fall."

Concerning the number of aircraft available to Naval Group Command, West the memorandum pointed out that only the Do-18 planes could be adapted for long-range reconnaissance. The fifty-six Do-18 planes available had flown 500,000 kilometers, that is 150 kilometers per plane per day. Ten planes had been lost; the monthly replacement figure had been three. "Therefore no increase in the number of planes available can be anticipated." The memorandum added that He-115 planes would be used for medium range reconnaissance and as multi-purpose planes.

The total requirements of Naval Group Command, West for purposes of reconnaissance within the area assigned to this command and under conditions of six miles visibility were listed as 126 planes in readiness, or a total of 378 planes including all reserves. Actual present strength was given as eighty-five planes (35 Do-18, 25 to 30 He-115, and 25 He-59).

Naval Group Command, West summed up the situation as follows: "From these figures it is evident, that the air reconnaissance required for naval operations cannot be carried out due to the lack of planes. In spite of favorable weather conditions there has been no possibility to get any information on enemy naval activities in more remote areas for days or even weeks. It is essential to increase the units under Commander, Naval Air

The prototype of the maritime reconnaissance version of the Dornier Do 18, the Do 18d D-AHDM, was the sole example of the family to have a twin-fin-and-rudder tail assembly. It was replaced by a single unit on production aircraft.

Obsolete by the outbreak of war, the Heinkel He 59 was employed on reconnaissance duties.

speedily. . . . Otherwise Commander, Naval Air, West is unable to carry out his task which is vital for naval operations."

If the request of Naval Group Command, West was justified, there was no authority to which this request could be submitted. In his conference with the Fuehrer, Admiral Raeder had limited himself to plead that no new organizational measures were adopted whereby Coastal Air Groups would be assigned to Air Force operations. Commander in Chief, Air transmitted his answer during a conference between the Chief of Staff, Naval Staff, and the Chief of the Air Force General Staff. This answer was phrased in technical terms and gave assurances of understanding for the mission of naval air. However, the net effect was that the Air Force now began to cut down on allocations of planes to the Navy, and at the same time to build up Air Force units for operations at sea. This conference took place on 24 October 1939. The protocol thereof stated:

"Concerning air operations in the North Sea. Commander in Chief, Air believes that the aim will be served best if of the twelve naval multipurpose squadrons in readiness or under construction, three are transferred to the X Air Corps. The planes can be assigned by this corps command to operations in the North Sea or against the English coast. Commander in Chief, Navy will retain six long-distance squadrons in addition to the ship planes. Later, carrier squadrons will be added. Commander in Chief, Air will give his very special attention to the maintenance and the personnel of these squadrons. In addition, Commander in Chief, Navy will retain the nine other 'M' squadrons, which should fully suffice for duty in the coastal waters of the North Sea area and in the Baltic. . ."

In a letter addressed to Goering, the Commander in Chief, Navy on 31 October 1939 rejected this proposal. He stated that minimum naval requirements up to 1942 called for 15 "M" and 9 "F" squadrons and that this figure already represented a reduction of three squadrons from the 1939 spring protocol. In addition the Commander in Chief, Navy pointed out:

a. Requirements of the Navy for long-distance naval aircraft with Navy trained personnel;
b. His approval of the assignment of the X Air Corps to operations in the North Sea Area;
c. The need for air support for naval operations against enemy merchantmen and for support of submarine operations;
d. The need for planes which, like destroyers, are capable of combining offensive operations with routine reconnaissance duty ("Waffeneinsatz aus der Aufklaerung heraus").

Finally, the letter raised the problem of mine-laying operations by air units and of the use of aerial torpedoes against units of the enemy fleet.

This letter by Raeder to Goering did not change the trend. On 31 October 1939, the Naval Staff informed the naval group commands that due to the current lack of sufficient aircraft, naval air operations were to be limited to reconnaissance, while offensive operations against enemy naval units were to be carried out "at present" by the Air Force, X Air Corps.

Developments of four months of war were summed up by Naval Staff in a memorandum dated 15 January 1940, dealing with "Organization and Expansion of the Naval Air Units of Commander in Chief, Navy" and signed by the Chief of Staff, Naval Staff, Vice Admiral Schniewindt.

The memorandum stated that at the outbreak of war fourteen squadrons were at the disposition of the Navy. It was therefore decided to transfer responsibility for offensive operations in the North Sea to the X Air Corps. While naval group commands were requesting additional air support, for instance for duty with destroyers operating in the North Sea, Commander in Chief, Air was trying to limit naval air units to six long-distance (F) and nine multi-purpose (M) squadrons. In addition, Commander in Chief, Air had informed the Naval Staff that the Navy could not receive planes of type Do 217, "due to the need for transferring all offensive air operations at sea to the X Air Corps," and that the Navy would receive instead planes of type He 115. Commander in Chief, Navy, in protesting this decision, had stated that He 115 was outdated already at the time it was delivered to the front, and that the requirements of coastal defense, reconnaissance, and anti-submarine patrol could not be carried out by the present coastal air squadrons even if eighteen such squadrons were available.

Beyond these general difficulties, the memorandum shows that by December 1939 naval air reconnaissance operations had come to a complete standstill. On 21 December 1939, "it became evident that no responsible command could assign planes of type He 111 J any longer to operations over the sea," due to technical shortcomings of this type. Thus the Naval Staff was unable to carry out any reconnaissance operations with the planes allocated by the Commander in Chief, Air. To overcome this sudden emergency, a temporary agreement was reached between the Air Force General Staff and the Naval Staff, whereby the X Air Corps was directed to carry out reconnaissance operations for Naval Group Command, West "within the limitations of what is possible". The Commander in Chief, Air then promised to adapt one group of planes type Do 17Z to naval requirements. The Naval Staff agreed to this proposal.

The memorandum concluded with the statement: "The Naval Staff is conscious of the shortcomings in quality and quantity but must yield to the material situation".

Conferences dealing with this situation continued all during spring

Technical shortcomings ruled out overwater operations of the Heinkel He 111J, it being ruled in December 1939 that 'no responsible command' could assign the type for such duties.

The Naval Staff agreed to the proposal that one group of Dornier Do 17Zs be adapted to suit naval requirements.

1940. However, the general picture remained the same. A further set-back for the Navy occurred when on 4 April 1940 the Commander in Chief, Air issued a revised armament program which provided for thinning out the air squadrons assigned to the Navy. When the agreement had been reached in spring 1939 which provided for assigning a definite number of squadrons to the naval command, each of these squadrons had been composed of twelve planes. In the meanwhile, the Commander in Chief, Air had reduced the number of squadrons to be assigned. Now the strength of the squadrons was reduced from the original twelve planes to: nine planes in each Ju 88 squadron, eleven planes in each Do 17 squadron, nine planes in each Bv 138 ship squadron.

Thus the decline of the Naval Air arm got under way.

The decline in figures is illustrated by the fact that the original 1939 agreement had provided for a "full strength" of forty-one squadrons or twenty-seven not counting ship and carrier squadrons. The greatest strength achieved by Naval Air in World War II appears to have been represented by the following figures, given as the actual strength of Naval Air on 15 January 1940:

C.A.G. 106 with squadrons	1/106	He 115 E
	2/106	Do 18
	3/106	He 59
C.A.G. 406 with squadrons	1/406	Do 18
	2/406	Do 18
	3/406	Do 18
C.A.G. 506 with squadrons	1/506	He 115 B
	2/506	He 115 B
	3/506	He 115 B
C.A.G. 606 with squadrons	1/606	at present being
	2/606	equipped with various
	3/606	sea plane types
C.A.G. 806 with squadrons	1/806	He 111 J
	2/806	He 111 J
	3/806	He 111 J
C.A.G. 906 with squadrons	1/906	He 59
	2/906	Do 18
	3/906	He 59

While the heading of this list stated that it included all naval air squadrons as of the given date, it appears that ship planes were not included in the above total of eighteen squadrons. By 1940 the two Ship Squadrons 1/196 and 5/196, each one equipped with Ar 196 planes, were under Naval Command.

The Arado Ar 196 shipborne reconnaissance seaplane entered service in the latter part of 1939. This variant, the Ar 196A-3, the principal production version, had heavier armament than the earlier versions.

This figure of eighteen Coastal Air squadrons now began to shrink rapidly.

7. New theaters create new shortages

In the beginning, the controversy between Navy and Air Force had been a struggle for jurisdiction and command. With the opening of the large campaigns of spring and summer 1940 a new element became evident. The Navy was faced with a greatly increased coastline which it had to defend and, if possible, to utilize for offensive operations. The Air Force was assigned the task of carrying out an "air blitz" against the British Isles.

On 9 April 1940 Germany started her campaign against Denmark and Norway. IL, the officer in charge of the naval air section in the Operations Division of the Naval Staff, communicated to the Chief of Operations Division, Naval Staff, on 29 April 1940 his views regarding the situation created by the occupation of the coast of Norway. "I do not see any way," IL stated, "in which the request of the Commander in Chief, Navy for a numerical increase in our coastal air units could successfully be submitted to the Air Force General Staff. However, Naval Staff can and must request that the formations allocated to us are fully maintained in accordance with agreement."

The Naval Staff did not fully accept these views of IL, but submitted a request to the Air Force General Staff on 24 May 1940, asking for an increase in the coastal air units in view of the situation in Norway. A total of twenty-six naval air squadrons, not including the carrier squadrons, was requested, to be composed of eight He 115 squadrons, three Do 17z, eleven Ju 88 and four Bv 138 B Ship Plane Squadrons. In addition the request was made to establish a new Commander, Naval Air, North (Fuehrer der Seefliegerverbaende, Nord), and to reestablish the Commander, Naval Air, East (F.d.F., Ost).

No direct answer to this naval request has been located in naval files. Instead, the Commander in Chief, Air, on 25 June 1940, transmitted the following communication to the Commander in Chief, Navy (given in excerpt):

"The collapse of France has created a new situation for the air command, All means available for air operations against England must now be concentrated by the most energetic means. Consequently, a new division of reconnaissance duties must be arranged between the Commander in Chief, Navy and the Commander in Chief, Air, necessitating the redistribution of available air units. I propose the following arrangement, and request agreement:

"The Commander in Chief, Air assumes responsibility for air

Four squadrons of Blohm und Voss Bv 138 flying boats were among the twenty-six naval air squadrons requested by the Naval Staff in view of the situation on Norway. This is a Bv 138A-1.

reconnaissance over Western England, the vicinity of the Orkney and Shetland Islands, along the East Coast of England and over the Channel south of 53° North.

"As reinforcements for offensive air operations I must use Group 806, which has just been fitted out with Ju 88, as well as Squadrons 3/106 and 3/906. I request that the naval personnel assigned to these units remain for the time being.

"Under my Command, the 2nd and 3rd Air Force are carrying out the air offensive against the British Isles from the Belgian–Dutch and the French coast. They are equipped with all means for reconnaissance and thereby assure surveillance of the coastal area occupied by us, as well as of the Channel. I request your agreement to this arrangement so that I can immediately issue all necessary orders. Goering".

The Commander in Chief, Navy answered this request on 3 July 1940. In his answer he protested against the arrangement as proposed by the Commander in Chief, Air. However, from this answer it appears that the Air Force High Command had issued orders in accordance with the Goering proposal prior to receiving an answer from Admiral Raeder.

Admiral Raeder pointed out that the frictions had become so troublesome that he had found it necessary to submit the matter to the Fuehrer for decision.* Admiral Raeder further indicated:

* Minutes of this Fuehrer conference available in the publication *Fuehrer Conferences 1940.*

a. Norway remains important for naval operations. Newly acquired bases on the French coast offer new operational possibilities. Operations in both sectors require intensive participation of air units.

b. Air units assigned to the Navy so far have been insufficient in strength and quality to carry out necessary operations.

c. This situation has led to countless frictions which in the end made it necessary to submit the whole problem to the Fuehrer, who shares the Navy's point of view and has clearly expressed his decision that the requirements of naval operations must be taken into account in the distribution and operational assignment of air units no less than the requirements of actual air warfare.

d. The Commander in Chief, Air bases his opinion on a wrong assumption when he believes that he can assign Coastal Air Group 806 and the two squadrons 3/106 and 9/106 to Air Force operations. These units are part of Naval Air which, as pointed out previously, is too weak in every respect to fulfill its own duties.

e. In view of pending submarine operations, the return of the two squadrons 3/106 and 3/906 is requested.

f. The request for the transfer of Group 806 is granted provided the following points are made part of the agreement:

(1) The transfer is to be of a temporary nature only. (2) Posts of Commander, Naval Air, North (Fliegerfuehrer (See) Nord), Commander, Naval Air, France, and Commander, Naval Air, East, are to be established in addition to the present Commander, Naval Air, West; these three commands are to operate under the General of the Air Force with the Commander in Chief, Navy. (3) All other naval air units which have temporarily been assigned to duty with the Commander in Chief, Air must be returned.

No direct answer to this communication has been located in the files of the Naval Staff. However, on 25 June 1940, one week after this Raeder letter was transmitted to Goering, the Command Staff of the Commander in Chief, Air (Ob.d.L., Fuehrungsstab I) sent the following wire to the Naval Staff:

"The Commander in Chief, Air suggests that the X Air Corps be left in charge of coastal and off-shore operations in Norway. Therefore, Group 506 as well as such other air units as may from time to time be assigned to operations on the Norwegian coast should remain under the command of the X Air Corps. The chain of command leading from the Commander Naval Air, West to naval air units in Norway has proven to be impractical."

8. Friction on all Fronts

The situation created by the Spring Protocol of 1939 had left relations between Navy and Air Force in a precarious balance. Immediately following the outbreak of the war this balance was upset by the actions of the Air Force High Command designed to cut down on allocations to the Navy and to build up units for sea operations under the Commander in Chief, Air.

With the progress of the war, the difficulties were no longer restricted to such controversies resulting from rivalry and difference of opinion. The problems which were created by the extension of coastal areas represent only one of the items of a steadily increasing list of difficulties in Navy–Air Force relations.

The naval files give the impression that by summer 1940 such an atmosphere of animosity had been created by inappropriate organization, that a clash of opinion occurred over almost every issue which had to be dealt with by the naval and the air command.

The documents show a serious controversy with regard to the use of aerial torpedoes. While the Navy had shown great interest in the development of this weapon, the Air Force disapproved at first of its general use as "uneconomical". It withheld from the Navy equipment necessary to fit planes for carrying aerial torpedoes. At a later time, when the importance of this weapon no longer could be debated, the Air Force set up its own torpedo squadrons.

The Navy was very much interested in using air mines as soon as this new weapon became available. Goering opposed this, stating that aerial mines would not be dropped until 5,000 such mines were available. At a later time, the Commander in Chief, Air suggested to the Naval Staff that Coastal Air Group 106 be transferred to the command of the 9th Air Division "so as to carry out the laying of air mines most efficiently." The Commander in Chief, Air simultaneously requested that all air mine operations be concentrated under the command of the 9th Air Division, since the Naval Air units lacked sufficient strength to carry out these operations. The Naval Staff agreed.

When, in the fall of 1940, the Naval Staff requested that air bases be established at Lorient and St. Nazaire for the support of submarine operations in the Atlantic, the Air Force replied that an inspection had been made of these harbors and that no facilities had been located there suitable for the construction of air bases. The Air Force communication added: "It cannot be assumed that other places more suitable for construction will be located in this vicinity."

The incessant conflicts over minor and major issues finally led to a violent clash between the Commander in Chief, Navy and the Commander in Chief, Air. The clash occurred with regard to the assignment of Coastal Air Group 606. According to a memorandum written by the IL of the Naval Staff, Major Gaul, and dated 8 September 1940, events were as follows:

"1. Reports submitted by Naval Group Command, West showed that between 24 August and 29 August the Coastal Air Group 606 was being used to carry out moderate to brisk attacks on England, especially in the Cornwall and Liverpool areas, as part of the 3rd Air Force. The Naval Staff pointed out in teletype No. 12 445/40 of 30 August that attacks during the day or even at night on strongly defended targets on the English mainland must be stopped in order to maintain the operational readiness of Coastal Air Group 606 for coming tasks.

"2. As Naval Group West made no alteration in the commitment of Coastal Air Group 606 after receiving these instructions, operations by this coastal air group on the English mainland were forbidden following a conference with the Commander in Chief, Navy. At the same time the imminent reconnaissance duties for Group West in connection with the requirements of naval warfare were pointed out. Following this, Coastal Air Group 606 was assigned for armed reconnaissance in the southern approach of St. George's Channel and the Irish Sea.

"3. During the night of 6 September the Air Force Liaison Officer of Naval Group, West, Col. Metzner, telephoned the Naval Staff and reported that the Reichsmarschall (Goering) had ordered that Coastal Air Group 606 was to take part in operation "Loge" (attack on London). However, the Group had the above mentioned definite order from the Commander in Chief, Navy, hence it requested a new decision.

"During the night Lieut. Cdr. Reinicke (Naval Staff) pointed out to Group West that the decision of the Commander in Chief, Navy still held good. About 0900 on 7 September the IL, Major Gaul, was again called up by Col. Metzner and asked for a favorable decision for the assignment of Coastal Air Group 606. IL referred to the views held by the Naval Staff which had been transmitted by Lieut. Cdr. Reinicke, and at the same time stated this decision had again been expressed in a teletype (No. 12901/40 Gkdos.) dispatched in the meantime.

"About 1000 IL was informed by the Operations Officer in the Air Force Command Staff, Major Christ, that after a report by Air Marshal Sperrle, Goering had ordered that Coastal Air Group 606 was to take part in the operation on London. He requested Naval Staff to agree to this decision now in order to avoid unpleasant friction. IL then informed Major Christ of the decision which Naval Staff had already transmitted to Group West by teletype. The order issued by the Commander in Chief, Navy was to be adhered to. IL added that the Reichsmarschall could not issue orders to a coastal air group that was tactically subordinate to the Navy. Major Christ was of a different opinion and stated that Group Commander 606 was an Air Force officer who was bound to carry out the orders of his most superior officer. IL regretted that this clash of opinions between the higher commands would be taken out on Coastal Air Group 606, as the Reichsmarschall simply was not entitled to give operational orders to other branches of the Armed Forces. Major Christ closed the conversation with an assurance that Group 606 would participate in the attack on London.

"IL reported the course of this discussion to the Chief of Operations Division, Naval Staff who saw no reason to change the decision expressed in the teletype and also emphasized that the Reichsmarschall could not issue any operational orders to this naval reconnaissance unit.

"4. About 1430 on 7 September, IL was informed by the duty officer that the Armed Forces High Command would settle the question of the commitment of Coastal Air Group 606 and that Naval Staff was requested to state its views. The Operations Officer, Capt. Wagner, was informed by IL of the state of the matter and was asked to inform the Chief of Operations Division so that the Armed Forces High Command could be convinced of the soundness of the Naval Staff order by personal representation.

"About 1900 IL was informed by Major von Falkenstein, Armed Forces High Command, that General Jodl had decided that Coastal Air Group 606 should participate in the attack on London as planned by the 3rd Air Force on orders from the Reichsmarschall. IL again pointed out that this was a regrettable decision, as it was quite intolerable that the Reichsmarschall should approve the issue of operational orders to flying units that were not tactically subordinate to the Air Force. Major v. Falkenstein then explained that according to the account from the 3rd Air Force the matter had taken the following course:

"The Navy had transferred Coastal Air Group 606 to Brest. Naval Group, West had given it hardly any assignments in connection with naval operations, so that the Air Group Commander had approached the Air Force and asked about the possibility of taking part in attacks on England. The 3rd Air Force had then taken over this commitment in agreement with Naval Group, West. After a time Naval Staff had forbidden the operations. This order was not complied with. On Thursday or Friday, Air Marshal Sperrle had reported to the Reichsmarschall along these lines and also added that it was obvious from the operational reports of Group 606 that the latter was not at all overloaded with work. He had therefore asked the Reichsmarschall for permission to include this Group in his Air Force for operation "Loge". In view of this account the Reichsmarschall agreed with the view held by Air Marshal Sperrle and gave permission to include Group 606 in the operation. The 3rd Air Force informed Group West of the Reichsmarschall's decision, and this had then led to the later developments.

"Major v. Falkenstein reported that he would inform the appropriate Air Force offices of the decision taken by General Jodl as the Fuehrer's representative, and he requested IL to inform Group West of this decision.

"IL reported the course of this conversation to the Chief of Operations Division, Naval Staff who sanctioned the dispatch of the following teletype to Group West:

'Coastal Air Group 606 is to participate in the proposed operation on London during the night of 7 September.'

"5. About 1100 on the night of 8 September Major Christ informed IL of a text transmitted by Armed Forces High Command concerning the decision on the commitment of Coastal Air Group 606:

'The Fuehrer has decided that Coastal Air Group 606 shall take part in operation "Loge".'

"About 1200 the Air Force Liaison Officer with Group West also informed IL of the text of this decision and added that Group West had received the Armed Forces decision through the Air Force two hours before the teletype from Naval Staff arrived. At the same time he stated that operation "Loge" was continuing and that Group 606 would continue to participate in the assignment of the 3rd Air Force.

"IL transmitted this message to the Operations Officer, who made a note thereof.

"6. About 1700 the duty officer stated that Group West had transmitted a message that in view of the Fuehrer's decision, Group 606 would also take part in the attacks on London during the night of 8 September, instead of only that of 7 September as sanctioned by the Naval Staff.

"IL asked the duty officer to inform the Operations Officer of this message."

9. The Fuehrer reorganizes Navy-Air relations

The conflict between Navy and Air Force had now widened to the extent that the Spring Protocol of 1939 no longer formed the basis for organization and command of Naval Air. A new agreement was needed. Since Navy and Air Force disagreed violently with one another, the Fuehrer stepped into the picture. He issued three successive directives which were to give a new basis and frame for Navy–Air Force relations. These directives differed from each other in scope as well as content.

The first directive dealt primarily with immediate matters. On 13 September 1940, six days after Jodl had directed Group 606 to take part in operation "Loge", Naval Staff received the following order, signed Adolf Hitler:

"The Fuehrer and Supreme Commander of the Armed Forces.

"Subject: Reconnaissance forces of the Navy.

"Intensified air warfare against England makes it necessary to concentrate all available forces in the hands of the Commander in Chief, Air and strictly to centralize their operational assignment. Aside from this, however, the Navy requires its own reconnaissance units which must be under its own tactical command in so far as the air operation is conducted in close tactical cooperation with our naval movements (off-shore patrol, support of submarines returning or leaving, protection of convoys in the North Sea and the Arctic, transfer of naval surface forces to the French Atlantic coast and, later on, operations based on this coast).

"However, in view of the fact that with the limited number of naval forces ready for action, naval operations are conducted at present only from time to time, there is danger that important air reconnaissance units under the tactical command of the Navy will be out of operation for lengthy periods. This danger must be averted by transferring these units from time to time from command to command between the Navy and the Air Force.

"I reserve for myself the right to issue such orders from time to time.

"For the time being, the coastal air units will operate as follows:

"Coastal Air Group 606 (Do-17z), Coastal Patrol Squadron 3/406 (Do-18), and Coastal Patrol Squadron 2/106 (Do-18) are to operate under the Commander in Chief, Air.

"Coastal Air Group 506 (He-115) reverts to the Commander in Chief, Navy as of 18 September. Two additional coastal air squadrons (Do-18) will go to the Commander in Chief, Air when the order to carry out operation "Seeloewe" (invasion of England) is issued. A fifth coastal air squadron (Do-18) will be assigned to the Commander in Chief, Air as soon as cruiser *Hipper* has been transferred to the operational area of Naval Group Command, West."

This order, while limited in its scope, greatly weakened naval air strength. The Navy now began to plan measures by which not only lost air support would be regained but by which also a more reliable basis for Navy–Air Force relations would be served.

By the end of November it was evident that for the time being operation "Seeloewe" was not to be carried out. The "air blitz" against England had not produced the results hoped for. The Naval Staff now requested the Armed Forces High Command to cause the re-transfer of Group 606 to the Navy. On 8 December 1940 answer was received from General Jodl, who stated that the Chief of the Air Force General Staff had rejected the Navy's request. The Naval Staff now requested Jodl to arrange for a conference between Raeder and Hitler on the "most important matter" of Navy–Air Force relations.

For this conference Naval Staff prepared the draft of a Fuehrer directive by which (a) return of Group 606 was to be ordered; (b) Commander in Chief, Navy was to be directed to carry out all aerial torpedo attacks; (c) air patrol activity over the Atlantic in support of submarine operations was to be intensified; (d) naval air units were to be permitted to take part in offensive operations against enemy surface forces. In the opinion of the Naval Staff, these proposals, if accepted, would have constituted a satisfactory basis for Navy–Air Force relations.

On 27 December 1940 Raeder attended a conference with the Fuehrer in which presumably these proposals were discussed.*

As a result of these efforts on the part of the Commander in Chief, Navy, and possibly also reflecting the loss of prestige suffered by the Air Force due to its inability to establish air superiority over England, a new order was issued by the "Fuehrer and Supreme Commander". The order was dated 6 January 1941 and stated in part:

"Subject: Air reconnaissance by the Navy.

"1. According to all information received from England directly and from neutral sources, the loss of merchant ships and the continuously decreasing English imports are at present the most serious problem for England. According to a report by the Navy (Commanding Admiral, Submarines), the sinkings of merchantmen can be increased considerably if air reconnaissance in sufficient strength is assigned primarily to the Commanding Admiral, Submarines, with orders to carry on a more systematic search for British convoys than has been done in the past and to direct submarines to these targets. Planes assigned to this duty must be fit for long-distance reconnaissance.

* Minutes of this conference available in the volume *Fuehrer Naval Conferences 1940.*

These planes should not be drawn from units assigned to the air offensive against the British Isles, since constant air attacks are the second means by which British resistance is made to dwindle.

"2. In view of these two considerations I herewith direct:

"a. The I/K.G. 40 (Type FW 200) is assigned to the Commander in Chief, Navy, to operate under Commanding Admiral, Submarines. Commander in Chief, Air will bring this squadron to a strength of at least twelve planes and maintain such strength, if necessary by assigning additional planes type He 111(5). Any exchange of personnel required will be regulated between the Commander in Chief, Navy and the Commander in Chief, Air.

"b. Coastal Air Group 806 reverts to the command of the Commander in Chief, Air as of 7 January. . . (signed) Adolf Hitler."

Only a very limited part of the Navy's suggestions was incorporated in this order, which again avoided laying down broad principles. However, the order pointed to the requirements of the Commanding Admiral, Submarines, and set down in definite terms how these requirements were to be satisfied. The Navy had scored one point.

In the following weeks Navy and Air Force alike seem to have made great efforts to gain from the Fuehrer a decision which would solve the Navy–Air Force controversy by establishing broad and long-term principles. These principles were to take the place of the scrapped "Spring

The long-range Focke-Wulf Fw 200 Condor, evolved from the pre-war airliner of the same name, became one of the Luftwaffe's most potent anti-shipping aircraft. This Fw 200C-4/U1 was Adolf Hitler's personal transport.

Protocol"; and they were urgently needed in view of the great number of disputed subjects. Some of the most urgent subjects had been discussed in a conference between the Chief of Staff, Naval Staff, Admiral Schniewindt, and the Chief of the Air Force General Staff, General Jeschonnek, during a conference on 4 January 1941. According to a written report by Admiral Schniewindt, the following points were raised by him:

1. An urgent request for support of naval operations by air attacks against British harbors, bases, docks, and yards. Reply by General Jeschonnek: Will be considered.
2. Protest against an order issued by the Air Force concerning the use of aerial torpedoes without previous consultation with the Naval Staff. Answer: It is conceded that the Naval Staff should have been consulted. The Air Force is interested in the further development of aerial torpedoes; while the Air Force believes that it is uneconomical to use such torpedoes against merchantmen, it has no objection against the occasional use of aerial torpedoes by naval air units.
3. A request for allocation of airplane types satisfying urgent naval requirements. Answer: The need for sufficient air reconnaissance support of submarine operations is fully recognized and will be provided in one form or another. The assignment of such reconnaissance units to the Commander in Chief, Navy will present difficulties ("die Form. . . wird dem Herrn Reichsmarschall schwer fallen"). Would it be sufficient to assign special units to the 3rd Air Force with the provision that they are to be used exclusively for the support of the Commanding Admiral, Submarines? It has been agreed that the Air Force is bound fully to supply naval requirements, and the Air Force is earnestly striving to keep this agreement. However, unfortunately weaknesses have often developed due to the urgencies of war. Nevertheless a serious effort is being made to alleviate the situation. Aside from this, it is believed that air reconnaissance operations in Norway for instance could be carried out simultaneously for the Air Force and the Navy, that is by Air Force patrol units.
4. Anti-air protection of the French coast. Answer: Everything possible is being done. Barrage balloons are not available. Assistance by the Navy will be most welcome.

The wide range of controversial subjects was brought to Hitler's attention anew in a conference with Raeder on 22 February.*

From naval files it appears that simultaneously with this Hitler–Raeder

* Minutes of this conference available in translation in the volume *Fuehrer Naval Conferences 1941.*

conference, the Air Force tried to win the support of General Jodl (OKW) for drafting a new Fuehrer directive. The Air Force aimed at a directive which would assure it not only administrative control but also tactical command of all German air strength. The naval record does not show what went on behind the scenes, that is between the representatives of the Air Force and the Chief of the Armed Forces Operational Staff, General Jodl. However, a new Fuehrer directive was prepared in an unusual manner as is evidenced by the following letter, which under date of 22 February 1941 (the date of the Hitler–Raeder conference) was sent to the Naval Staff by General Warlimont, the Chief of the section of the Armed Forces High Command making top policy (section "L").

"The Chief of the Armed Forces Operations Staff (Gen. Jodl) just informed me of the Fuehrer's decision pertaining to the re-organization of air reconnaissance. Enclosed I am forwarding an excerpt of this decision. The Chief of the Armed Forces Operations Staff is interested to learn prior to issuing this order whether the Naval Staff wants to make any comments for tactical or technical reasons. . . The Chief of the Operations Staff requests keeping in mind that the basic decision of the Fuehrer must be viewed as final. Since the new organization shall be set up as of 10 March, I am to transmit to Berchtesgaden any comments by Naval Staff as soon as possible, but not later than 23 February."

The "decision of the Fuehrer", comment to which was requested within less than 24 hours, and which was attached to Warlimont's letter, appears to have been a draft drawn up by Jodl. It stated in part:

"I therefore give the following order:

"1. Reconnaissance over the North Sea north of 52° N, at the Skagerrak and the exits of the Baltic Sea remains the task of the Navy.*

"2. Reconnaissance off the Norwegian coast, over the northern North Sea including the Orkney, the Shetland and the Faroe Islands will be conducted by the Air Force, which will set up a special Commander, Reconnaissance, Norway (Fuehrer der Aufklaerung, Norwegen).

"3. Reconnaissance in the Channel area south of 52° N, remains the task of the Air Force except for reconnaissance for the protection of our convoys.

"4. Reconnaissance over the Atlantic and air protection of our convoys in that area is transferred to the Commander in Chief, Air. For this task he will set up a special Commander, Air, Atlantic (Fliegerfuehrer, Atlantik) who will be charged with:

* The Navy reconnaissance area thus established extended from 52° N., that is north of a line Harwich-Rotterdam, along the coast of Holland, Germany and Denmark, to the southernmost tip of Norway which barely touches 58° N.

Reconnaissance for the Commanding Admiral, Submarines;
reconnaissance and patrol during operations of naval surface forces in
the Atlantic or for the protection of convoys;
meteorological patrol;
Such offensive air operations against targets at sea and in such areas
as will be agreed upon between the Air Force and the Navy."

This point "4" of the draft of the directive represented a reversal of the
directive issued by Hitler six weeks previously. It also made point "1" of
the directive practically meaningless. If enacted, this directive would
transfer tactical command of most air units operating in support of naval
warfare to the Commander in Chief, Air.

The Navy's reaction to this plan was expressed in a communication
which the Commander in Chief, Navy, Admiral Raeder, sent on 24
February 1941 to the Armed Forces High Command. This communication
stated in part:

"I must assume that the memoranda I presented and my reports have
not found acceptance. However, as Commander in Chief, Navy, my responsibility for the conduct of the war at sea causes me to lay down once more
my opinions concerning the importance of air reconnaissance for the
requirements of naval operations. . .

"During the past months of the war, the Naval Staff has kept the Armed
Forces High Command informed by various means of communications,
reports and memoranda on the difficulties resulting from the insufficient
allocation of naval air units. On 25 January 1941, I stated in a memorandum that I believe the situation can be remedied satisfactorily by returning to the Navy at once all naval air units which were put at the disposal
of the Commander in Chief, Air. . .

"The long-term settlement which now has been ordered by the
Fuehrer indicates that no account has been taken of these principles
which I hold to be essential, especially the right of the naval group commands to give orders to the naval air units under their command
("Einsatz durch die Marinegruppenbe-fehlshaber auf Grund eines
Unterstellungsverhaeltnisses"). I point to the serious limitations and
dangers which will result from this for naval operations, and to other possible consequences."

The Raeder memorandum then recorded in great detail the ill effects
observed in the past. Yet, his efforts proved of no avail.

On 28 February 1941 an order arrived from Fuehrer Headquarters,
which was in effect the beginning of the end of the air arm under the
command of the Navy. Point "C" of this order stated: "I therefore order:"
There followed the text of the draft previously submitted by Jodl.

Section one of this draft, dealing with reconnaissance by naval air units in the North Sea was enlarged by the following sentence:

"In addition, the Navy will carry out air patrol for the protection of submarines in the Channel area as far as Cherbourg. For these assignments the Commander, Naval Air, remains under the tactical command of Naval Staff."

For the rest, the directive followed the text submitted previously by Jodl. Added was a section (5) which ordered Commander in Chief Air, to set up, in preparation of operation "Barbarossa" (Invasion of Russia), a Commander, Naval Air, Baltic (Fliegerfuehrer Ostsee). This order was preceded by more general statements of the Fuehrer which read in part as follows:

"A. Reports and memoranda of the (two) Commanders in Chief have acquainted me with the divergent and opposing ideas of the Navy and the Air Force concerning the organization of air reconnaissance in the coastal areas and over the sea.

Both the Navy and the Air Force agree as to the importance of the task which is to be carried out by such reconnaissance and as to the strength required. The Navy, however, citing the agreement which was concluded in the spring of 1939 between the Commander in Chief, Air and the Commander in Chief, Navy, asks that all coastal air units set up for the operational requirements of the Navy are to operate under naval command.

"The Commander in Chief, Air is of the opinion that only those air units are to operate under naval command which are assigned exclusively to duty with the Naval Staff. . .

"B. With regard to this difference of opinion I state:

"1. The agreement concluded in the year 1939 between the two Commanders in Chief cannot be viewed as a contract which excludes any other agreement in the course of the war.
"2. An arrangement whereby each branch of the Armed Forces has at all times full command over those units which are required to carry out specific duties, is wasteful and uneconomical.
"3. Reconnaissance operations and air offensive operations of the coastal air units and of the Air Force in the majority of cases are carried out in the same sea area ('Seegebiet'). For this reason they must be concentrated in the hands of the Air Force."

Point C gave the order quoted above.

Point D concluded: "This directive considers only the critical situation which arose in the course of this spring. It does not lay down the principles for a future organization of the Naval Air arm."

10. The Last Coastal Air Group is detached from Naval Command

The Fuehrer directive of 28 February 1941 established a new basis for the relations between the Navy and the Air Force. Administrative problems which arose were discussed in a conference between Admiral Schniewindt and General Jeschonnek on 5 March 1941. On 8 March, Commander in Chief, Air issued an order in regard to the command over air units engaged in naval activities which established the following new organization for air units assigned to coastal and sea duty:

A. The Navy is in charge of the Commander, Naval Air (F.d. Luft) who acts under Naval Group Command, North. Under Commander, Naval Air: six squadrons and one reserve squadron of ship planes. He is responsible for air reconnaissance in the North Sea between 52° N and 58° N, over the Skagerrak, and the Baltic, and for anti-submarine patrol from the Danish coast to Cherbourg.
B. The 5th Air Force is in charge of the Commander, Air, North (Flieger-fuehrer Nord) who with three naval air squadrons, is responsible for reconnaissance over the Norwegian coast, Northern England, and the North Sea north of 58° N.
C. The 3rd Air Force is in charge of Commander, Air, Atlantic (Fl. Fu. Atlantik) who with ten squadrons is responsible for reconnaissance in the Atlantic and for anti-submarine patrol from Cherbourg to Spain.
D. Naval Group Commands and the Commanding Admiral, Submarines are authorized to make requests and give directions with regard to reconnaissance assignments.

The Air Force order listed in addition two (naval air) squadrons assigned to the XI Air Corps.

This organization was kept intact only for a short time. Soon the Commander in Chief, Air ordered changes which further depleted air strength available for operations in the Atlantic and the North Sea. In April 1941, the X Air Corps was transferred to the Mediterranean Theater to support operations in North Africa. The Commander in Chief, Air ordered the following planes transferred to the X Air Corps: six torpedo planes from the Commander, Air, Atlantic; five torpedo planes from the Commander, Air, North; and five torpedo planes from the Commander, Naval Air. A new and sharp clash followed, since the Commander in Chief, Air had again ordered the transfer of planes under the command of the Navy without previously consulting the Naval Staff. No change in the order resulted.

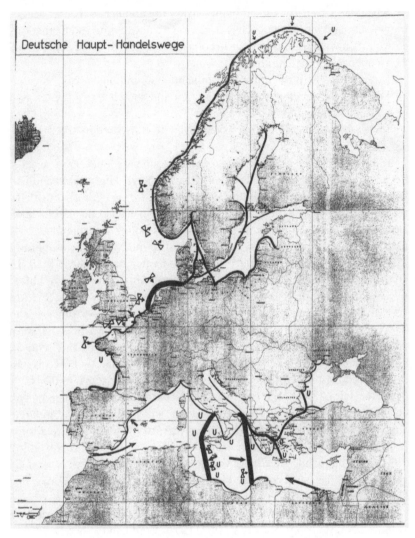

Germany's maritime routes and the threat of air, surface (arrow) and submarine (U) attack, as seen in November 1941. (Korvettenkapitan Assmann, Aufgaben und Probleme der Deutschen Seekriegfuhrung, 11/1941, USNARA RG 547 Box 52)

By 1941 the lack of cooperation between Navy and Air Force had reached such a degree that consequences became apparent in fields no longer directly related to air operations. On 12 November 1941, the Quartermaster, Naval Staff pointed out that the Air Force now was increasing construction of its own seagoing vessels. The adverse consequences thereof were stressed in a memorandum which stated in part:

61

"Since the Air Force is steadily increasing the number of its own seago-ing vessels, and more particularly is setting up naval units and formations as well as navigation schools, it becomes necessary to clarify this issue. Consequences at present are:

"Interference with the unity of command in operational areas.

"Diversion of manpower with instinct for and knowledge of the sea, and of personnel trained for sea duty.

"Increasing occupation of yard facilities with construction orders of the Air Force."

Additional problems arose with regard to air personnel. Ever since it began to build up a German naval air arm, the Naval High Command had held the view that naval training was required for any Air Force officer assigned to duty over the sea. A great number of naval officers had been assigned to naval air units in pursuit of this policy. By summer 1941, however, command over these units was lost to the Navy. The units were assigned more and more to duties of limited value to the Naval Staff. In addition, submarine warfare drained the reserve of physically qualified naval officers. Naval Personnel therefore informed the Air Force Staff on 13 November 1941 that it was forced to recall 80 to 100 naval officers who had been transferred to duty with the Air Force, but who now were required for submarine duty. The Air Force at first rejected this request, stating that once the officers had been transferred to the Air Force, it was up to the officer himself to decide whether he wanted to return to the Navy.

By the fall of 1941, the Commander, Naval Air was in charge of one coastal air group (506), one depleted air squadron (1/706), and one squadron of ship planes. This was in contrast to the forty-one squadrons promised to the Commander in Chief, Navy for 1942. Early in November 1941, the Commander in Chief, Air requested that the last full coastal air group still under naval command be transferred to the 3rd Air Force. The Commander in Chief, Navy agreed.

An immediate protest was wired to the Naval Staff by the Commanding Admiral, Naval Group, North, Admiral Carls. Commander, Naval Air was operating under this naval group command and it was his primary task to support naval operations designed to interfere with the Murmansk convoy traffic. Admiral Carls wired:

"If the Naval Staff stands by its surprising decision to relinquish command over Group 506, then there remain under Commander, Naval Air only the five planes of Squadron 1/706 and the Arado planes of Ship Plane Squadron 1/196. This would proclaim the verdict of death over the naval air arm. I most urgently request. . ."

In answer, Admiral Raeder wrote personally to Admiral Carls:

"On 19 November I decided that Coastal Air Group 506 should be trans-

The cruiser Prinz Eugen*'s Arado Ar 196A-3 is preserved at Naval Air Station Willow Grove, Pennsylvania, in the USA. (AAHS from Ray Wagner)*

ferred to the 3rd Air Force in accordance with a request from the Air Force Command Staff. I fully respect all the considerations which you have pointed out, and I underline that in principle our views are in full accord. . . I most sincerely regret this development. . . Now as always I believe that the needs of naval operations will be served best by a naval air force which has developed out of the ranks of the Navy and which works in closest cooperation."

11. End of the Independent Naval Air Command

As soon as the last coastal air group had been transferred from naval to Air Force command, the question arose whether there was any further justification for keeping the "Fuehrer der Seeluftstreitkraefte", the Commander, Naval Air, and his staff in charge of a naval air arm which no longer existed.

On 1 December 1941, the General of the Air Force with the Commander in Chief, Navy, conferred with Grand Admiral Raeder on this matter. A record of the conference gives the following details (in excerpt):

"General Ritter stated:

"With the transfer of Coastal Air Group 506, the Commander, Naval

Air, with his staff of sixteen officers and of about 100 enlisted men, is in charge of only Squadron 1/706 and Ship Plane Squadron 1/196. Of these two squadrons, 1/706 is for all practical purposes commanded by the Commanding Admiral, Defenses, East, while those planes of the Ship Plane Squadron not aboard ship have orders to cooperate with naval units or coastal commanders for anti-submarine patrol. This results in a situation whereby the whole staff of the Commander, Naval Air is inactive, waiting for the vague possibility that Group 506 might temporarily return in connection with a specific naval operation. Reduction of the staff of the Commander, Naval Air appears unavoidable. I propose to suggest to the Commander in Chief, Air, that all air operations in the North Sea be combined under the command of a "Commander, Air, North Sea" (Fliegerfuehrer Nordsee). This staff would be formed by the Commander, Naval Air. At the same time it should be pointed out that in the event of a later increase of ship and carrier plane squadrons, the complete staff would return to the Navy. I believe I am justified in assuming that the Commander in Chief, Air would welcome such a proposal. If the Grand Admiral feels that he must reject this proposal, then a reduction of the staff of the Commander, Naval Air will take place by force of circumstances. . .

"The Commander in Chief, Navy replied as follows:

"In this affair I can only see a continuation of the past policy of stripping naval air ("Auspluenderung der Marineluftwaffe") regardless of all serious consequences for naval operations. If the necessary number and types of planes were made available to the Commander, Naval Air, he could carry out all the assignments you describe just as well without having to be separated from the Navy. Under no circumstances can I give my agreement to this proposal. I cannot keep you from submitting your proposal to the Commander in Chief, Air ("kannich. Ihnen nicht verbieten"), and I shall not even view this as an unfriendly act. I fully realize that in the end I probably shall again be forced by the Commander in Chief, Air to agree to this solution. That would be only in keeping with past procedure. However, in the face of naval history I will not accept the responsibility of having lent my hand to the dissolution of the Command, Naval Air."

Naval records show that the Naval Staff did not share this view of the Commander in Chief, Navy, but held that a dissolution of the staff would be unavoidable and that it therefore would be wise to try to save whatever might be saved.

The subject appears again in the record of a conference between General Ritter and the IL of Naval Staff, Major Gaul. Notes on this conference taken by Major Gaul show that the Air Force Personnel Section, without awaiting a final decision, had started to dissolve the staff of the

Commander, Naval Air by withdrawing the Operations and the Intelligence Officer (Ia, Ic).

The same record shows that the General of the Air Force with the Commander in Chief, Navy had submitted his proposal to the Air Force Command Staff, suggesting that Commander, Naval Air be transferred from naval to Air Force command and be assigned to form the new staff "Commander, Air, North Sea". The Air Force Command Staff, however, had rejected this proposal on 29 January 1942 and demanded that the staff of Commander, Naval Air be reduced to the strength of an Air Group Command.

Major Gaul concluded his notes on this conference with the statement: "Herewith the struggle for naval air units comes to an end. The present situation is untenable. I see no way in which the complete liquidation of Commander, Naval Air could still be opposed."

On 18 February 1942, Grand Admiral Raeder sent a final plea to Reichsmarschall Goering not to dissolve the staff of Commander, Naval Air. This plea was caused by the request of the Air Force to reduce the staff to the strength of an air group. In trying to avoid such a move, Raeder was now willing to accept the suggestions previously made by General Ritter. When the Grand Admiral two and a half months earlier had stated that he would not submit these proposals, he had added that the time might come when Commander in Chief, Air would force him to do so. The time had now arrived. In his letter, the Commander in Chief, Navy stated in part:

"I wish to ask you most urgently, Herr Reichsmarschall, to revise your present plan for the solution of this problem. From the beginning the Commander, Naval Air has been the center for the unified training of air units operating over the sea and in immediate cooperation with naval forces. The activities of this command concerned reconnaissance, security patrol, and the use of aerial torpedoes. Numerous units of your Air Force have received most valuable officer personnel from this command. They were thereby enabled to carry out their missions over the sea in accord with the over-all requirements of the war. Through the channels of Commander, Naval Air, ideas of the Navy have passed on to the Air Force to the best advantage of both branches of the Armed Forces. If this staff should disappear, its valuable experience too will soon be lost.

"This staff cannot remain for a lengthy period of time without units of the Air Force, and it will be of no future value to the Navy if it loses its close contact with the front. On the other hand it is impossible for me to relinquish the staff which is responsible for collecting, evaluating and pre-serving the experiences gained in the cooperation between Navy and Air Force. The future development of the Navy and the appearance of aircraft carriers at a later date will call for a naval air arm, and naval air units will be necessary. At such a time officers must be available who have grown up in both branches of the Armed Forces. . . I therefore propose:

"a. Setting up a new Commander, Air (Fliegerfuehrer) for the Baltic Coast and the North Sea. I ask that the staff of Commander, Naval Air be assigned to this command. In addition to such forces as you might give to this staff, it would remain in charge of Coastal Air Group 506 and Ship Plane Squadron 1/196. This new Commander, Air would be under the 3rd Air Force in every regard. . .

"b. Since I am not in a position to estimate your plans for assignment, the following solution appears equally possible: The North Sea area south of the line Hanstholm-Newcastle will be assigned to the 3rd Air Force. Coastal Air Group 506 is to operate under the 3rd Air Force. Commander, Naval Air takes the place of the present enlarged staff of Combat Group 1./K.G. 26; he is then made Commander, Air, North, equipped with Squadron 1/708 and assigned to the 5th Air Force. . .

"I hope that you, Herr Reichsmarschall, will agree to one of these proposals, which will mean that the staff, Commander, Naval Air is kept intact in a different form. At the same time you will acquire in addition to administrative control full tactical command over this staff, which has excelled in every respect. Raeder."

No answer to this plea has been located in naval files. On 7 April 1942, the Operations Section of the Command Staff of the Air Force transmitted by wire the following order (given in excerpt):

"1. In accordance with the Naval High Command, Commander, Naval Air is transferred immediately to the command of the 3rd Air Force in every respect.

"2. The 3rd Air Force will make the assignment of tasks to the Commander, Naval Air, direct him to his battle station, and allocate his forces to him. Among the duties of the Commander, Naval Air will be the following:
 (a) Reconnaissance and offensive operations in the North Sea;
 (b) Close cooperation with the "E-boats" of the Navy;
 (c) Reconnaissance and security patrol for operations of naval surface forces. This will be carried out in preference to offensive missions.

"3. On the same date, Coastal Air Squadron 1/706 is assigned to the command of the 5th Air Force in every respect."

The document carries a Naval Staff marginal note which states:
 "In general in accordance with the proposal made by the Commander in Chief, Navy to the Commander in Chief, Air."

With this order, the independent German naval air arm had ceased to exist.

12. Summary of the Development of Naval Air under Grand Admiral Raeder

The Commander in Chief, Navy sent a personal letter to Colonel Schily, the Commander, Naval Air, when this officer was detached from duty with the Navy. The letter, dated 17 April 1942, recapitulated part of the history of the German naval air arm. . . "The war years", Grand Admiral Raeder wrote, "have brought a changing fate to the naval air arm. My original intention to make your unit a strong instrument of naval warfare by steadily increasing its numbers and making use of technical advances could not be realized. By order of the Commander in Chief, Air, issued in accordance with my proposal, you are detached from your tactical relation to the Navy and are transferred to the command of the 3rd Air Force. This does not bring to a final close the efforts of the Navy to develop its own air arm. The Fuehrer will make a decision about this matter at a later date. . . I express my sincere hope that in your new post you will maintain your interest in the Navy and in our common tasks at sea."

Naval records show that the Commander in Chief, Navy sincerely

The German aircraft carrier Graf Zeppelin *after launch and ready for fitting out. It was never made operationally ready.*

believed in the possibility of gaining the Fuehrer's consent for the re-establishment of a naval air arm at a later time. Such hopes had been renewed as the result of an order by Hitler, dated 13 March 1942, by which the aircraft carrier *Graf Zeppelin* was to be completed "in the shortest possible time in view of the vital importance of such a unit." The same order stated that the carrier was to be equipped with fighter, reconnaissance and torpedo planes, and directed "Commander in Chief, Air to assure the availability of planes and personnel at the given time."

A memorandum drawn up in the fall of 1942 clearly showed the hope of the Commander in Chief, Navy that carriers might provide the Navy with a new air arm of its own. This memorandum was to be used by Grand Admiral Raeder during a conference with the Fuehrer. It pointed out the following:

"The order has been given to complete the carrier *Graf Zeppelin*, and to convert the cruiser *Seydlitz* and so far three merchantships into auxiliary carriers. Under favorable working conditions the Navy will thereby acquire five additional front line units by the end of 1944 or early in 1945. Through their assignment for reconnaissance and offensive operations the airplanes aboard these carriers become an instrument of naval warfare. The Air Force units which will then be part of the Navy will be so strong in personnel as well as material, that a new line of demarcation will have to be drawn between Navy and Air Force interests with regard to personnel and ground organization. The Naval Staff therefore considers creation of a fleet air arm essential. With the organization of this fleet air arm the ship plane squadron could revert from the Air Force command back to the Navy. The future fleet air arm would then be composed of carrier and ship plane squadrons. They would operate under the over-all command of the Navy High Command. Administrative jurisdiction would be exercised by the Fleet Command. Training and operation would be carried out by an Admiral of the Fleet Air Arm under the Fleet Command."

This draft, which had been drawn up by IL, Naval Staff, was sent on 4 November 1942 by Naval Staff to the permanent deputy of Commander in Chief, Navy at Fuehrer Headquarters, Admiral Krancke, with a note saying that the matter had not been reported to the Fuehrer by Grand Admiral Raeder "due to the general situation," but should be taken up at an opportune time.

Such a time, it appears, never arose. Two months later the Fuehrer ordered all carrier construction halted. By 30 January 1943, Grand Admiral Raeder resigned as Commander in Chief, Navy.

The years during which Admiral Raeder had stood at the helm of the German Navy had seen the establishment and growth of a German naval air arm, its weakening, and its final absorption by the Air Force. The over-all developments were summed up in a communication which the IL, Naval Staff sent on 2 February 1942 to Naval Group Command, North in answer to one of the many protests. This memorandum was written with the obvious desire not to criticize but to explain what had taken place. It pointed out:

1. Since the creation of a German air force, Naval Staff has advocated a naval air arm.
2. The rapid development of all air units made it necessary to realize this aim in the form of a compromise. Naval Air units assigned to the tactical command of Commander in Chief, Navy were manned mostly by naval personnel. For equipment, ground organization, and all other requirements they were dependent upon the large organization of the Air Force.
3. Up to 1939 the naval air arm was built up according to plan. It was planned that the development should be concluded by 1942–43, by which time the naval air arm was to be composed of sixty-two squadrons, including seven ship and twelve carrier plane squadrons.
4. The war had its effects on this program. After the Norwegian campaign had been concluded, the focal point of operations shifted to the west. The North Sea became almost a dead sea. It was therefore natural for the Commander in Chief, Air to combine all air units. In the course of intensified air warfare against England, Coastal Air Groups 106, 606, and 806 one after another went to the Commander in Chief, Air. Other squadrons or groups were assigned to the tactical command of higher Air Force command staffs; thus Coastal Air Group 506 was assigned to the 5th Air Force.
5. The development of the war situation necessitated the assignment of considerable air strength to the Mediterranean, and with the preparation for the war against Russia the center of gravity shifted in that direction. By order of the Supreme Commander "Commanders, Air" were established as a temporary solution.
6. New sea areas in the operational zones (Baltic, Black Sea) necessitated the creation of new air units for duty at sea (Group 125 and 126) since the other air units were tied down in support of ground operations. This reduced further the personnel and material resources available to Commander, Naval Air. This strained situation was not relieved in 1941. New British activities in the northern North Sea and the Arctic Ocean called for an increase of our defensive strength in Norway. Again units were withdrawn from the Commander, Naval Air, this time from the central and southern North Sea, and assigned to the 5th Air Force (Squadron 1/406, Ship Plane Squadron 1/196).

7. In support of submarine operations it became necessary to give additional air strength to the west. The Commander, Naval Air therefore agreed to the transfer of Coastal Air Group 506 to the command of the 3rd Air Force.

8. The difficulties for cooperation (in the field) are well known to the Naval Staff. They are the result of a lack of proper basic training for duty over the sea, of an absence of schooling in cooperation with the fleet, and finally of the differences between the two branches of the Armed Forces in the means and technique of communication. Up to 1939 the basic training of the Air Force units for cooperation with naval units was conducted only at Naval Air units. The knowledge acquired in this training was systematically broadened by extended training exercises once or twice a year. All officer personnel assigned to naval air units had served for several years with the Navy and especially with the Fleet.

9. After 1939 only the joint basic training program remained; joint operation with the Fleet became impossible. The Air Force tried to increase its contingent of naval officers, but the Navy could not concede this; on the contrary, in the course of the submarine program many naval officers were withdrawn from duty with the Air Force. The Air Force now is assigning its own personnel to naval observation schools.

10. The joint training of Air Force and fleet units was taken up again by October 1941. It soon became evident that the same mistakes were being made in tactical assignment and in carrying out air missions as had characterized such training before the war.

11. The Air Force is now conducting training of its own for bombing missions against naval targets, including attacks from high altitude as well as Stuka-attacks.

Col. Gaul concluded his communication with the statement: "The two branches of the Armed Forces will work together more successfully if each side endeavors to understand and respect the given situation with regard to strength and assignment. Such an attitude will bring about better results than the clinging to command prerogatives which can only partially be based upon war experiences."

This opinion of the IL, Naval Staff was in marked difference to the views stated by the Commander in Chief, Navy, Grand Admiral Raeder.

13. The Doenitz Era

The change which took place in the Naval High Command on 30 January 1943 had its effect upon Navy–Air Force relations.

The retiring Commander in Chief, Grand Admiral Raeder, had been the sponsor of an independent naval air arm. He had seen this arm grow and develop. He had become entangled in arguments with the Commander in Chief, Air, first with regard to allocation and administration, later with regard to tactical command. In these arguments Raeder had fought with formal and legal reasons against a man who had little respect for formality and who was used to making his own laws. Raeder continued his up-hill struggle even when he must have realized full well that in arguing with the No. 2 Nazi about rights and prerogatives, he was on the losing side.

With Admiral Doenitz a different personality entered the scene. Since the days of World War I the submarine had been Doenitz's predominant interest. In working on submarine construction plans between the two World Wars he, like Goering, had learned how to stretch legal regulations, and how, at all times, to keep his eye on what is most essential – and that to his mind meant air support for submarine operations. As soon as he took over the Naval High Command, he set out to get this support. Approaching the naval air question as an operation problem, he was successful in establishing some understanding and better relations with many Air Force officers.

Doenitz's campaign to get adequate air support for his submarine operations started almost at the moment he acquired the rank of Commander in Chief, Navy. On 20 February 1943 the Naval Staff sent a memorandum to the Air Force Command Staff. The subject given was "Air operations in the Atlantic area." The memorandum stated in part:

"Recently, set-backs have occurred while blockade-runners were being brought into harbor. Our submarines are operating in steadily increasing numbers without positive results. This situation directs the attention of the Naval Staff again to the Atlantic and causes the following considerations:

"It is an established fact that the war on merchant shipping is of prime importance. All efforts of the Naval Staff to maintain contact with the enemy convoys by assigning more submarines or by repeatedly changing the operational areas are limited by the vast distances of the Atlantic and by the resulting difficulty of establishing contact with convoys far away from their point of assembly or port of destination. We must continue to gain a maximum of information about the course of the enemy convoys if the Battle of the Atlantic is to remain successful. This can be done only by means of air reconnaissance. Airplanes must penetrate to mid-Atlantic; airplanes must locate the convoys; airplanes must keep contact with these convoys; and airplanes must lead the submarines to the target and destroy it in joint action. This represents the tactical requirements which must be fulfilled by the airplanes the Naval Staff is requesting from the Commander in Chief, Air for Atlantic operations.

71

"It cannot be the task of Naval Staff to request a definite type of airplane for these operations. However, a type appears desirable which would be capable of combining very long-distance reconnaissance with active participation in an engagement.

"In view of the urgency of the subject, it is requested that types already available be assigned as fast as possible to carry out a maximum of long-distance reconnaissance and combat missions in cooperation with the Commanding Admiral, Submarines.

"The Naval Staff considers it essential that the problem of constructing airplane types for Atlantic operations be made the subject of a thorough study, and requests the Air Force Command Staff to transmit its views. Fricke."

This memorandum set the line which the Naval Staff henceforth was to pursue in dealings with the Air Force: operational requirements were pointed out, and satisfactory action was requested. The rest was left to the Air Force to decide.

The trend of the new policy is shown by a personal letter which was sent to Admiral Doenitz by the (Air Force) Commander, Atlantic, Maj. Gen. Kessler, on 3 May 1943. General Kessler's assignment called for close cooperation with the Commanding Admiral, Submarines. In this, as in all other assignments, he operated under the 3rd Air Force. Having requested reinforcement from the 3rd Air Force, General Kessler sent a copy of this request to Admiral Doenitz, together with the following personal note (in excerpt):

"I hope that the 3rd Air Force will be convinced by the statement that it is possible to multiply the loss of enemy shipping ten to twelve times, as compared to the figures for 1942, if the air strength available in the West is properly assigned against the convoys. The reinforcement which was promised to me has not yet arrived. The strength of my units probably decreased instead of increased between 1 March and today in view of the great losses resulting from needed repairs and the forced assignments for Naval Group Command, West. This lack of strength threatens to endanger the success of the current cooperation with the Commanding Admiral, Submarines. For it is evident that all gasoline has been spent for nothing, if after three to four days of unsuccessful reconnaissance I have to ground my unit due to lack of planes. The following 24 to 36 hours of inactivity may be decisive, for during this period the enemy convoy may slip through unnoticed. . . Yours most obediently, Kessler."

On 11 June 1943, IL suggested to the Commander in Chief, Navy that far-reaching new requests should be made to the Air Force. These requests were transmitted by the Naval Staff on 12 June in a memorandum to the Chief of the Air Force General Staff, General Jeschonnek. The memorandum stated in part:

"A. In a note on 8 June Naval Staff expressed the view that henceforth it will be essential for the German conduct of the war to continue sinking a maximum of enemy shipping. Measures proposed toward this aim culminated in the suggestion that all German air units be assigned to direct or indirect participation in operations against the enemy's sea power, in so far as planes are not absolutely needed for the defense of the European continent.

"1. Indirect participation of the Air Force in the war against the Anglo-American sea power must take forms which will assure our submarine operations of a maximum of success. Required are:

    a. Air protection over the Bay of Biscay;

    b. Support of submarine operations by locating enemy convoys and guiding the submarines to the target.

Minimum requirements for (a): one long-distance fighter-bomber squadron with sufficient reserves for assignment to fast bombing missions; one long-distance fighter group.

"Minimum requirements for (b): Twelve long-distance planes in daily readiness, that is one squadron of modern planes.

"2. Direct participation of the Air Force must take the following form:

"Attacks against convoys and single ships in the open sea, Required: two squadrons of He-177.

"Attacks against convoys and single ships off the enemy coast. Required: one squadron of fast attack planes.

"Large-scale mining operations in the area of the British Isles. Required: one squadron of He-177, one squadron of medium fighter planes.

Heinkel's He 177 Greif heavy bomber, with its coupled pairs of engines driving two propellers, was counted on for a number of maritime roles, as a dive-bomber, guided-missile platform and even as a long-range fighter against Allied ASW aircraft. Most of these missions proved beyond the troubled design's capabilities, however.

"Attacks against harbors, yards and docks in the British Isles. Required: two squadrons of He-177.

"B. Only joint training can bring about good tactical cooperation. The Naval Staff therefore proposes to set up in the Baltic near Gdynia a training center for air operations at sea. Here, all personnel which is to take part in air operations over the sea is to be made ready for front line duty in joint training.

"C. Operations against the Anglo-American sea power represent the one single objective for the assignment, equipment, and training of these air units. The center of gravity of these operations is in the West. The organization of air units in the West is to be adapted accordingly. The Naval Staff therefore proposes to reorganize the 3rd Air Force into an air force for sea operations, and to train and assign this force exclusively for operations against the enemy's sea power. The size of this air force makes it advisable to consider a division of duties between an Air Corps A and an Air Corps B. The chain of command should run: Naval Staff – Group West – 3rd Air Force – Corps B; and: Naval Staff – Commanding Admiral, Submarines, Operations – Commander, Submarines, West – Corps A."

With this memorandum the Naval Staff extended its suggestions and requests from the operational to the administrative field. However, in keeping with the new policy all suggestions were based on operational requirements. This policy bore fruit, and Commander in Chief, Air was ready to consider this proposal.

However, in his considerations the Commander in Chief, Air tried to shift the emphasis. The Doenitz proposal had asked for primary support of submarine operations; the Goering reply stated that the Air Force would now concentrate all its strength on air operations against the enemy's sea power. On 30 July 1943 the Chief of the Air Force General Staff transmitted to the Naval Staff "Excerpts of an Air Force proposal to which the Reichsmarschall (Goering) had agreed in principle. This proposal stated:

"If one accepts the view that a naval power can be decisively defeated only at sea, then no ways or means must be left untried to:

a. Compensate for the decrease in sinkings by submarines by utilizing other weapons whenever possible;

b. Do everything possible in defense against the enemy's anti-submarine operations and in support of our own operations.

"The focal point for the assignment of the German Air Force must be shifted to enemy shipping. Henceforth, the German Air Force must be assigned at all times and with all means at its disposal to operations against the enemy supply lines, that is against shipyards, docks, harbors, and ships in harbors and at sea. Exceptions are to be made only when air units must be assigned to the support of Army ground operations, or in defense against large-scale enemy landing operations.

"The successes which can be expected from such air operations can also considerably increase the successes of our submarines for the time being. It is true that air operations alone will have no decisive influence on the submarine campaign as such, due to the limited range and fire power of our planes, which at present are not well suited for such assignments. However, the presence of our planes at sea will in itself distract the enemy's anti-submarine air patrol and air defense. Thereby the difficult task of our submarines will be eased, and joint successes in the war on merchant shipping will increase.

"All operations against the British sea power will be carried out by the 3rd Air Force. Under the 3rd Air Force operate: the III Air Corps (Commander, Air, Atlantic) and the IX Air Corps (Attack-Commander, England). Requirements in strength which have to be fulfilled by the summer of 1944 are as follows: III Air Corps is to be composed of one long-distance reconnaissance group, two long-distance sea reconnaissance squadrons, one sea patrol squadron, two and 1/3 long-distance combat squadrons, one fighter-bomber squadron, one fighter squadron. The IX Air Corps is to be composed of three combat squadrons, two fighter groups (He-177), two fast fighter squadrons."

This Air Force proposal differed in many points from the plan submitted by Naval Staff. However, Navy and Air Force now had a common aim: in view of the general war situation, all available strength was to be concentrated upon operations against the enemy's sea power. The air strength available for such assignment was to be increased as rapidly as possible.

14. The Decline of the Air Force

This program for combined submarine and air operations held great promises. However, only few of these promises ever became reality. By the time the agreement was reached in summer 1943, the Allied war potential had been built up to such an extent that the initiative was rapidly being wrested from the Germans.

Evidence of new difficulties arising from this situation in Navy Air Force relations is amply contained in the *Fuehrer Naval Conferences 1943* and *Fuehrer Naval Conferences 1944*. The IL files of the German Naval Staff too reflect this situation. Many difficulties, such as manpower and raw material shortages, loss of production facilities through air raid damage, capture of occupied territories, etc., began to beset the Germans. Navy–Air Force relations remained on a fairly cooperative basis, and there are strong indications that the new difficulties arising did not result so much from actual differences of opinion, as from the increasing shortages confronting the German Air Force in 1944.

A Naval Staff conference on 28 April 1944 dealt with some of these new difficulties. Present at this conference were the Commander in Chief, Navy, the Chief of Staff, Naval Staff, the Liaison Officer with the Air Force, Capt. Moessel, and the IL, Col. Gaul. According to the handwritten minutes by Col. Gaul, the Chief of Staff, Naval Staff stated the following:

"The good relations which by now have existed for about a year between the Air Force and the Navy would be most seriously threatened by an effort to straighten out in a sharp manner the differences of opinion between the Commander in Chief, Navy and the Reichsmarschall. The Chief of Staff, Naval Staff therefore advises against an exchange of letters in this matter. He suggests that for clarification of the problem the Air Force Command Staff be requested to issue a statement to the effect that the Air Force, due to its present strength and assignments, is unable to carry out the Fuehrer directive.

"The Commander in Chief, Navy once more described what happened at Fuehrer headquarters. He concluded by saying that a misunderstanding in this affair was impossible. The Fuehrer ordered that additional units should be assigned to 5th Air Force. The Commander in Chief, Navy points out that he subscribed unconditionally to the factual arguments, but that he must reject most strongly the possibility of a so-called misunderstanding. Capt. Moessel was ordered to cause the Air Force Command Staff to send a teletype message in the above sense."

From this note it appears that the differences of opinion between Doenitz and Goering resulted from the inability of the Air Force to assign air units as directed by the Fuehrer. The precarious situation of the German Air Force, and the implications of this situation for air operations in the Atlantic are shown by a message which IL, Naval Staff sent on 29 June 1944 to Capt. Assmann, the naval representative in the Operations Section of the Operational Staff of the Armed Forces High Command – that is in Hitler's field headquarters. The message read in part:

"On 13 June, the General, Reconnaissance Planes, informed the Air Force Command Staff as follows with regard to Air Force armament program #226:

"Planes available for reconnaissance in the Atlantic as of 1 June 1944: two squadrons, that is fifteen Ju-290.

With the termination of Ju-290 construction, planes available will decrease from fifteen to eleven by the end of 1944. By June 1945 the squadrons will have ceased to exist. The only possible type available at present as a substitute is the He-177B-5F. The construction program of this type should permit one such squadron, that is twelve He-177 to be ready for action by 1 May 1945. Thus the following over-all development would be given:

1 Sept.   44 – 11 Ju-290
1 Dec.   44 – 11 Ju-290
1 March 45 – 11 Ju-290 and   7 He-177B
1 June   45 –   2 Ju-290 and 14 He-177B
1 Sept.   45 –   18 He-177B

"The present figure of 15 to 11 Ju-290 does not permit any systematic reconnaissance over the Atlantic in support of submarine operations, but only occasional reconnaissance in support of (air) combat units. The present range of 1,800 to 2,000 kilometers is insufficient for submarine operations. He-177 can cover these same distances only if its armament is

As of 1 June 1944 fifteen Junkers Ju 290s were available for reconnaissance in the Atlantic. Seen here at the Junkers works at Dessau on 23 March 1944 is Ju 290A-5 WNr0180, with the nose-mounted aerials for its FuG 200 'Hohentwiel' radar clearly in evidence.

A close-up of the FuG 200 antennae on the nose of a Ju 290A-5 of FAGr 5.

reduced to one four-barrel MG 131 each forward and aft. This situation with regard to air reconnaissance must considerably limit the possibilities for a renewed submarine campaign unless the Navy can adjust submarine tactics to these circumstances. Sixty planes were requested for Atlantic reconnaissance with a range of about 3,500 kilometers, strong defensive armament, and high altitude radar equipment capable of locating targets within a radius of 200 kilometers. Me-264 had been chosen as the basic type for a plane fulfilling these requirements.

"Comment by Naval Staff to the above information:

"The Commander in Chief, Navy has repeatedly pointed out that a primary condition for a renewed successful submarine campaign is long-distance reconnaissance by planes in sufficient numbers and of satisfactory type. The new submarines, even more so than the earlier types, depend on planes for observation at sea. Their main strength rests in the ability to travel with greater speed under water and thereby to operate successfully under water. Facilities for observing the water surface in order to locate targets are poorer than was the case with the former submarine types. He-177 represents only a poor solution. Meisel."

At the time of this communication, the end of June 1944, the German conduct of war at sea and in the air was fast reaching a stage where operations were limited to paper plans. A final re-organization order, issued on 26 September 1944 by the Air Force General Staff and probably drawn up in an effort to concentrate all air reserves for the defense of the Reich territory, appears to have been of little practical consequence. It read as follows:

"I. As of today the following posts are abolished:

General of the Air Force with Commander in Chief, Navy; Inspector with the General of the Air Force with Commander in Chief, Navy.

"As of today the following posts are established:

General for Sea Affairs of the Air Force, with an Inspector of the sea and sea rescue service of the Air Force.

"The General of Sea Affairs of the Air Force (General des Seewesens der Luftwaffe) holds the rank of a divisional commander. Administratively he is under the Air Force Command, Reich. He will receive directives concerning his authority in matters of supply and inspection directly from the Quartermaster General of the Air Force High Command.

"II. The following duties which have become free as the result of this order are assigned as follows:

"Liaison to the High Command, Navy in all matters of interest to both branches of the Armed Forces: to the General Staff Officer of the Air Force on the Naval Staff (IL);

"Tactical command of air reconnaissance squadrons including Ship Plane Group 196: to General, Air Reconnaissance.

"The courier squadron of the Naval High Command will operate under the orders of the General Staff Officer of the Air Force in the Naval Staff; in every other regard it will be under the authority of the Commander, Air Base Staaken.

"III. Simultaneously with acquiring the function of a commander for sea reconnaissance units, the staff of the General, Air Reconnaissance will be increased by an Inspector, Sea. Date of transfer: 1 November 1944."

By the time this order went into effect, German air operations at sea had ceased for all practical purposes. The war was drawing to a close.

Chapter 2

THE GERMAN NAVAL AIR FORCE, 1933 – SEPTEMBER, 1939

by Oberst (i.G.) Walter Gaul

(1) 1. From 1933 onward Germany was rearming. During this period, the German Naval High Command had begun to realize the possibilities of developing the airplane, within a measurable time, into a potential factor affecting sea power.

In all the contemporary memoranda and in conferences with the planners of the future German Air Force, the Naval War Staff repeatedly emphasized the following ideas on the constitution, command and training of air units:

(a) A single command for all the forces employed would provide the most efficient means of conducting sea warfare.
(b) The success of naval operations is in large measure dependent on an air arm, experienced in conditions at sea and trained in the art of naval warfare.
(c) The aircraft is one of the most important weapons in the conduct of naval warfare. Its ability to scout for naval forces over a wide area lessens the chances of surprise attack; because it can deliver swift counter attacks it has become an invaluable offensive and defensive weapon; it can no longer be regarded as only suitable for ancillary functions, it has become an integral force in naval warfare.

The ultimate aim of all naval planning was therefore to build up a strong naval air arm consisting of reconnaissance, coastal fighter, carrier-borne and ship-borne units as a component part of the Navy.

2. The point of view of the German Air Force High Command was different. C-in-C German Air Force felt that he was responsible for the arming of Germany's air forces and he made it quite plain that he would control all air actions, even over the sea and against naval targets. The need for a single command at sea was only considered necessary when the opposing naval forces were in tactical contact.

The gap occasioned by a dual command in the operational area could be bridged by identical training, combined exercises and a special close liaison between the two commands. It was up to the German Air Force to form and train a single officers' corps, capable of dealing with any task in the air.

(2) In 1935, the German Air Force had not the means to deal successfully with the problems of naval warfare. The views of the Air Force High Command regarding the balance between air and sea power were insufficiently formed. C-in-C German Air Force therefore agreed in principle to build up the Naval Air Force. Thus, in 1935, when the German Air Force was assuming its individual character as the third branch of the Armed Forces, the Air Force Command (Navy) known as Luftkreis VI (See)* was established and an Air Marshal,** who had begun his career as a naval officer, was put in command. He had jurisdiction over the coastal areas of the Baltic and the North Sea with their air personnel, air defenses (fighter and anti-aircraft) and the G.A.F. signals service with its L/T network and radio communications.

In theory, this officer was subordinate to the C-in-C German Air Force, to whom he was responsible for the efficiency of personnel and equipment and for close cooperation with the Navy, but in practice, with his naval outlook and interest in his former service, he tended to rely principally on C-in-C Navy.

A Naval Air Commander,*** as an Air Force Officer commanding naval air operational units and flying personnel was operationally under his command. This officer was to come under the tactical direction of C-in-C Fleet in war time.

The first naval estimate put forward in 1935 was that the Naval Air Force should consist of 25 Staffeln:

3 mixed Coastal Gruppen: 1 close reconnaissance Staffel, 1 long-range reconnaissance Staffel, 1 multi-purpose Staffel for attacks with bombs, mines, torpedoes.

2 ship-borne Gruppen: Each Gruppe consisting of two seaplane Staffeln.

3 mixed carrier-borne Gruppen: Each Gruppe consisting of 1 Fighter Staffel, 1 multi-purpose Staffel, 1 Stuka (Dive-bomber) Staffel.

3 Seaplane Coastal Fighter Staffeln.

Except for use on aircraft carriers, it was intended at that time that the following types of seaplane were to be supplied:

* Later renamed Luftwaffenkommando (See) = Naval Air Command.
** Lieut. General, later General der Flieger Zander.
*** Major General Geisler, also a former naval officer.

For long-range reconnaissance: the Do-18, a twin-engined flying boat of high endurance, seaworthy and defensively well armed but of medium cruising speed.

For close-range reconnaissance and coastal patrols: the single-engined seaplane He-60 and the He-114, both of which could be catapulted and carried in ships. They could develop a high speed, were seaworthy and were armed with two fixed machineguns and one rear gun.

The twin-engined He-59 was to be used for torpedo attacks, for bombing and for the laying of mines and smoke screens. With its high endurance, ample bomb load, dependable seaworthiness and strong armament, it was considered very suitable for these offensive tasks.

For the coastal fighter type the He-51 seaplane was selected.

It was intended that aircraft carriers should carry the following types of planes to be supplied by the German Air Force after conversion:

1. Dive-bomber (Stuka) = Ju-87T ⎫
     ⎬ undergoing tests.
2. Fighter Bf-109T ⎭

3. Multi-purpose plane Fieseler Fi-167 – under construction.

The Heinkel He 60 seaplane, which could be carried in ships and catapult launched, was used for close-range reconnaissance and coastal patrols.

Heinkel's He 114 performed similar duties to those of the He 60, which it was designed to succeed. Improvements included an all-metal fuselage, in place of the He 60's largely fabric-covered structure.

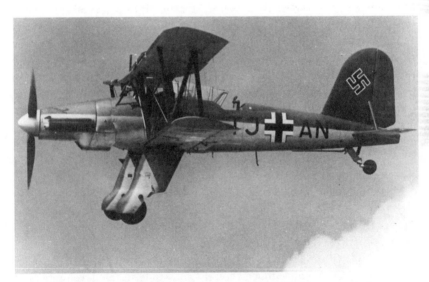

If prizes were awarded for inelegance, the Fieseler Fi 167, represented here by an Fi 167A-05, would be a prime candidate. The aircraft was designed as a carrier-borne multi-purpose attack aircraft when Germany's first aircraft carrier, the Graf Zeppelin, *was under construction. Although no carriers were completed, coastal trials of the Fi 167 were undertaken in the Netherlands, but all were withdrawn by 1943.*

The planes, special equipment and weapons, except mines and torpe-does, were designed and developed by the German Air Force construction departments according to naval specifications; they were built in German Air Force factories and supplied to the Naval Air Force by the Air Ministry.

In the first stage of the expansion program, the ground organization for the Baltic and North Sea areas included the seaplane bases of Pillau, Nest, Swinemünde, Bug auf Rügen, Grossenbrode, Kiel, Wilhelmshaven, List, Hörnum, Norderney and Borkum; it was planned to use Bremerhaven and Kiel-Holtenau as carrier bases.

Schools were opened at Warnemünde and Bug auf Rügen for the train-ing of aircrews and ground personnel.

The Navy transferred to the German Air Force 60 to 80 naval officers to fill the various command posts and to provide pilots and observers. Naval officers on the reserve and retired lists were recalled to take up administrative and other posts in the ground organization.

To protect the interests and requirements of the Navy, officers were appointed to the German Air Ministry in the Personnel, Organization and Supply Divisions.

The liaison between the two services was carried out by their respective War Staffs through specially appointed liaison officers; a typical example was to be found in the Operations Division of these staffs.

The German Air Force Staff Officer appointed for liaison duties to the Naval War Staff was an ex-naval officer. He presented the naval specifica-tions regarding technical developments and tactical improvements in flying equipment and weapons; he furthered the expansion of the supply, training and ground organization and made arrangements for the partic-ipation of German Air Force formations in fleet exercises. His counterpart in the Air War Staff was a naval staff officer.

In 1935, therefore, a naval air service was coming into existence, entirely manned by naval personnel and supported by a supply and ground organization, naval in character. C-in-C German Air Force thereby recog-nized the need for a special branch of the German Air Force to serve the German Navy in naval warfare and undertook to maintain and expand this force in line with the Navy's expansion.

From 1935 to 1938 the Naval High Command planned a further expan-sion of the fleet and gave much thought and study to the development of the Air Force in naval warfare. The Naval War Staff came to the conclu-sion that the 25 Staffeln program was no longer adequate, especially in the event of war with a naval power such as Great Britain. Fast aircraft were required to reconnoiter and attack the Channel harbors and bases in the west and those of the eastern Baltic in the east. Furthermore, the Naval

Staff was not satisfied with the naval air situation in the event of war and they considered that the German Air Force, whose main preoccupation was a continental war, could not at all times fulfill the requirements of German naval strategy. They considered that the Navy should be in a position to deal independently with the naval air situation and control their own naval air forces.

In pursuit of this policy, Naval High Command proposed to C-in-C German Air Force, first in 1936 and later in 1938, a modified form of the 62 Staffeln program. This program* provided for:

29 multi-purpose Staffeln	(He-115)
9 flying-boat Staffeln	(Do-18)
3 long-range reconnaissance Staffeln	(later types of land aircraft)**
6 long-range bomber Staffeln	(later types of land aircraft)
7 ship-borne Staffeln	
12 carrier-borne Staffeln	(for the two aircraft carriers in project)

(3) On 11 January, 1935, C-in-C Navy proposed to C-in-C German Air Force a scheme for the training of Naval Air Observers.

In this scheme 80% of the observers were to be drawn from officers of the Naval Officers' Corps who had the following qualifications:

1. Graduation from Naval College after three years' training.
2. Three years' service at sea as a Lieutenant and qualification as Officer of the Watch in minor units.

Subsequently, these officers were to serve as observers in the Naval Air Force for three years; 20% would then be transferred on a voluntary basis to the German Air Force while the rest would revert to naval duties.

An amendment to this scheme was proposed by C-in-C Navy on 5 May during a conference. He proposed that 100%, rather than 80%, of the Naval Air Observers should be drawn from the Navy. This scheme would be in full operation by 1940, up to which time a temporary plan would operate, by which officers would be selected after passing their final examination for Lieutenant and part of their sea training would be omitted. An additional entry of 140 Naval Cadets per year was contemplated to replace the officers selected for the Naval Air Service.

* In 1936 the German Air Force made it known unofficially that the expansion of the Naval Air Force might be completed in two stages by 1942 within the framework of the total rearmament.
** Later types of German Air Force bomber and reconnaissance aircraft for use in the Channel and in attacks on fleet bases.

This proposal was unacceptable to the German Air Force, whose aim was to make use of the Navy's training facilities to build up an adequate number of aircrews capable of dealing with air problems over the sea.

No decision could be reached and the outbreak of the war made other arrangements necessary.

(4) The German Air Force did not feel inclined to give up control of aerial warfare in any of its aspects. They made a very detailed study in order to gain a practical approach to the air/sea problem in their training establishments and schools during war courses.

On the practical side, the Navy helped in the training by founding the "Naval Training Staff for the Air Force", in which Air Force officers of the first line air units were instructed in relevant naval subjects, strategy and tactics. The aerial exercises with the fleet in which Air Force formations took part were performed principally by the "Greifswald Training Geschwader".

From these maneuvers, no doubt, part of the background for the general air policy was evolved at that time, and its application was envisaged in a war with the western powers. This policy, together with the production capacity of the German aircraft industry, influenced the reaction of the Air Force to the "62 Staffeln program" and brought about a definite statement of policy regarding the Naval Air Force.

On 24 November, 1938 a meeting was called between representatives of the Operations Division of both War Staffs. The Chief of the General Staff of the Air Force* stated:

"The projected expansion program of the German Air Force, due to be completed by the spring of 1942, provides for the formation of 58 bomber Geschwader, 16 fighter Geschwader and a sixfold increase of the anti-aircraft defenses.

Thirteen of these bomber Geschwader are earmarked for air/sea warfare.

In view of the productive capacity of the German Aircraft Industry, the long-term policy of the Air Force can be carried out only if construction is entirely concentrated on two types of aircraft for the future air forces, namely, Ju-88 and He-177.

A simultaneous expansion of the Naval Air Force from 25 to 62 Staffeln is impossible and appears unnecessary since the Air Force is prepared to take over all offensive tasks and part of the reconnaissance duties with its thirteen bomber Geschwader detailed for air/sea warfare . . . . ."

The Chief of the General Staff of the Air Force also announced impending changes in general organization, by which the Naval Air Command

* General Maj. Stumpf.

86

would be abolished. This change of Air Force policy meant that the Navy would have to give up independent control of the Naval Air Arm, thus placing the Naval War Staff in a very difficult position. They protested vigorously against the change in organization and the reduction of forces, but found the Air Staff uncompromising.

(5) This clash of opinions could only be settled by the C's-in-C of the two services, who met in conference on 27 January, 1939.

The agreement reached and decisions made at this conference were issued in the memorandum of that date and signed by both C's-in-C.

In this conference, agreement was reached on the following matters:

(1) Operational areas: England and those sea areas in which naval forces were unable to operate were to be regarded as the Air Force operational areas.

(2) Responsibility for air reconnaissance at sea: the Navy was responsible for the execution of their own reconnaissance in the course of operations; it was recommended that there should be a constant exchange of information, which would be facilitated by having the two headquarters close to one another.

(3) Participation of the Air Force in naval actions: it was decided that tactical intervention by the Air Force in naval actions should take place only when requested by the Navy or if generally agreed upon beforehand.

It was decided that each minelaying operation should have the previous concurrence of the Navy, with the proviso that the Air Force should have freedom of action in waters beyond the reach of naval forces.

The Naval Air Force would be brought up to the following strength by 1941:

9 long-range reconnaissance Staffeln,
12 multi-purpose Staffeln,
12 carrier-borne Staffeln,
 2 ship-borne Staffeln.

C-in-C Air Force gave the assurance that a further increase might be expected after 1941.

Moreover, it was decided that the air defense of the naval fortress areas, except for fighter forces and the Air Reporting and Warning Service, should be the responsibility of C-in-C Navy.

The following decisions were made regarding changes in the organization:

(1) On 1 February, 1939, the position of Air Marshal on the Staff of C-in-C Navy* would be created; thereby Naval Air Command would be abolished and its activities would cease at the latest on 1 April, 1939.

(2) The administration and supply of the entire naval air ground organization would be abolished and taken over by the Air Force Administrative Commands I, III, XI from 1 April, 1939. This applied also to the naval air training establishments, but not to the Naval Air Equipment Branch, which remained in existence and would come territorially under Air Force Administrative Command XI.

(3) C-in-C Air Force further approved the appointment of a general staff officer of the Air Force who would act as adviser to C-in-C Navy on tactical questions and would be responsible for liaison between the two staffs.

(6) The decisions and agreements reached in the memorandum meant that the Navy had to give up their ambition to set up an independent Naval Air Force. With the abolition of the Naval Air Command, the Naval Air Force had lost its naval character and such forces as were left were relegated to the functions of an auxiliary service.

Perhaps the assurance which C-in-C Air Force gave C-in-C Navy that 13 bomber Geschwader would be detailed for naval warfare, together with the weight which C-in-C Air Force carried in German political and economic circles may have influenced C-in-C Navy in his acceptance of the terms and implications of this memorandum.

By its terms, the Air Force took over the reconnaissance of enemy naval bases and coastal areas and undertook to attack the Home Fleet and its bases and Britain's sea-borne trade. Therefore, in a future war with Britain, the Navy would not only have to rely on the capability and fighting efficiency of the Air Force air crews, but would also have to ensure Air War Staff's co-operation.

The Naval High Command had therefore to revise their policy; they had to gain the interest of the Air War Staff in order to obtain a favorable consideration of all naval air problems, and they assisted the Air Force theoretically and practically by providing training facilities in the form of fleet exercises and above all, helped to expand and perfect the communications systems between the two operational headquarters. The Air Force, on the other hand, by getting the terms accepted, had established the right to exert air power over the sea and had stretched their tentacles in to the realm of sea power. They shouldered greater responsibilities from now on

* See appendix No. I – Organization

and continued in their efforts to cope with the tasks which would confront them in the event of a war with England.

In the spring of 1939, Lieut. General Geisler, who had been Naval Air Commander, was transferred to Luftflotte 2 for special duties. His instructions were to investigate all questions relative to the preparation for and conduct of naval air warfare and to determine the requirements for training organization and command in accordance with Air Officer Commanding Luftflotte 2's instructions. His findings, which led to selection of targets in the event of a war with Great Britain, were approved by the Air Force High Command. They can be summed up as follows:

"The main target for the Air Force is the destruction of the British fleet, but, in 1939, this objective is out of the question as the number of available aircraft with the required radius of action is insufficient, their armament is not yet adequate and there are not yet enough well trained aircrews for the assignment. The immediate alternative target within our reach is the crippling of the Aircraft Production Industry, by bombing of aircraft factories and by stopping the flow of supplies to the British Isles, thus contributing to the blockade of the British Isles."

(7) Neither the Air Force nor the Naval Air Force was ready for war when Britain declared war on Germany on 3 September, 1939.

As the building programs were not due to be completed till 1941, most units were not up to strength.

The Naval Air Force had immediately available:

14 Coastal Staffeln consisting of He-59 and Do-18. Certain types were undergoing trials such as He-115 and Blohm Voss 138 (BV-138). One ship-borne Staffel of Ar-196 was available. Four carrier-borne Staffeln were in process of formation.

The forces were divided between the North Sea and Baltic and were commanded by the Naval Air Commanders, West and East respectively, who, for tactical purposes, came under the Naval Commanders in those areas, i.e. C's-in-C Groups West and East.

After the completion of operations against Poland, the main war effort switched to the west. Naval Air Commander West's forces were increased to eleven Coastal Staffeln, consisting of five long-range reconnaissance Staffeln and six multi-purpose Staffeln.

It was estimated that 90 to 130 seaplanes were ready for service; owing to the conversion to He-115, one to two Staffeln could not be brought into the front line.

The personnel were efficient and their morale high, whilst the general state of the equipment could be considered good.

On the other hand, the state of readiness for offensive operations could not be regarded as satisfactory because the He-59 were thought to be too slow for offensive bombing and the aerial torpedo had not been sufficiently perfected for use under service conditions.

Minelaying was in abeyance on the express orders of Naval War Staff.

The German Air Force held the following forces in readiness for naval air warfare with Great Britain:

(1) From Luftflotte 3, for targets on the mainland, a total of 3 bomber Gruppen from the Third and Fourth Fliegerdivisionen, plus the requisite reconnaissance Staffeln.

(2) From Luftflotte 2, for attacking naval targets, 2 bomber Gruppen from Bomber Geschwader 26, 3 bomber Gruppen from Bomber Geschwader 27 and one bomber Gruppe from Bomber Geschwader 28 as far as the proficiency of the flying personnel would allow.

On 3 September, 1939 General Geisler received orders to form the Tenth Fliegerdivision.

It consisted of First and Second Gruppen of Bomber Geschwader 26 and Bomber Geschwader 30, which was in process of formation, and represented a total of 50 to 60 serviceable He-111 and ten to fifteen serviceable Ju-88.

In an emergency, the units of the Greifswald Training Geschwader which were sufficiently trained could be called upon, supported by the reconnaissance planes provided by Luftflotte 2.

The fighter forces available in northwestern Germany and its coastal areas consisted of Fighter Geschwader 1 and 26.

One Gruppe of Fighter Geschwader 26 was being converted into twin-engined Me-110; this was considered an important and necessary measure for the protection of the fleet in the Heligoland Bight.

The Memorandum of 27 January, 1939

At the conference held on 27 January, 1939, C-in-C Air Force and C-in-C Navy discussed the following points and decided as follows:

I. Operations

(1) *Operational areas*

It is agreed that the main effort of the Air Force is to be directed against England and those sea areas where naval action is impracticable. Should the radius of action of the Air Force units permit of operations beyond those areas, and should there be an encroachment on the

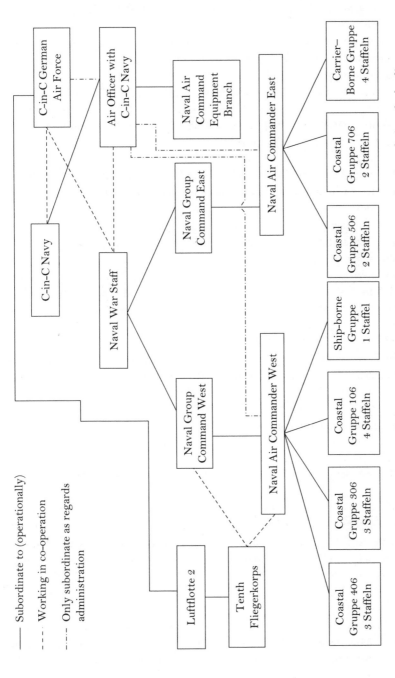

Key:

— Subordinate to (operationally)

--- Working in co-operation

--- Only subordinate as regards administration

C-in-C German Air Force

Air Officer with C-in-C Navy

C-in-C Navy

Naval Air Command Equipment Branch

Naval War Staff

Naval Group Command East

Naval Group Command West

Naval Air Commander East

Naval Air Commander West

Luftflotte 2

Tenth Fliegerkorps

Carrier-Borne Gruppe 4 Staffeln

Coastal Gruppe 706 2 Staffeln

Coastal Gruppe 506 2 Staffeln

Ship-borne Gruppe 1 Staffel

Coastal Gruppe 106 4 Staffeln

Coastal Gruppe 306 3 Staffeln

Coastal Gruppe 406 3 Staffeln

Organization of the Navy and the German Air Force at the outbreak of war, September 1939, showing relation of subordinate Commands and co-ordination naval operational areas, an understanding with the Navy must be reached.

(2) *Reconnaissance*

C-in-C Air Force is in no way responsible for naval reconnaissance. Any sea reconnaissance carried out for naval purposes is a naval commitment.

(3) A constant and reciprocal exchange of information is to be ensured by placing the headquarters close to one another. This constant co-oper-ation is intended to achieve co-ordination and mutual support in the military measures of both services.

(4) *Participation in naval actions*

The tactical participation of the Air Force in naval actions (actions between ships) is only to take place when requested by the Navy or by general consent. The planned participation in naval actions, within measurable time, refers only to the Naval Air Force, as this force is trained within the framework of the Navy for naval actions.

(5) *Minelaying*

All minelaying operations will be performed in agreement with the Navy. From the outset, certain coastal areas, closed to naval forces, can be assigned to the Air Force for minelaying operations.

II. Strength and equipment of the Naval Air Force

Cs-in-C Navy and Air Force are in agreement as to the strength of the establishment, namely, that C-in-C Air Force will provide, up to and including 1941, the following forces for the purposes of naval air warfare:

9 long-range reconnaissance Staffeln
18 multi-purpose   "
12 carrier-borne   "
2 ship-borne   "

C-in-C Navy requests that, in principle, only those types of planes known to be suitable be supplied for naval air purposes. C-in-C Air Force agrees to increase the efficiency of the Naval Air Force in accordance with the wishes of C-in-C Navy and to ensure that the aircraft provided will satisfy naval requirements.

III. Coastal Air Defense

C-in-C Navy concurs in the arrangements for the air defense of coastal areas contained in the top secret order "Az IIb 13 Nr 1400/38 g.K." of C-in-C Air Force General Staff, 2nd Division (IIIb) issued by the Air Ministry on 18 June, 1938.

In accordance with this order, C-in-C Navy retains the responsibility for the air defense of the naval fortress areas. The Aircraft Reporting Service at sea is a naval commitment. All reports of enemy aircraft are to be passed direct or routed via the Naval Defense Reporting Service to the Aircraft Reporting Service.

IV. Changes in the Organization

C-in-C Air Force informs C-in-C Navy that an Air Force Officer will be attached to C-in-C Navy on 1 February. The Naval Air Force Command will thereby be abolished and will cease to function at a date to be determined (not later than 1 April). The Air Force Officer attached to C-in-C Navy is, in peace time, tactically subordinate to C-in-C Air Force, and in war time to C-in-C Navy. In peace time, he will be in command of all naval air personnel. He is at the same time Inspector of Air Force flying personnel. As such he will work under the direction of the Head of the Training Division of the Air Ministry.

In order that C-in-C Navy's training requirements may be satisfied in full, the Air Force Officer attached to C-in-C Navy is directed to work in closest co-operation with the Navy; he is also to attend carefully to the wishes of C-in-C Navy. Any instructions issued by the Head of the Training Division of the Air Ministry on the training of naval air personnel are to be submitted to C-in-C Navy before being forwarded to C-in-C Air Force.

C-in-C Air Force concurs in C-in-C Navy's proposal that in addition to the Air Officer attached to C-in-C Navy, a General Staff Officer be appointed to the Naval High Command. The Naval Air Command, planned to function up to 1 April, 1939, will be abolished. The administration and supply services of the Naval Ground Organization are to be transferred to the Air Force Administrative Commands I, III and XI on a date to be fixed later. The same applies to naval air training establishments but not to the Naval Air Equipment Branch, which is to continue to function and will come territorially under the Air Administrative Command XI. The Air Force Officer attached to C-in-C Navy is authorized, both in peace and in war, to issue direct orders to the Equipment Branch regarding supplies for the naval air units.

Should any amendment to the above decisions and organization be necessary, a meeting will be arranged to take place in six months' time.

PART II

THE AIR WAR AT SEA –
NAVY AND LUFTWAFFE VIEWS

This section gives two overviews of how Germany waged the air war at sea, one from a Navy perceptive (done postwar) and one, done in 1944 when most of the operations had been concluded, from a Luftwaffe perspective (intended for internal use only). Together, they provide the broad course of these air operations.

Chapter 3

A SURVEY FROM THE NAVAL POINT OF VIEW OF THE ORGANIZATION OF THE GERMAN AIR FORCE FOR OPERATIONS OVER THE SEA, 1939–1945

By Eberhard Weichold, Vice Admiral of the former German Navy.

A. Development of the Luftwaffe Organization

1. The origin of the problem

1. In war each side pursues the object of imposing its will on the opponent, using force. This force must be sufficiently effective to persuade the opponent to submit to the political conditions of the other side. In previous wars such means of force could be applied against men and equipment either on land or on the sea, and the army and the fleet were thus the agents of the force. Weapons were evolved which suited either of these two methods.

2. The discovery of the aircraft involved a new means of war, with the air as its medium. As this medium extends equally over the land and the sea, the new weapon could be used to support the old means of warfare on land and on sea, thus increasing their effectiveness, and reducing the effectiveness of the opponent's weapons. On this principle an aircraft necessarily becomes a weapon of land and sea warfare. This combination led to increased offensive power on land and at sea, and showed the old weapons of land or sea warfare to be decisively inferior. The association of offensive power on land, or on the sea, with air power against a battle target demands the closest co-operation between the forces concerned; in other words an aircraft, as a means of war, is a weapon of land or sea warfare. Resulting from this there will have to be definite types of aircraft, of training, of tactics and especially of organization for each branch of an Air Force.

3. On the other hand the air, as the third medium, possesses an independent character, and air weapons offer an independent opportunity of action against land or sea targets. As a result the enemy's defensive

96

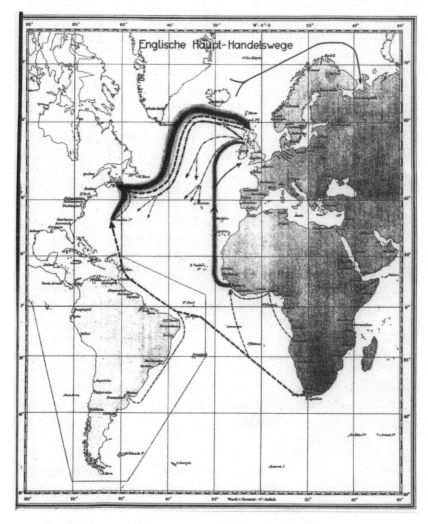

Britain's maritime lifelines as they were viewed by the Kriegsmarine during the war. (Korvettenkapitan Assmann, Aufgaben und Probleme der Deutschen Seekriegfuhrung, 11/1941, USNARA RG 547 Box 52)

capacity on land or at sea against attacks in the same medium will be considerably affected. The speed and range of aircraft enable this means of pressure to be exerted over extensive areas and against the greatest number of people. This new offensive power has thus become an independent factor in warfare, possessing the character of an independent third fighting service. The organization of this part of an Air Force requires very different treatment from the parts of the Air Force attached to the other two fighting services.

97

4. Regarded from this point of view, the organization of air-power for these two different functions would require entirely separate treatment, and yet there are serious objections to this. The aircraft, considered as an aerodynamic instrument, is fundamentally the same for both these functions, and its development as such is still in a fluid state. Developments in construction, ground organization, flying training, and the considerable concomitant resources and material, are largely similar for both functions. Thus, technical considerations would seem to impose a unification of both parts of the Air Force. Similarly, the purely military requirement of maximum concentration of associated offensive weapons imposes uniformity, and theoretically these considerations lead to the desire for a single Air Force.

5. The variety of the above-mentioned factors shows that the organization of an Air Force must take into account fundamental, numerous and often contradictory points of view. Moreover, individual countries have to consider their widely varying geographical conditions, war aims, concentration of resources and other factors. Thus individual requirements emphasize the fundamental divergences, and the organization of an Air Force will vary from one country to another.

6. The only conclusion theoretically, and from practical experience, is that there is no ideal solution or standard, and the organizer must study the individual case in an unprejudiced manner, in order to arrive at a compromise solution which will suit present reality.

    To perform this task, knowledge of the problems of other organizers and of their experiments will be important. It is well known that practice and theory often diverge, and that the practical experience of other people with other views often enriches one's own thoughts. In the light of these thoughts an appreciation of the organization of the German Luftwaffe in its operations over the sea between 1939 and 1945 will now be given. It must at once be admitted that this appreciation from the naval point of view will not be free from a certain bias, however much one may try to remain unprejudiced.

2. The development of the German Air Force in peacetime

7. From 1933 onwards two opposed principles marked the employment of the Luftwaffe. On the one hand the Navy required the use of aircraft as a means of sea warfare, and on the other the High Command of the Luftwaffe required aircraft for operations of the independent Air Force.

    The Navy wanted the creation of a powerful Naval Air Arm, embracing all aircraft types, as a functional branch of the Navy. The aim was to create an organization which would possess single control of all methods of naval warfare, including surface, submarine and air operations. In this respect the aircraft was not an independent weapon over the sea, neither was it merely an aid to naval operations, but an integral part of sea-power. This conception led to the demand for flying formations manned by men drawn from the Fleet, whose tactical training must take place within the framework of the Navy, and whose flying personnel and ground organization must conform to the needs of the naval warfare.

8. On the other hand the High Command of the Luftwaffe took the extreme opposite view, by aiming at single control of all the tasks that would be required of aircraft, including operations over the sea and against targets at sea. No departure from this principle was envisaged, except for air operations connected with tactical contact of naval forces at sea. However, the High Command of the Luftwaffe, in the first years of the development of this new arm, had no adequate authority to insist on these views, which were opposed to those of the Navy, and in 1935 agreed temporarily to a compromise solution, which largely met the wishes of the Navy. A special branch of the Luftwaffe for naval operations was constituted in co-operation with Navy; in war the Navy was to control and operate this branch.

9. However, in the succeeding years the High Command of the Luftwaffe again made a fundamental claim to its own conduct of operations over the sea. Starting with the premise that it would necessarily have to conduct air operations over the sea against harbors and armament centers of an island country, the operational Luftwaffe included among its targets (also targets of the Navy) the merchant ships and warships of this island opponent. This extension of targets encroached on the claims of the Navy for responsibility at sea, and constituted a radical departure from the principle of single control in the war at sea. To implement this development, particular units of the Luftwaffe were allocated for war across the sea and in the sea areas. In January 1939 an agreement between the Navy and the Luftwaffe secured for the High Command of the Luftwaffe the responsibility for mining operations in the enemy's coastal waters, and for action against enemy ships at sea; also for participation in the tactical actions of naval forces when requested by the Navy, and for air reconnaissance in connection with these operations. Naval air formations of the Navy were confined to reconnaissance tasks for naval forces, and to operations when two fleets were in contact.

This radical renunciation by the Navy of single control of all the means of warfare at sea marked the abandonment of the compromise solution of 1935, and led to a further withdrawal of the Navy from control of air operations in its own areas. Because of the personal position of the Commander-in-Chief Luftwaffe within the National Socialist state, the Navy found itself unable to resist this development.

10. This shifting of responsibility consequently made itself felt in the field of equipment. In the middle of 1939 the Navy disposed of only 14 coastal reconnaissance Staffeln, and one ship-borne Staffel, for use in tactical operations under their control, whereas for air war against England the operational Luftwaffe was to have 27 Staffeln, or nearly double, of which 7 Staffeln were for operations against targets at sea. Thus, apart from the weak German naval forces, it was the Luftwaffe that possessed the offensive weapon which appeared most competent to attack England, in spite of her sea-superiority. And the intention was considerably to increase these forces of the Luftwaffe; consequently in case of war with Great Britain the principal operations would become a main responsibility of the operational Luftwaffe. The recognition of the value of this new offensive weapon, and the temporary German ascendancy in this field led to an under-estimation of the influence of British sea-power. Undoubtedly this erroneous estimate also encouraged Germany to pursue political aims which bore no relation to the current orthodox estimate of land and sea power throughout the world. This misinterpretation of the relative importance of the three fighting services characterizes not only the last years of peace, but also the decisive part of the war of 1939/45.

3. The development of the Luftwaffe organization in the early part of the war

11. The tendency of the immediate pre-war period was for the High Command of the Luftwaffe to assume responsibility for all air operations, and when war came, the operational Luftwaffe conducted operations in sea areas, with the Navy working alongside them. Operational tasks of aircraft over the sea were regarded as the sole responsibility of the Luftwaffe, as were operations against ship targets, which were also targets of the naval forces. Even when air units took part in naval operations the conduct of the air operations was controlled by the Luftwaffe. Air mining operations off the enemy's coast, which to a great extent encroached on the functions of naval forces, were regarded by the Commander-in-Chief, Luftwaffe, as his own responsibility. He could not, however, hinder the initial mining operations by units of the Naval Air Arm, which had been specially trained for this purpose.

The Luftwaffe thus controlled the tasks of air formations over the sea, although the Navy was also controlling its own aircraft. In one operational area there was thus dual control of air operations. The resulting difficulties provided the first test of the existing organization of the German Air Force.

12. As the war proceeded, preponderating control of the Luftwaffe over air operations increased to the disadvantage of the Naval Air Arm, and soon the latter were no longer able to carry out the strictly naval reconnaissance tasks, which had to be allocated to formations of the operational Luftwaffe. Thus, in the first few months of the war the Navy had already lost its fight for the operational and technical control of air operations over the sea. The winter of 1939/40 was marked by a further decline in the influence of the Naval Air Arm, for the German Naval Staff was forced by the necessities of the naval war to demand a progressively increasing participation by the operational Luftwaffe in operations over the sea. This brought increased prestige to the Luftwaffe in its fight against Great Britain, at the cost not only of the Naval Air Arm, but also of the Navy itself.

13. This effect came not solely from the development of the Luftwaffe as a factor in the fight, but also from the apparent inactivity of the German Fleet. In the first phase of the war, characterized by the actions in the North Sea, German naval forces were able to carry out very few effective operations against the British Navy. Only the U-boats in the Atlantic, and destroyers on the east coast of England, could be employed. The larger German surface units, which could only gradually be brought to a state of readiness for action, found no scope in the North Sea; for because of the unequal forces a fleet action could not be sought, neither was vital British shipping to be found in this area.

Moreover, there was no compelling necessity for co-operation between naval and air forces, as had been advocated by the Navy during peace exercises. There was not one instance of naval forces being brought in contact with an enemy through air reconnaissance. From this the Luftwaffe concluded that war experience had not confirmed peacetime conception of the importance of the Navy. On the other hand the employment of the Luftwaffe on and across the sea appeared to prove its merit in interrupting the enemy's imports and even in attacks on sea targets. This overrating of its own possibilities and under-estimation of the purely naval means of war caused the Luftwaffe increasingly to undervalue the importance of the Naval Air Arm. Moreover the inferiority of float planes of the Naval Air Arm compared with land planes of the operational Luftwaffe, and the concentration in the first year on new types for the latter only, emphasized the difference in practical performance between the two kinds of aircraft. Since all the tasks of the Naval Air Arm had also necessarily to be performed by units of the operational Luftwaffe, the continuance of the former seemed to be unjustified, a view which was upheld by the High Command of the Luftwaffe. Advocates of a single Air Force hoped shortly to overcome the only previous advantage of the Naval Air Arm, namely that it had enjoyed specialized training in naval warfare. The further course of the war, beyond the North Sea, with its new problems of fighting British sea communications, would show whether joint naval operations between naval forces and air formations of the operational Luftwaffe would be necessary. This point of view was the second test of Luftwaffe organization.

14. The transfer from the Naval Air Arm to the operational Luftwaffe of the principal tasks over the sea had another result. In practice the development of a single Air Force strengthens its power of operational concentration. Air units normally allocated for naval tasks, could equally be used for land tasks, just as the main body of the operational Luftwaffe could be temporarily concentrated for tasks over the sea. This theoretically universal application of the operational Luftwaffe was claimed by the advocates of the single Air Force as its greatest advantage. Assuming that the operational Luftwaffe could be effectively trained for naval tasks and that it could be quickly diverted from land to sea tasks under the ever changing circumstances of sea warfare, it would still only be possible to apply this principle if involvement in land operations did not prejudice support for naval operations. Heavy wastage or unavoidable commitment of the single Air Force on the land fronts would vitiate the advantage of universal employment, whereas the Naval Air Arm, whose aircraft could not be used over the land, would always be a part of the naval forces.

The third test of the Luftwaffe organization in relation to naval requirements lay in the practical working of the idea of a single Luftwaffe.

15. Finally the creation of a single Luftwaffe had a further psychological consequence. Advocates of this idea aimed at the creation of a single corps of air officers and a single tradition for which they claimed many advantages. Since these advocates believed principally in an operational use of the new Air Force on the lines of Douhet's teachings, and as nearly all the officers of this third arm were drawn from the Army, and thought in terms of continental warfare, there was little hope that the importance of naval air operations would be duly appreciated. The fourth and most important test of the soundness of the Luftwaffe organization lay in the practical consequence of this psychological approach to a world war, which was therefore essentially a sea war; for this attitude governed all associated questions of the employment of

an Air Force. There is no doubt that a powerful Naval Air Arm, manned by officers conversant with naval problems, would have constituted a counter-weight to the operational conception of the High Command of the Luftwaffe.

16. The Navy did not give up the operational control of the Naval Air Arm until April 1942, but already in the first phase of the war the operational Luftwaffe had assumed preponderating control of air operations over the sea. In practice this meant that a single Air Force, embracing the extreme theoretical principle of unity of control, had been established. The Luftwaffe, as the third branch of the fighting forces with an independent status, led an entirely separate life; and its use in conjunction with the other two services, especially the Navy, depended entirely on its own appreciation of the necessity. This considerable independence was further increased by the fact that the third branch of the German Armed Forces was not subjected to higher control. The Supreme Command of the Armed Forces (OKW) was merely a working advisory staff for Hitler, which had no executive power, least of all over the Luftwaffe.

But with this far-reaching independence the High Command of the Luftwaffe bore full and sole responsibility for the success or failure of its own operations, including operations of the other services insofar as aircraft were needed. In the field of naval warfare this implied responsibility for air participation and for the provision or failure to provide air resources for the proper exercise of seapower.

B. The Achievements of the Luftwaffe in cooperation with naval warfare

17. We will now consider the achievements of the Luftwaffe in association with surface and submarine naval warfare; this does not include air operations across the sea, or air warfare over England. It will be shown that even the complete operational use of a single Luftwaffe is incapable of replacing sea power or of eliminating that of the opponent.

Independent operations of the Luftwaffe on the sea and against ship targets are not considered here, because they have no connection with operations of naval forces. The considerable effects of the Luftwaffe's naval operations were not conditioned by the organization of a single Air Force, for similar successes could have fallen to the units of a Naval Air Arm. Though the operational Luftwaffe was in a position to concentrate its forces more extensively, this advantage would have disappeared through the greater suitability for sea-air operations of a properly equipped and tactically trained Naval Air Arm. Although the

*Photographed in Norway in the spring of 1942, this late-production
Heinkel He 115C-1 of 1./Kü.Fl.Gr.906 has a fixed 20mm MG 151
cannon beneath the port side of its nose.*

achievements of the Luftwaffe against sea targets were considerable
throughout the war, and influenced the naval situation, (as during the
Norwegian campaign and the occupation of Crete) yet these operations cannot form a criterion in relation to naval operations.

The following examination is therefore confined to that aspect of
the conduct of the naval war in which the Luftwaffe definitely affected
the use of naval forces.

18. 1. *The air mining war against the coast of Britain*

In the first phase of the war, mining operations against the east coast
of England were one of the few means of attacking British shipping in
the North Sea. From the middle of October 1939 this mine warfare
was conducted by the destroyers of the German Navy, and showed
visible results. The effect was even bigger than was shown by actual
sinkings. The German Naval Staff then regarded the intensification of
this method of warfare as the most effective means of attacking the
British war economy, and endeavored to obtain the participation of the
Luftwaffe. The Navy first used its own multi-purpose aircraft, but as
there were few of these available, the total effect of mining from the

air could only be small. The Naval Staff pressed for support from the Luftwaffe for mining operations, which the Commander-in-Chief of the Luftwaffe regarded as his responsibility. But as for technical reasons, a large effort by the operational Luftwaffe would not be possible for a considerable time, the air staff at that time fundamentally opposed an early use of air mines. After lengthy argument between the Navy and the Luftwaffe, the Staff of the latter at the end of February 1940 obtained from Hitler an order to stop air mining operations, even by the Naval Air Arm, until such time as the operational forces available would be sufficient to carry out a large-scale mining operation.

But in the meantime the British authorities had examined the new firing mechanism of an unexploded mine, which enabled them to prepare technical, protective and sweeping methods and to organize against the later extensive use of this weapon.

Viewed as a whole it is very doubtful whether it was right to employ the weak Naval Air Arm in 1939 for the first dropping of air mines, but on the other hand the postponement required by the Luftwaffe was equally unsuitable, in view of the British discovery. Since air mines were first used to increase the effect of minelaying by surface forces, this support should have been continued with such Luftwaffe forces as were available at the time. But the air mining campaign, whose chief value lay in surprise and concentration, lapsed into spasmodic undertakings, and met with the most varied obstructions.

Without being categorical as to which of the two centers of control – the Navy, or the High Command of the Luftwaffe – was right, it can be asserted that the existence of the dual organization prevented effective action against British sea communications, and this could have been avoided with single control of operations.

19. 2. *Development and use of the torpedo-bomber*

The use of this weapon by the British had brought them decisive success, such as the heavy losses of the Italian Fleet at Taranto and at Matapan, the interruption of German Atlantic warfare through the torpedoing of *Gneisenau* in Brest on 6 April 1942, and of *Luetzow* off the Norwegian coast on 13 June 1941, and finally the sinking of the *Bismarck*.

On the other hand the Germans had difficulties in developing this weapon. The dual organization of the aircraft used for war against Britain envisaged the torpedo as a weapon of the Naval Air Arm, and in view of the heavy commitments for torpedoes for U-boats, the production of torpedoes for aircraft was marked by difficulties and delays.

A Heinkel He 111H-6 with a brace of practice LT F5b torpedoes mounted on PVC underfuselage racks.

An L10 glider torpedo, showing the detachable wing and tail surfaces.

This Heinkel He 111E-4 carries a glider torpedo, fitted with wings and tail to enable it to be released at greater heights and ranges. The flying surfaces detached before the weapon entered the water.

And yet the first months of the war revealed torpedo-bombers of the Naval Air Arm as a practical weapon.

Already in the first phase of the war the Naval Air Arm had been replaced by the operational Luftwaffe as the agent for offensive air action against sea targets, and no further development took place in types or weapons for naval air warfare. But the Luftwaffe itself had not yet provided torpedoes for its own units engaged in sea warfare, since it had not appreciated the value of the weapon and was convinced that better results could be obtained by bombs than by tactically difficult

107

This Junkers Ju 88A-4 was evaluated at Gotenhafen as a carrier for a pair of L10 glider torpedoes, one being carried beneath each wing.

Focke-Wulf Fw 190A-5/U14 torpedo fighter WNr 871, the first of two prototypes, carries an LTF 5b torpedo on an adapted ETC 501 fuselage rack. The fighter required an enlarged fin, strengthened undercarriage and a lengthened tailwheel leg to enable it to carry the weapon.

torpedo attacks. The Commander-in-Chief of the Luftwaffe actually obtained from Hitler a temporary order forbidding the further provision of air torpedoes, and did not alter his mind until the further operations of British torpedo-bombers had demonstrated the great effectiveness of this weapon. Even then the Luftwaffe was able to carry out its program only because it was the inheritor of the Naval Air Arm, with its trained personnel. There is no doubt that this dual development of the air torpedo prevented its effective use, as had occurred with the dual control in the air mining campaign. Recognition of the value of the weapon came so late that its full exploitation was no longer possible owing to the armament situation.

20. 3. *The air war on shipping*

In view of the decisive inferiority in numbers of the German Navy there was no question of contesting British sea power by using surface forces. The only possibility of damaging the opponent lay in attacking British shipping with U-boats, through mining operations, and through raider activities by individual surface units. Intensification of the effects of naval action by using the Luftwaffe was most desirable. British ship targets were to be found at sea and in the harbors, docks and shipyards, and from the outbreak of war the German Naval Staff pressed for participation by the Luftwaffe in the war on shipping, so as to intensify the effect. Accordingly at the end of 1939 and the beginning of 1940 Flieger Korps X was effectively used against British shipping in the North Sea and off the east coast, though this correct method of attack occurred only spasmodically. The operational staff of the Luftwaffe considered that the main target in Britain was the aircraft industry, and regarded the blockade of England as a secondary task, to be carried out by occasional attacks on the principal ports and shipping.

21. Preparation and execution of the Norwegian campaign interrupted participation by the operational Luftwaffe in the war on merchant shipping, until the beginning of the campaign in France. The successful Luftwaffe operations against shipping in the summer of 1940 were again interrupted by preparations for the Battle of Britain, which involved concentration on air and land targets. The directives for targets in this operation expressly stated that sea attacks on warships and shipping must take second place to military objectives. This shows the extent to which the German Command hoped for decisive results from purely air warfare and from attacks on land targets. However, effective participation by the operational Luftwaffe in the war on shipping, which the

Navy regarded as the decisive factor against England, did not eventuate. Thus the German announcement on 18 July 1940 of a total blockade of the British Isles was not implemented. Not until the beginning of 1941 did the German High Command begin to recognize that, contrary to earlier conceptions, the greatest damage to the British war economy had occurred through the heavy shipping losses caused by sea and air attacks. Resulting from this, Hitler on the 6 February 1941 directed that future air attacks were to be concentrated on those targets whose destruction was also the aim of naval warfare. Accordingly the first quarter of 1941 was marked by a shifting of targets for the operational Luftwaffe to British coastal centers, and to shipping westward of Ireland, and this caused considerable losses in British imports.

22. Thus it had taken 18 months for the operational Luftwaffe to initiate the right method of attacking Britain, which harmonized with the operations of the German Navy, and represented an ideal concentration of the German Armed Forces against their principal enemy. But even this late recognition did not bear fruit, since further continental commitments of the Luftwaffe precluded adequate use of its forces in sea warfare.

If a Naval Air Arm had existed, the Naval Command would have employed it principally against shipping. Thus it can be asserted that the German organization of a single Luftwaffe was not propitious for direct attack on British shipping or imports.

23. 4. *Air reconnaissance for U-boat warfare*

Apart from its independent war on shipping, the Luftwaffe also had the opportunity of supporting the U-boat war. In addition to protection of U-boat bases and exit routes, the main possibilities lay in reconnaissance for U-boat operations, and indeed this was the decisive problem of the U-boat war.

The launching of the U-boat war regarded by the German Admiralty as the principal means of attacking Britain, was countered by the British Admiralty's re-introduction of the convoy system. This caused the formerly busy traffic routes in the Atlantic to become deserted, and all shipping was concentrated into a few protected convoys. In the immense sea area there was unlimited choice of routes for these convoys and the possibility of large diversions of shipping to avoid the approach of U-boats. The finding of these convoys was therefore the problem of the U-boat war. The small height of eye in U-boats and their low speed made them poor agents for reconnaissance, and the few boats available made it difficult to adopt broad searching formations. This serious handicap could have been remedied by air reconnaissance, which would have decisively increased the successes of the U-boats.

24. At the outbreak of war the Luftwaffe possessed in the trans-ocean aircraft of Lufthansa an excellent means of long distance air reconnaissance. Though these were not war aircraft, and their number was small, yet, if when war started, the type had been further developed and manufactured on a large scale and had been co-ordinated with the new U-boat building program, a long distance reconnaissance service could have been established within a reasonable time. Operating from the French Atlantic bases the aircraft could have surveyed an area up to 1,000 miles in depth in the Atlantic from 40° N to 60° N, and up to 25° W. It was through this area that the main North–South traffic

One way to provide air reconnaissance for U-Boats was to equip them with the Focke Achgelis Fa 330 Bachstelze (Water Wagtail) unpowered rotary-wing kite. This device could be stowed aboard a submarine and assembled or disassembled in minutes. When towed behind a U-boat it would ascend to a height of 300-500ft, enabling its pilot to see as far as 25 miles on a clear day.

111

Once aloft in the Fa 330, the pilot could report his sightings to the parent U-Boat through a telephone line that ran down the towing cable. These rotorcraft were used operationally in the Indian Ocean and the South Atlantic.

from the South Atlantic and the East–West North Atlantic traffic to the British Isles would have to pass. The later types of long distance reconnaissance machines had a penetrating range of 1,600 miles, which would have made it practically impossible for British shipping to escape observation. But the number of this type of aircraft put into production by the Luftwaffe was so small that there was hardly ever sufficient air reconnaissance for U-boat operations.

25. From the summer of 1940, with the occupation of France, U-boat bases began to be used on the Atlantic coast. But the concentration of the Luftwaffe in the autumn for the Battle of Britain interfered with the demands of the Naval Staff for air reconnaissance of the East

Atlantic in support of U-boats. It was not until the beginning of 1941 that for the first time a Hitler directive satisfied the fundamental requirements of the Naval Staff, but the demand of the Admiral Commanding U-boats for daily reconnaissance by at least 12 aircraft (for which he had been pressing for a whole year) was never fulfilled. There were times when not more than two or three aircraft were available. The monthly production of long range reconnaissance aircraft was hardle sufficient to replace losses.

When the further course of the war showed that a decision on the Continent was not attainable, the importance of the naval war came to the fore, insofar as the continental commitments still permitted. Hitler and the Luftwaffe now appreciated the necessity for supporting U-boat operations with air power. But increase in production of long distance sea reconnaissance types was not possible, as building resources were already fully applied to the requirements of the operational Luftwaffe, and alteration of the program would have caused interference with the overall production which was unacceptable to the conduct of the land war.

26. In contrast to this meager support for the U-boat war, the British Air Force played a decisive role in fighting U-boats. The British also faced urgent demands for air units in the various theaters of war, but clear and prompt recognition of the danger points led them to dispose and direct their air power in such a way that the Atlantic was under control. This supervision of the sea areas, using radar, forced U-boats under water, and prevented large scale operations by groups of U-boats against convoys, for such operations could only have been carried out on the surface. As the U-boats on operations had to remain submerged, and their number was small in relation to the tasks, their effective days were over. Locating the enemy, which even before the build-up of the enemy's air threat was the chief problem, became even more important, and operations without air reconnaissance offered no prospect. In spite of all efforts, the extremely small forces of Fliegerfuehrer Atlantic could no longer carry out their tasks. When eventually the Luftwaffe declared its readiness to give priority to Atlantic reconnaissance over its other commitments, it was already too late. The time for U-boat warfare had passed. It is true that there were other causes beside inadequate help by the Luftwaffe, and yet if U-boat operations between 1940 and 1943 had been adequately supported by air reconnaissance, they could have had a much greater effect on the course of the war than was the case with the U-boats thrown back on to their own resources. It can therefore be said that the failure of air power to come to the help of the U-boat war during its

most favorable period prevented the campaign from having the maximum success, and that the prevailing organization of the single Luftwaffe lost the Germans the chance of decisive results from this weapon.

5. Air reconnaissance for naval surface forces

28. Sea-air reconnaissance for naval surface forces appeared at the beginning of the war to be the only problem of co-operation with the Luftwaffe which, from a naval point of view, had been properly dealt with. In its naval air formations the Naval Command possessed suitable types and trained personnel for this task, and even with the development in the early half of the war that brought the Luftwaffe into operational prominence, reconnaissance tasks for naval forces were left entirely to the Naval Air Arm.

29. But because of technical and other disadvantages of the float planes, particularly in the winter, it had become necessary to use the more efficient land planes of the operational Luftwaffe on these tasks. Though the Naval Command was increasingly dependent on the results of the Luftwaffe's air reconnaissance, it had no influence over the employment of these aircraft, but could only make applications, which the Luftwaffe handled according to its own estimate of their importance. For the most part the reconnaissance reports that the Luftwaffe provided for the Navy were a by-product of the former's own reconnaissance in connection with bomber operations. Reconnaissance reports by the operational Luftwaffe did not possess the degree of accuracy as regards position, identification and types, sighting and contact reports etc. that prevailed with the trained observers of the Naval Air Arm. The Luftwaffe normally accepted no responsibility for the accuracy of the reconnaissance reports which it provided. This was not a serious disadvantage to the Navy in the early days of the war, when for other reasons large-scale naval operations were not carried out, but in the long run this state of affairs was not acceptable. The Navy did not achieve the desired aim of exercising tactical control over the reconnaissance forces of the Luftwaffe.

30. Not until February 1941 did Hitler settle the long-standing conflict between Navy and Luftwaffe regarding reconnaissance outside the area of the Naval Air Arm. In practice this decision made the operational Luftwaffe responsible for all reconnaissance over the sea. It was an improvement on the previous condition in which the Luftwaffe accepted no responsibility for results of reconnaissance outside the operational area of the Naval Air Arm. But Hitler's decision did not fundamentally solve the problem, since the Naval Staff generally

regarded reconnaissance at sea as a responsibility of the particular Naval Commander. War experiences up to this date had shown that the personnel for Naval reconnaissance must be drawn from the Navy, and that the aircraft must be suited to sea warfare. This unalterable requirement was not satisfied by Hitler's new instructions.

31. The Luftwaffe now had sole responsibility for the two reconnaissance functions, firstly reconnaissance in connection with its own bomber operations, and secondly for Naval operations. It was often the case that the same air formations could not carry out both tasks, and the reconnaissance forces had to be divided. It was understandable, and not always avoidable that in such cases the Luftwaffe Commander gave priority to reconnaissance tasks for his own operations, and relegated the naval tasks to second place, since he did not clearly understand their importance. The geographical distance between control centers increased the difficulties. The unsuitability of an organization which made naval operations dependent on the provision of air reconnaissance by the Luftwaffe is shown up in the fight against British–Russian convoys in Northern Waters; these operations, which had an independent character were vital to the war against Russia. During this period the reports of the Naval Commands revealed a constant series of complaints about poor results or inadequate reconnaissance, making the employment of naval forces difficult or resulting in failure of operations. Ultimately it was lack of information about the enemy which caused the failure of operations of both surface forces and U-boats in northern waters. It was not always merely a shortage of aircraft that caused inadequate reconnaissance for the Navy, but frequently this was due to an unavoidable lack of understanding among the commanding officers of the operational Luftwaffe of the nature of naval warfare. It is comprehensible that the Luftwaffe attached greater importance to their successes in sinking ships, than to the indirect pressure by a fleet in being, which was not immediately apparent.

32. German operations in northern waters which required the closest operational and tactical contact between the Navy and the Luftwaffe, provide the best material for evaluating the efficiency of the organization created by the High Command of the Luftwaffe. It is evident that a Naval Air Force would have held an entirely different conception of its reconnaissance duties for naval purposes, and the training and operations would have been under naval control.

6. Combined operations between Luftwaffe and naval forces

33. In addition to air reconnaissance, combined air-sea operations had been a particular feature of peace-time training for the Naval Air Arm.

These tasks required a high degree of mutual knowledge of the weapons and the tactics, and the closest co-ordinated training of the sea and air units, as parts of the same offensive weapon, as well as smooth functioning of a mutual communications network. The specialized operational and tactical training of the Naval Air Force aimed at fulfilling these difficult requirements. But this direct co-operation was taken over early in the war by the operational Luftwaffe. It was not as easy to integrate the requirements between two different parts of the armed forces as in the case of a common organization of the sea and air forces of one service. And such improvements as the proximity of the control centers, direct communications and personal contact were not sufficient to remove this disadvantage.

34. It was not until the third phase of the naval war, during operations against British convoys in northern waters, that the opportunity arose for this close co-operation between naval and air power. The difficulties of air reconnaissance have already been mentioned, and it is not surprising that the difficult tasks in this theater could not be satisfactorily completed. This cannot be laid at the door of the operational Luftwaffe, since the opponent's naval forces made only the shortest contact with our own, and it was not the German intention to seek decisions in naval actions. But if a Naval Air Arm had been able to work in close contact with our naval forces, it would not have regarded the destruction of enemy convoys as its chief objective but would have afforded valuable support to the German naval forces in their fight against British superiority at sea.

35. There was another theater of war where combined sea and air operations would have been of the greatest importance, namely the Mediterranean, where the German Luftwaffe should have worked in with the Italian Navy. In home waters there was perhaps the excuse that there was no German Fleet wanting to seek action, or requiring support from the air, but this excuse could not apply in the Mediterranean. The strength of the Italian Fleet was such that a fleet action with the British Mediterranean Fleet was entirely possible. Even if the Italians had psychological reasons for not seeking a decisive action, there were nevertheless times and opportunities when the Italian Command was ready to use its naval forces against formations of the enemy. But, in view of the low capacity of the Italian Air Force in relation to naval operations, this would have required assistance in reconnaissance, air cover, and bomber forces by the German air formations stationed in the Mediterranean.

36. In any case these German air formations had independent possibilities of action against enemy movements, and were frequently used in

support of Italian forces. But support for the Italian Fleet, when other operations might produce results, was a commitment which they were not prepared to undertake. All the outstanding tactical successes of the Luftwaffe against Malta and British Mediterranean shipping only went to prove the limitations of an independent air force operating in the sea area.

37. There is no question that the Italian Fleet failed because of its own inactivity, but it is equally true that the lack of air support for naval operations was a principal reason for the ineffectiveness of the Italian Fleet in the face of a naval opponent who enjoyed outstanding support from the air.

38. The axis war in the Mediterranean was lost principally because of the dual control of naval operations by the Navy and the Luftwaffe. If there had been available an efficient Naval Air Arm of either of the Axis partners, the Italian naval forces would have had positive operational possibilities and would have made it far more difficult for the enemy to achieve successes. Thus the German Luftwaffe organization also showed itself to be unsuited for naval operations in the Mediterranean, a theater of war vital to the whole issue.

7. The air cover for naval forces

39. Air protection for naval forces, whether at sea or in harbor, is an essential task of air warfare. For this purpose aircraft do not require any characteristics peculiar to sea warfare. Fighter formations of the operational Luftwaffe successfully provided air protection for naval forces as far as circumstances allowed, e.g. the Brest group's dash through the Channel 11 February, 1942.

In the course of the war ships increasingly had to do without air cover, and this was not due to defects in the existing organization, but rather because the fighter branch of the Luftwaffe lacked sufficient forces to meet all its commitments.

Thus the inclusion of fighter aircraft in a Naval Air Arm is not a fundamental necessity, as in the case of reconnaissance and bomber aircraft. And yet the subordination of fighter forces to naval operational control is desired so as to avoid any delay in coping with sudden air attacks, and also in order to establish an all-round Naval Air Arm, whose reconnaissance and bomber forces require fighter protection just as ships do. There is therefore no objection to incorporating fighter protection into the Naval Air Arm, particularly for heavy fighter tasks over the open sea.

8. The use of aircraft carriers in connection with long distance naval operations

40. The aircraft carrier clearly showed its war value for all purposes of long distance operations. The aircraft carrier is obviously an integral part of sea-power and the High Command of the Luftwaffe never disputed this, though there were some differences of opinion between it and the Navy as regards conduct of operations and manning of the aircraft.

That the two aircraft-carriers under construction at the beginning of the war were never completed is attributable to various obstructions and difficulties, none of which, however, originated with the operational Luftwaffe. The failure of air reconnaissance, bomber support and air protection in support of the trade war by German surface forces in the Atlantic, and the ensuing difficulties of German naval operations, are not a consequence of the organization of the German single air force. But it goes without saying that aircraft carriers and shipborne aircraft form the nucleus of a Naval Air Arm. It can be said that in any future naval war, a Naval Air Arm is essential to any country wishing to aspire to the full use of sea power.

9. The effect of dwindling air power on the naval war

41. Consequent on the disappearance of the Naval Air Arm on the taking over of naval air tasks by the Luftwaffe, the German Navy was anxious lest the tying down of the operational Luftwaffe to land operations should mean a very limited practical use of air forces for naval requirements. The further course of the war confirmed these fears. The involvement and losses of the Luftwaffe in the continental campaign, particularly in Russia, contributed more and more to their failure to participate in the naval tasks. Thus the operational Luftwaffe, far from making good the disappearance of the Naval Air Arm, failed especially in its main task of air reconnaissance for naval purposes, which decisively affected naval operations. This weakness in the Luftwaffe's organization directly contributed to the loss of freedom of action by the surface forces and by U-boats. The naval control centers had to work mostly in the dark, at a time when inferior naval forces and the small number of available U-boats demanded particularly good information about the enemy. On the other hand the enemy, already superior at sea, was operating with the help of a superior and outstandingly trained and equipped naval air reconnaissance organization. This disparity ultimately caused the failure of German naval operations, not so much in the North Atlantic, where within the limits of range the Luftwaffe could have given some help in spite of the opponent's better opportunities, but especially in Northern Waters, where the proxim-

ity of German aerodromes facilitated support for naval operations in an area far removed from the enemy's air bases, where he would have to operate from aircraft carriers.

42. More important still was the fading of the Luftwaffe in the Mediterranean theater. This applied equally to air operations across the Mediterranean (Cyrenaica and the Tunis campaign) and to the use of the air forces at sea (elimination of Malta and air operations against British convoys). But the principal cause of the enemy's control of sea communications was the elimination of the Italian Fleet through failure to provide active and passive air support for it. And yet, in view of the geographical characteristics of the theater of war, the survival of the Axis armies across the Mediterranean depended on superiority in that sea. It is true that strong air support for the Italian Fleet would have correspondingly reduced support for the various other air and land operations, and would have prevented the launching of several ambitious plans of the Italo-German armies in North Africa; but on the other hand the catastrophic loss of sea-power in the Mediterranean, with its fatal consequences for the North African campaign, would have been avoided. If there had been some security for supplies to North Africa, it would at least have been possible for the Axis powers to maintain a defensive position in Africa much longer. The effect on the general war situation is obvious, for the loss of the Mediterranean was one of the principal factors in the decline of Germany's strategic position.

43. This development can be attributed to the under-estimation of the importance of sea-power by the German High Command. The availability of a powerful Naval Air Arm in the Mediterranean, which in the circumstances could only have been a German force, would certainly have provided the Italian Fleet and the Axis naval war with much greater power, both active and latent. Such a Naval Air Arm would not have been whittled away through losses and commitments in land operations, as was the case with the Luftwaffe.

44. To sum up, the practical effects of the atrophy of the operational Luftwaffe in the naval theaters of war show that the organization of the single air force was not suited to the conduct of a naval war.

C. Comprehensive appreciation of the organization of the Luftwaffe for purposes of naval warfare

45. It is not the purpose of this paper to examine the effect of the formation of a single Luftwaffe on the conduct of air and land operations, or air operations in sea areas independently of the Navy. Unquestionably

the actual organization had considerable advantages for these types of operations. The advantages were apparent in the Continental campaigns in Poland, France and Russia, and permitted the inception of successful operations across the seas, which would not have been feasible without this all-round employment of the whole air force.

46. The High Command of the Luftwaffe was confident that its forces had proved themselves through their decisive role in the occupation of Norway and Crete, which had shown that the conception of a single Luftwaffe was right. In these operations of the Wehrmacht, the Luftwaffe, in closest co-operation with the Army and the Navy, and also in independent operations, carried out the most useful tasks. Theories on the use of paratroops and air-borne troops, until then untested, proved their value in operations across the sea, and the opponent's sea-power was prevented from interfering with the extension of the German zone of operations.

47. While fully appreciating the performance of the operational Luftwaffe during the Norwegian operations and still more in the occupation of Crete, one must not forget the specialized nature of these operations in relation to naval warfare. Both these cases were concerned principally with land operations and air supply tasks across limited sea areas, and in all cases the actions took place in coastal waters where the full power of land-based bombers and fighters could be launched against naval forces, who themselves had no air support except from aircraft carriers. Thus these two successful operations by the Luftwaffe merely prove the power of an air force operating against enemy naval forces in extended coastal areas. They produced no instance of common operations with our own naval forces, who in both cases were used only for transport tasks, and whose purpose was to avoid any engagement with enemy forces.

48. The above mentioned special cases involving particular coastal areas show that a naval force can to some extent be replaced by an air force. Nevertheless such lessons cannot be applied to the normal conditions of naval warfare or extended to the high seas, where the object of the employment of naval forces remains, as before, the destruction of the enemy's shipping. This main function of naval warfare was not performed principally or solely by the Luftwaffe, whose aircraft had to be integrated with the other weapons of sea warfare. It is the purpose here to evaluate the aircraft for sea operations, and the organization for this kind of warfare. In conclusion it must again be emphasized that the effective operations of the Luftwaffe in Norway and Crete are no proof of the value of the Luftwaffe organization for purposes of naval warfare, that is, for the normal tasks of naval forces in areas outside coastal waters.

49. On the other hand the above examination has shown that the unavoidable disadvantages of a single air force had serious results on the conduct of the naval war. Continental warfare, fully and successfully exploited by the operational Luftwaffe, was not sufficient to ensure victory. But failure to exploit opportunities in the naval theaters of war, due to insufficient use of the Luftwaffe, was the principal cause of losing the war.

50. Though mention has been made of the defects of a single operational Luftwaffe and the resultant lack of support for naval operations, this in no way implies a lack of appreciation of the esprit de corps of the formations employed on naval tasks, particularly by Flieger Korps X. There is no question that these forces showed devoted enthusiasm in action over the sea – an element foreign to them – and this forms an admirable chapter in the German history of the war. Neither can it be maintained that the operational staff and commands of the Luftwaffe were permanently unaware of the importance of the naval theater. The events of the war, with their hard blows and bitter lessons, were the best educator in the meaning of the sea and of sea-power. But the resulting experience reacted unilaterally on the Luftwaffe, who alone assumed responsibility for meeting the requirements and necessities of naval operations. Under the existing circumstances this function could not be achieved, and the energetic action and good intentions of the operational Luftwaffe produced tactical results, but no strategic effects in the area of the naval war.

51. This appreciation transcends the problem of evaluating the organization of the Luftwaffe, for the operational objectives of an air force are principally a strategic problem, and to a lesser extent an organizational one. But there is no doubt that the existing organization and the spirit which it produced contributed to operational judgments and decisions. A different form of organization, with an adequate part of the Luftwaffe in close contact with the Navy and its idea of global naval warfare, would have influenced the operational Luftwaffe's views in this direction, and would have ensured an impartial conception of air strategy.

52. The ultimate answer as to the influence of the Luftwaffe organization on the conduct of the naval war can be summed up from the naval point of view as follows:

"The German organization of the single Luftwaffe in the war of 1939/45 was unable to give the naval war that measure of support which could have been expected from a Naval Air Arm. The resulting inferiority in the means of naval warfare on and under the surface robbed the Navy of decisive successes in the U-boat war, in the

Mediterranean and in Northern Waters. The advantages of a single Luftwaffe for an independent air war and for land warfare were not sufficient to make good the disadvantages which the Navy had to suffer. In a world war, which was fundamentally a sea war, decisions on land and in the air did not achieve final victory, whereas German reverses in the naval theaters of war multiplied to an extent which lost Germany the whole war."

Chapter 4

THE OPERATIONAL USE OF THE LUFTWAFFE IN THE WAR AT SEA, 1939–43

by OKL, 8th Abteilung, January, 1944

I. The Situation in 1939

The following considerations were of primary importance when the Luftwaffe was being built up:

1) The elimination of the threat of air attack on the Reich by neighbouring countries, arising from the central position of the Reich,
2) The elimination in the shortest possible time of continental powers directly threatening the Reich on land, and barring access to the Atlantic in the west.

There had never been any doubt of the possibility and the necessity of using the bulk of the Luftwaffe in full force for strategic purposes on land, and later also at sea. The strategic idea was present in the leadership as well as in the technical development of the bombing forces, which were created for and completely suited to these purposes. It was therefore in accordance with the situation to concentrate on this "strategic air force" and to make only parts of it available for direct support of the Army and Navy. The weaker the Luftwaffe formations used for "cooperation" with other branches of the Service, were, the stronger would be the strategic force which could be built up and trained.

These views proved to be absolutely correct then as now, when considered from a long-term aspect.

Owing to these views the German Navy in the West could expect direct support only from a few coastal reconnaissance Gruppen and from aircraft carried on board. In addition, carrier units were being formed for the aircraft-carrier under construction.

These forces had to suffice for the direct support of naval operations, which were necessarily limited to the Baltic and North Sea for the time

being, always considered from the view-point of first building up a strategic air force, the effect of which would be felt later on the entire conduct
of the war and consequently on strategy at sea.

The exercises for the use of strategic air forces, planned and carried out
by these formations before the war, indicated the long-term policy of the
Luftwaffe Command regarding the strategic possibilities of air forces used
at sea.

History will one day draw special attention to the fact that all these theories were expressed so early in Luftwaffe policy although officers and
men were then fully occupied with its re-formation, which (after years of
military stagnation on a large and small scale) proved exceptionally difficult as regards personnel and technical matters.

The resultant possibility of Luftwaffe operations in strength over sea
areas had also affected maritime air forces since the beginning of the war.
Mixed coastal reconnaissance Gruppen were reformed into Gruppen with
one type of aircraft, and a bomber Gruppe set up in September 1939 was
equipped with Do–17 Z landplanes.

Head of the maritime air forces was termed Luftwaffe General at Naval
H.Q. Maritime Luftwaffe H.Q. ceased to exist after 1 April 1939. He was
subordinate to C. in C. Navy in matters relating to command and to C. in
C. Luftwaffe in all other matters.

His duties in 1939 were as follows:

1) To prepare the Maritime Air Forces for operational use in cooperation
   with the Luftwaffe General Staff and Naval Command.
2) To supervise serviceability, supply and training of Maritime Air
   Forces in cooperation with the Luftwaffe Q.M.G.

The Maritime Air Forces were divided into the formations of the
"Commander of Maritime Air Forces, West" and "Commander of
Maritime Air Forces, East" and were tactically subordinate to the Naval
Commanders West and East.

Their primary task was to carry out coastal and sea reconnaissance, to
support naval forces in mercantile warfare and, as far as possible, to carry
out independent mercantile warfare.

Although the main reconnaissance aircraft, the Do-18 flying-boat, did
not always appear equal to British aircraft then being used at sea against
Germany, the capture of shipping by the Navy resulted from reconnaissance by the Maritime Air Forces during this period.

The coastal multi-purpose Staffeln did not engage in any important
actions during 1939.

On the other hand, bomber formations soon attacked the British fleet at

Scapa Flow with good results considering their experience at that time. In addition, they were on the alert to repel enemy naval operations against the German coast.

However, the Luftwaffe and the Maritime Air Force did not yet have a decisive influence on the situation at sea. Neither did the strategic position (still as in 1914) provide the preliminary conditions, or overall strategy permit the use of strong forces for this purpose. Preparations were being made first to break open the necessary jumping-off areas to the gates of the world.

II. The Acquisition of the Strategic Position in the Atlantic

With the capture in 1940 of the strategic position from Spitzbergen to the Bay of Biscay, the preliminary conditions for inter-continental warfare by Germany began to take shape. For the first time strong Luftwaffe forces, i.e. not only Maritime Air Forces, were used at great distances over land and sea for decisive land operations.

Strategic cooperation between all three arms of the Wehrmacht introduced in this operation proved successful and led to a complete victory. Above all, it was obvious that the policy of Luftwaffe Command to make the Air Force an independent arm of the Services as regards command and employment and provided with all the necessary auxiliary branches had been correct.

The Luftwaffe compensated for the weaknesses of the German Navy, due to the Versailles Treaty, and by tactical and strategic air transport operations made the holding of territorial gains possible, particularly in Norway.

The strategic situation at sea, which was characterised by British mastery of the North Atlantic as in 1914, was completely changed by this operation. The dreams of 1914–18 became reality in 1940 in a few days.

The strategic situation which had been produced by surprise could more-over be maintained in spite of an inferior Navy, as the Luftwaffe commanded coastal areas and rendered them practically invulnerable.

In the initial major operation by all three branches of the Services, the Luftwaffe was seen at the peak of its performance. There can be no doubt that without the Luftwaffe the attack on the Danish Islands and on Norway would not have resulted in a lasting success.

The conquest of Denmark and Norway will therefore be entered in war history as a classic example of how combined strategy and in particular naval strategy were influenced by the strategic employment of the Luftwaffe.

This impression is further strengthened by the capture of the Channel and Atlantic coasts, achieved by the three branches of the Service acting together.

Considered from the aspect of world-wide operations in this war, the conquest of Holland, Belgium and France in itself can actually be regarded only as a means to an end. The establishment of ocean bases was the vital factor in the war against England, and later probably against America as well, for if Germany did not exploit these bases she could neither exist in this war nor be in a position to strike the enemy where he was weakest.

It was of primary importance that Army operations aimed at capturing these bases should be set in motion as quickly as possible. The collective strength of Luftwaffe operations greatly facilitated the achievement of these aims from the point of view of combined strategy.

Through the preceding operations in northern Europe and present operations in Western Europe, the Luftwaffe now thinks in terms of intercontinental strategy both in questions of command and in operation.

If it did not succeed in decisively blocking the British withdrawal across the Channel from Dunkirk, this was due to unfavourable weather conditions. In any case, the Luftwaffe inflicted such heavy losses on the enemy there, that there was no question of a renewed British strategic threat to the occupied western areas until the end of 1943.

The change in the strategic situation in a main British sea supply area was now regarded as a basis for future Wehrmacht operations against British supply shipping.

III. The commencement of strategic employment of the Luftwaffe against British supply shipping in 1940

From the end of the summer of 1940 combined strategy had to consider the probability of the situation in the east developing into a future war with Russia and assume that the United States would also enter the war at a given time.

A decisive blow had to be struck against Britain, Germany's main enemy, before this happened. First therefore it was necessary to eliminate England as a major factor in the war.

This resulted in the following methods of forcing England to recognise the situation created in Europe by the German Wehrmacht, which was an essential preliminary for later military operations on other fronts:

1) to take the island fortress by storm,
2) to destroy centres of vital importance to the British people,
3) to paralyse gradually the supply of the island by cutting sea communications.

Immediate occupation of the island would doubtless have had a decisive effect, but in view of the strength of the British fleet and the imperturbability of the R.A.F., an invasion would in all probability have been met by a resistance which would have resulted in a strategic disadvantage for Germany with incalculable consequences.

Thus it was decided to use the Luftwaffe in mass operations against England to break down first of all the economic and military strength of England at its root.

At the same time the Navy, now in a more favourable position, would pursue intensified operations against shipping bringing supplies to the island.

The Luftwaffe participated very effectively in this plan of campaign, first of all by dropping magnetic mines.

The 9th Fliegerdivision (later IX Fliegerkorps), which was formed from small units on 1 February 1940 and whose formations were constantly increasing, first became operational by using elements of the Maritime Air Forces (K.Fl.Gr. 106) and was reinforced by bomber formations (K.G. 4, elements of K.G. 30 and 40 and K.Fl.Gr. 100 and 126) in 1940.

There can be no doubt that this first aerial mine-laying operation not only seriously handicapped the enemy's supply shipping by endangering

A Focke-Wulf Fw 200 Condor of KG 40 with the unit's 'ringed globe' emblem displayed prominently on its nose.

river estuaries and entrances to ports, but also forced him to use a large number of men and ships for mine-sweeping. And so personnel and material available for productive supply shipping was reduced by a not inconsiderable percentage. Only the Luftwaffe was capable of mining distant ports on the north-west coast. During the period from 1 April 1940 to 31 December 1943, 693 vessels totalling 1,408,947 tons were sunk, probably sunk or damaged.

The Luftwaffe continued to pursue the strategic air campaign at sea by aerial mine-laying operations.

The aerial mine-laying campaign was conducted with increasing success in the years that followed and also helped not only to facilitate the task of the Navy itself, but to exercise an important influence in the economic war on enemy military and economic strength. The aerial mine can no longer be ignored in Luftwaffe operations over sea areas. Much attention will continue to be devoted to the constant technical and tactical improvement of this factor in the air campaign.

During these years the Luftwaffe could also point to successes in operations against enemy naval forces. However, decisive successes could not yet be achieved owing to lack of forces, the large number of other tasks necessarily resulting from combined strategy, as well as the fact that the aerial torpedo arm was not yet completely ready for operational use. Nevertheless, the Luftwaffe shared in the losses inflicted on the enemy by making effective attack on transport vessels and warships. Not until 1944 will remote-controlled bombs bring about a change of tactics in this type of operation.

In addition to IX Fliegerkorps, which carried out anti-shipping operations as well as mine-laying, Fliegerfuehrer Atlantik and Fliegerfuehrer North, later North-East, North-West and Lofoten as well, appeared in 1941 in Luftflotte and Luftflotte 5 Command Areas respectively as Luftwaffe Operations Staffs for marine warfare.

The Fuehrer der Luftwaffe West had already been renamed Fuehrer der Seeluftstreitkraefte on 27 August 1940. From March 1941 he was responsible for reconnaissance over the North Sea between 52° and 58° north. Reconnaissance north of this parallel was carried out by Fliegerfuehrer Nord. Fliegerfuehrer Atlantik was responsible for reconnaissance in the Channel and west of the Scilly Islands–Ouessant.

The continued conversion of Maritime Air Forces into bomber formations was also to be seen in the gradual re-equipment of Coastal Reconnaissance Staffeln with Ju 88's. The strategic air force was reinforced by them.

On 7 April 1942 the Commander of Maritime Air Forces was subordinated to Luftflotte 3. The 506 Coastal Reconnaissance Gruppe, which was still under his command, was re-equipped as an aerial torpedo formation, trained and renamed III/K.G. 26.

On 17 July 1942 the Commander of Maritime Air Forces was transferred to Chantilly and participated in the bombing attacks from 27 July to 6 August on the British Isles as commander of three Bomber Gruppen of IX Fliegerkorps. He was also in charge of organising defence for the event of a British landing on the Atlantic coast. When this happened at Dieppe on 18 August 1942, he successfully commanded operations by six bomber Gruppen of IX Fliegerkorps.

When these formations were subordinated to IX Fliegerkorps on 7 September 1942 the post of Commander of Maritime Air Forces ceased to exist.

From 25 April 1940 the Luftwaffe General at Naval H.Q. was responsible for sending up reinforcements and supplies to Coastal Reconnaissance formations and shipborne Staffeln equipped with seaplanes.

Thus the years 1940–1943 saw the gradual absorption of the Maritime Air Forces into the Luftwaffe and also the concentration of all formations suitable for sea as well as for land operations under C.-in-C. Luftwaffe. The Luftwaffe Supreme Command was therefore in complete control of air operations at sea. Close co-operation with the Navy was assured.

It can justly be said that this adjustment was in complete accord with combined strategy. The entire development of the combined strategy practised by the Navy and Luftwaffe in the western part of the European theatre of operations led inevitably to this solution. This enabled the air forces, under a unified command, and with an allocation of personnel and material according to its total requirements, to exploit even more the potentialities of air warfare, to give operational support to the Navy and to lay the foundations of independent air warfare at sea.

The Luftwaffe was preparing itself technically and in its training for this task, which would probably increase still further later in the war.

As most of the Luftwaffe was required for the Eastern Campaign in 1941, Luftwaffe forces in the West found it extremely difficult to carry out tasks allotted to them, such as sea reconnaissance, anti-shipping and aerial mine-laying operations and attacks on land targets in England. Numerical weakness was an important factor in this instance. Training for operations over sea areas had to be further intensified, particularly in the case of formations which arrived temporarily from the Eastern front. Owing to losses and employment for other tasks, formations were not always able to acquire a full knowledge of air warfare at sea. Thus it is all the more noteworthy that in spite of this the numerically weak air forces in the West scored successes.

For the above reasons, however, the development of combined strategy still prevented the Luftwaffe from concentrating on cutting off British supplies with newly supplemented strength and decisive technical improvements.

However, like Germany, the enemy had also extended the development of his air forces in the direction of operations over the sea, but in addition he had recognised the great importance of air forces in operations over the sea for offensive and, in particular, for defensive purposes and had reinforced and trained his formations accordingly.

Thus for a long time both sides accepted the fundamental idea that the air force should be the deciding influence if not the dominating factor in sea warfare also.

Sea warfare without concentrated air warfare over the sea is no longer conceivable. Swift movement by strong forces over large areas, the annihilating effect of bombs, torpedoes and other modern weapons, long-range reconnaissance and fighter cover are the means by which the Luftwaffe is changing the whole aspect of sea warfare.

The air forces of every country have recognised this line of development. One must assume that they will pursue these lines to their ultimate conclusion, as Germany herself has done.

IV. Characteristic Luftwaffe operations in direct support of operations by German surface forces, 1942/43

1. Cruiser operations in the Atlantic

The first submarine put into Lorient as early as 7 July 1940, but more than six months passed before the first German battleship formation could be transferred to Brest. Consequently, cruiser operations against British supply shipping were first carried out from North Sea bases during 1940.

On 27 October 1940 the *Admiral Scheer* left Brunsbüttel and succeeded in breaking through the Shetland Firth from Stavanger into the open Atlantic to attack shipping on the Halifax convoy route, unobserved by the enemy. The cruiser could not locate the expected convoy without air reconnaissance. When on 5 November the weather at last permitted shipborne aircraft to operate, the convoy was observed from an altitude of 600m, 30 to 40 sea miles away. The *Admiral Scheer* sank 11 vessels of this convoy totalling 117,400 tons.

The damaged battleships *Scharnhorst* and *Gneisenau* were not ready to put to sea until the end of December 1940 and eventually left Kiel on 22 January 1941.

In the first attempt to break through south of Iceland on 28 January, the formation encountered British patrols. The breakthrough was successfully carried out through the Denmark Strait (between Iceland and Greenland) on 4 February, the C.-in-C. Fleet using air reconnaissance reports on the situation at Scapa Flow and acting accordingly. Thus, for the first time in the history of naval warfare, German battleships had succeeded in breaking into the Atlantic.

For weeks on end the two battleships carried out mercantile warfare in the Atlantic without overseas bases and maintained only by depot ships, making the raids on the Canada—Britain route, and after sinking 22 vessels totalling 116,000 tons, put into Brest unmolested on 22 March 1941.

The appearance of the two battleships in the Atlantic forced the British to use strong Home Fleet forces piecemeal for convoy escort duties, which relieved strategic operations in the Atlantic to the advantage of the Germans.

The ship-borne aircraft proved extremely valuable for close reconnaissance and courier operations, but could not operate at long range.

There is no doubt that if long-range reconnaissance aircraft had been used the successes achieved would have been even greater. In future cruiser operations will be supported by long-range reconnaissance and bomber formations.

The appearance of the two battleships in the Atlantic also forced the British to make heavy air attacks on them in their bases.

2. *The* Bismarck *Episode*

The successes achieved by the *Scharnhorst* and the *Gneisenau* led to the decision taken by the Naval Staff on 2 April 1941, to put the recently-completed battleship *Bismarck* and the heavy cruiser *Prinz Eugen* into commission at once, so that British naval units employed on convoy escort duties could be opposed by German ships having commensurate fire-power.

In the absence of long-range reconnaissance by the Luftwaffe, such operations had to be carried out by U-boats and disguised motor vessels.

The British Admiralty was informed by agents on 20 May of the break-out of the German ships through the Great Belt. This was confirmed by reconnaissance aircraft flying over the Skagerrak on 21 May. The battle formation steamed out of Grimstadt Fjord at midnight on 21 May. At daybreak it was joined by 40 twin and single-engine fighters of Luftflotte 5 which provided aircover to the limit of their range. Furthermore during the night of 21/22 May British aircraft using flares searched the area at Bergen where the German ships had been anchored.

Four British battleships and six cruisers at anchor in Scapa Flow were sighted by Fliegerfuehrer Nord, during reconnaissance on the afternoon of 22 May. The C.-in-C., Fleet, believed that he could assume from this report that the main body of the Home Fleet had certainly not yet put to sea and that thus it could not reach the southern tip of Greenland ahead of the German force. Marinegruppe Nord (Naval Group Command, North) still believed on the evening of 22 May that the enemy was so far unaware of the movement of the German ships. Actually, as a result of British air reconnaissance of 21 May, the cruisers *Norfolk* and *Suffolk* were able to make contact with the German force at 19.22 hours before nightfall on 23 May and to maintain it throughout the night. The battleships *Hood* and *Prince of Wales* had been approaching by the shortest route south of Iceland since early morning of 22 May and at 05.45 hours on 24 May they closed in on the German formation in the Strait of Denmark. In the ensuing engagement at a range of between 20 and 30 km the *Hood* was sunk by hits in the after magazine and the *Prince of Wales* was shaken off. However, the *Bismarck* was hit in the oil tanks and left a wide trail of oil in its wake, thus making it easier for the enemy to maintain contact.

As he did not know the whereabouts of the battleship *King George V* and probably hoped to be able to recommence his assigned task after putting in to St. Nazaire for repairs, C.-in-C., Fleet decided against returning to Norway through the Strait of Denmark where the Luftwaffe could have provided cover for the *Bismarck* halfway between Iceland and Norway.*

On the night of 24/25 May the aircraft carrier *Victorious* and the flagship of the Home Fleet, the *King George V*, sailing from Scapa Flow, had been brought up far enough under the guidance of the cruisers shadowing the German ships, for an attack to be launched by carrier-borne aircraft against the *Bismarck*. The attack was made in two waves at midnight but was without noteworthy result. According to British sources, contact was lost with the German force after this attack, though the German C.-in-C., Fleet, was quite unaware that this was the case.

The British units passed to the west of the German warship. Under the mistaken impression that the enemy knew its position anyhow through the ships by which it assumed it was being shadowed, the *Bismarck* betrayed itself by a W/T exchange which lasted for an hour and a half and enabled the enemy to pinpoint its position. The *Bismarck* proceeded all day on 25 May without interference and hopes of saving the ship rose accordingly.

A decisive event occurred on the morning of 26 May: a Catalina flyingboat of Coastal Command 600 sea miles from its base, that is to say, at the utmost limit of its range, sighted the *Bismarck* at 10.30 hours on its dash for the Bay of Biscay. The report from the flying-boat summoned the aircraft-carrier *Ark Royal* from Gibraltar whose aircraft in turn maintained

---

* According to British accounts, the *King George V* was about 300 sea miles south-west of the *Bismarck* and not, as the C.-in-C. supposed, north-east of him in the Straits of Denmark.

contact with the *Bismarck* until the cruiser *Sheffield* was able to take over. As the slower warships of the British Home Fleet lay astern and the only battlecruiser of the Gibraltar Squadron, the *Renown*, was no match for the German battleships, the Commander of the British Fleet launched an attack by torpedo-carrying aircraft of the *Ark Royal*. In a second attack at 21.15 hours they scored two hits. The steering gear of the *Bismarck* was damaged so that the ship could only go round in circles.

Luftflottenkommando 3 received word at 16.00 hours on 24 May from Group Command West that the *Bismarck* would dock at St. Nazaire. The Commander of Luftflotte 3 accordingly reinforced Fliegerfuehrer Atlantic (comprising one long-range reconnaissance Staffel, one bomber Gruppe and two coastal command Gruppen) on 26 May by two bomber Gruppen* and on 27 May by three further bomber Gruppen.** In addition, balloon

Scourge of the Atlantic; the menacing silhouette of an Fw 200 Condor on long-range patrol in search of Allied shipping.

* I/KG 28 (Nantes) and KG 100 (Vannes).
** I/KG 77, II/KG 54, III/KG 1 (Lannion).

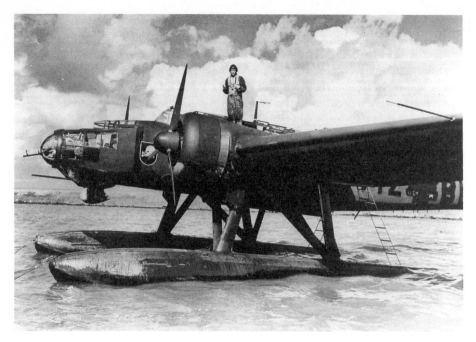

A Heinkel He 115C-1 of 3./Kü.Fl.Gr.106, with the unit's skull-and-crossbones emblem clearly in evidence.

barrage units and a battery of anti-aircraft artillery were sent to St. Nazaire.

Fliegerfuehrer Atlantic then initiated extensive sea reconnaissance operations to pin down the British naval forces that were cutting off the escape route of the *Bismarck*. On 26 May, a FW-200 of I/K.G.40 on a twelve hour flight sighted a British battleship at 15.45 hours at 19° 15′ W and 50° 30′ N – that is, almost at the limit of the aircraft's range. This battleship was taken to be either the *Rodney* or the *Nelson* and was escorted by four destroyers. The formation was steering a course of 170°.

Thanks to the preparatory measures that had been taken, on 27 May a force of 3 FW-200s, 8 Ju-88s and 10 He-115s was able to take off on armed reconnaissance beginning at 03.07 hours, while it was still dark. At 9.45 hours two battleships were sighted at 17° 5′ W and 48° 20′ N. From the appearance of their funnels they were taken to be the *Renown* and the *Repulse*. They were accompanied by two destroyers and the aircraft-carrier *Ark Royal*, in other words the Gibraltar Squadron, steering a course of 40°. The reconnaissance aircraft immediately notified U-boats of the position of the British units by D/F signals. At 10.43 hours W/T messages giving exact information were discontinued.

A widely reproduced German wartime propaganda photograph of a test torpedo launch from a Heinkel He 111H. The He 111H became the Luftwaffe's primary torpedo bomber, but was never used in this role in decisive numbers or with effective radar. (US National Archives)

At about the same time 5 JU-88s of the 606th Coastal Group observed the *Bismarck* being engaged by 2 heavy and 2 light units at 15° 45′ W and 47° 25′ N. The aircraft joined battle but a dive-bombing attack on a cruiser was frustated by the strong defensive action of Gladiator aircraft.

Its steering gear out of action, the *Bismarck* was within easy target range and was badly hit by the combined fire of the *King George V*, the *Rodney* and the heavy cruisers *Dorsetshire* and *Norfolk*. When its guns had been silenced the *Dorsetshire* moved in to make a short range attack with torpedoes. The defenceless *Bismarck* went down at 11.01 hours, its flag still flying.

In view of information obtained during reconnaissance operations the previous day, a further force of

17 He-111s of I/KG 28 and
12 He-111s of KG 100

Junkers Ju 88 bombers en route to a target.

based at Nantes and Vannes, was sent out at 05.48 hours (first light in Lorient 05.38 hours) to attack the British naval units.

I/KG 28 reached the battle area about 11.00 hours, probably shortly after the *Bismarck* capsized, and sighted an aircraft carrier, a battleship and a destroyer in line ahead. The attack on the aircraft carrier did not succeed owing to strong defence. KG 100 missed the British fleet altogether.

At 15.37 hours further bomber formations were sent out to follow the enemy ships:

13 Ju-88s of I/KG 77,
 5 Ju-88s of II/KG 1 and
16 Ju-88s of II/KG 54.

An aircraft of 3(F)/123 (long distance recce) sighted at 16.10 hours the homeward-bound Gibraltar fleet at 17° 10′ W and 48° 10′ N on a course of 210°.

The bomber formations were unable to find the enemy ships owing to bad visibility.

The returning Home Fleet was not sighted by reconnaissance aircraft on this day until dusk. 8 aircraft of the 406th Coastal Command Group sighted:

20.40 hours, 13° 30′ W and 50° 10′ N, 4 large ships and 8 destroyers, course 30°

21.40   ”   12° 15′ W and 51° 25′ N, 1 destroyer, course 50°.

22.30   ”   12° 15′ W and 50° 50′ N, 1 battleship and 2 cruisers, course no longer determinable.

Two British battleships, the *King George V* and a ship of the *Nelson* class escorted by seven destroyers on a course of 60°, were sighted on the morning of 28 May by long-range reconnaissance aircraft at 10° 10′ W and 54° 10′ N, 150 km west of the Irish coast. In an attack made by the bomber formations, which had been sent out in pursuit of the enemy formations since the early morning, a British cruiser and a destroyer were heavily damaged.* The destroyer was observed to be going down at 10.20 hours 100 km from the Irish coast. It was the destroyer *Mashona*, the loss of which was admitted by the British. The search for survivors of the *Bismarck* on 27 and 28 May was fruitless.

The reasons for the unhappy outcome of the *Bismarck* episode were: the more favourable strategic position of the British Navy in the Atlantic to the west of its home bases, and hence its ability to deploy aircraft carriers at short notice, secondly the prompt transmission of agent's reports, and lastly, the luck attending British air reconnaissance.

The reports of British air reconnaissance on 21 May and on the night of 21/22 May were largely responsible for the correct deployment of the British naval units. This applies particularly to the contact that was maintained on the course round the north of Iceland and to the fact that the British battleships set a straight course from Scapa Flow to the west in order to intercept the German battle formation. What decided the fate of the *Bismarck*, however, was being sighted by a Catalina flying-boat on 26 May and the resultant summoning of the aircraft carrier *Ark Royal* from Gibraltar.

It was not British naval power which sank the *Bismarck* but the reconnaissance and torpedo-carrying aircraft of the Royal Air Force.

Working in close co-operation with the command of the German Navy, the Luftwaffe did everything it could by using the forces available, which were tactically and technically suited, to ensure the safe passage of the *Bismarck*.

* A total of 63 bombers took part in the operations on 28 May 1941.

V. Survey of operational use of the Luftwaffe against enemy supply shipping, 1941/43

At the turn of 1940–41, preparations for the defensive battle against the Russian threat in the east began to take shape. This necessarily lead to a transfer of air power eastwards.

The favourable strategic position on the Atlantic and the plans for Luftwaffe operations in strength against British supply could not be used.

There are three large sea areas for future air operations

1) the central Atlantic as area of main effort,
2) the Northern waters as supply for the Soviet Union,
3) the Mediterranean as the main battle area for the German and Italian Armed Forces in this sea area itself and in Africa.

These sea areas, particularly the central Atlantic, would develop into the main battle areas of combined strategy following the entry of the U.S.A. into the war, which was expected sooner or later. The enemy realised this and made every effort to secure air superiority over the Atlantic and in coastal areas. The effect produced by his air forces on German submarines and the Luftwaffe was of decisive importance to combined strategy on both sides.

1. In the Atlantic

In March 1941 the Fliegerfuehrer Atlantik was appointed by order of the Fuehrer and made subordinate to Luftflotte 3.

His task was to co-operate closely with the C.-in-C. Submarine Fleet in operations against enemy supply shipping in the Atlantic, that is on the convoy routes from the Mediterranean to Britain and on the eastern part of the U.S.–Britain line, as well as on the eastern, southern and western coasts of Britain.

At first successes were surprisingly great, particularly in the Atlantic, as the attacks on enemy shipping encountered only slight opposition, whether from A.A. or aircraft.*

---

* During the period from 15 March – 31 October 1941 the Luftwaffe reported 56 convoys and shadowed many of them for several days at a time, thus enabling submarines to close in. Through close co-operation between submarines and air reconnaissance 74 merchant vessels totalling 390,000 tons, 1 aircraft-carrier and 1 destroyer were sunk. Between 13 March – 31 December 1941 bombing attacks by aircraft under the command of Fliegerfuehrer Atlantic produced the following results:

Sunk:	161	vessels	totalling	903,000 GRT
Probably sunk:	7	"	"	31,000 GRT
Damaged	113	"	"	590,000 GRT

However, in six months this situation had already undergone a radical change.

Owing to strong enemy defensive armament, low-level lateral attacks by Condors which until then were the usual and only possible method of attack owing to the equipment of this aircraft, had to be discontinued, first against convoys and then also against single vessels.

However, the Condors still had a useful task in carrying out reconnaissance for C.-in-C. Submarine Fleet so that submarines could be directed towards convoys.

Attacks on convoys escorted by destroyers and to an increasing extent by aircraft were now presenting even submarines with a difficult task.

The submarines transferred their point of main effort beyond the range of the Condors to attack the important convoys from America and operated exclusively in American waters from the late autumn of 1941.

Thus in the middle of December 1941 co-operation with C.-in-C. Submarine Fleet in the joint campaign against enemy shipping in the eastern Atlantic came practically to a standstill. Some of the Condor Staffeln were used in other theatres of operations. Owing to their limited range, the aircraft still at the disposal of the Atlantikfuehrer (K.Fl.Gr. 106) could be used only for operations against convoys around the British Isles.

For this reason IX Fliegerkorps also took over anti-shipping operations in the waters off the eastern coast of England.

During the period from July 1940 to 31 December 1943 bombers of the IX Fliegerkorps scored the following successes:

Sunk:	42 vessels totalling	167,000 GRT
Probably sunk:	38 vessels totalling	171,000 GRT
Damaged:	118 vessels totalling	439,000 GRT
Total:	198 vessels totalling	777,000 GRT

Fliegerfuehrer Atlantic confined himself to the area off the English south and west coasts. There were no extensive successes as for reasons of combined strategy torpedo aircraft were used on other fronts and the

---

(*footnote continued*)

During this period the following warships were sunk or damaged:

Sunk	Damaged
2 destroyers	1 battleship
1 mine-layer	3 destroyers
1 submarine	1 A.A. cruiser
1 M.T.B.	1 light cruiser
	1 anti-submarine trawler

available bombers had to be concentrated for attacks on the British mainland.

In May 1942 C.-in-C. Submarine Fleet again requested the assistance of Fliegerfuehrer Atlantic, but at first only for protection against the rapidly increasing threats to U-boats moving into and out of the Bay of Biscay by enemy anti-submarine craft. During the whole of 1942 and part of 1943 this was Fliegerfuehrer Atlantic's main task of co-operation with the C.-in-C. Submarine Fleet.

The twin-engined fighter formations set up by the Fliegerfuehrer Atlantic succeeded in driving British anti-submarine craft out of the Bay of Biscay into the Atlantic.

For the purpose of bringing blockade-runners in or out, cooperation in reconnaissance over the Atlantic was transferred from C.-in-C. Submarine Fleet to Marinegruppe West.

During reconnaissance operations carried out between 1 March and 22 April 1943 by a daily average of 6 aircraft over a sea area from 38° to 49° north and 10° to 20° west approximately 4,000,000 tons of merchant shipping and warships totalling about 300,000 tons were observed, the convoys moving within the effective range of German long-range bombers for at least four to five days. During these 6 weeks about one seventh of the enemy's serviceable merchant shipping lay within reach of long-range bombers, but as there were no formations available for a concentrated attack owing to the predominance of reconnaissance operations for Marinegruppe West, only a few vessels were sunk by aircraft on armed reconnaissance. Moreover, high-altitude bombing operations could not be carried out owing to low cloud.

Since the summer of 1942 the Fliegerfuehrer Atlantic had urged that the Fw-200 be equipped with bomb-sight C-7D and that crews be trained in dropping bombs. The results obtained in the spring of 1943 after the reequipment of III/K.G. 40 show that extensive successes are possible in the greater Atlantic area if the necessary forces, suitably equipped and with properly trained crews are available.

At first it was estimated that it would take 10–12 months to re-equip Condors with radio bomb control sets (Kehlgeraet). Today the Fw-200 has been fitted in a considerably shorter time.

The more dangerous mercantile warfare became for Great Britain, the greater were the efforts to organise defensive measures, particularly in the air.

The enemy provided his convoys from Britain to Gibraltar with air cover in addition to moving them further and further out of range of the Fw-200. New location equipment and methods made U-boat operations more difficult.

The importance the enemy attached to keeping the Bay of Biscay under observation can be estimated by the fact that in one month during the spring of 1943, 2,070 aircraft were picked up by radar.

2. Northern Waters

During 1942 rather more than half of the Soviet Union's supplies from overseas passed through Northern waters.

A total of 2,300,000 tons were imported as follows:

through White Sea ports (Murmansk, Archangel):   1,200,000 tons
through Persian ports (Karachi, Bushir, Bender-Schrapur): 600,000 tons
through Far-Eastern and northern ports (Vladivostok,
    Nikolajevsk, Lena, Jenissei):   500,000 tons

Supplies brought into the White Sea during 1942 fell into the following categories:

210,000 tons of war material	= 18%
1,600,000 tons of industrial raw materials	= 49%
240,000 tons of food	= 20%
160,000 tons of mineral oil	= 13%

The war material comprised:
1,880   aircraft,
2,350   tanks,
8,300   trucks,
6,400   other vehicles,
2,250   field guns.

Cooperation between Naval H.Q.s and Luftflotte 5 in Norway became extremely cordial. Moreover, the Luftwaffe had an extremely large share in the successful operations against convoys to Russia during the summer of 1942.

a) Between 25 and 30 May 1942 311 sorties were flown in cloudless weather against convoy PQ-16, which consisted of 30 transports, 2 heavy cruisers and 8 destroyers. 16 merchant vessels totalling 111,000 tons were sunk.

b) Between 9 and 10 July 1942 the Luftwaffe flew 212 bombing and torpedo sorties against convoy PQ-17, which comprised 30 merchant vessels and was protected by a double cordon of escorts (1 cruiser and a large number of destroyers), inflicting the following losses:

24 merchant vessels totalling 156,000 GRT,
1 cruiser of 9,000 tons

c) Convoy PQ-18, consisting of 40 transports and escorted by an aircraft-carrier and a large number of destroyers, sustained the following losses between 13 and 19 October 1942 in 337 sorties carried out
with cloud at 300 to 1,000 metres:
24 merchant vessels totalling 170,000 GRT,
1 destroyer of 1,200 tons,
2 escort vessels of 2,000 tons

The aircraft-carrier was badly damaged.

Thus in 860 sorties, of which 243 were made by torpedo-carrying
aircraft, the Luftwaffe inflicted the following losses on the three
convoys:
437,000 GRT
1 cruiser,
1 destroyer and
2 escort vessels sunk.

In addition 42 torpedo and 49 bomb hits were scored, badly damaging
a large number of other merchant vessels.

A comparison of successes obtained by torpedo-carrying and bomber
aircraft is very revealing.

For each ship sunk the following sorties were made:

a) in the case of the PQ-16 convoy under the best weather conditions for
dive-bombing attacks:
9.8 torpedo sorties as compared with
23.6 dive-bomber sorties.

b) in the case of the PQ-17 convoy, similarly in the best weather conditions:
7 torpedo sorties as compared with
9.2 dive bomber sorties.

c) in the case of the PQ-18 convoy in unfavourable weather conditions for
dive-bomber attacks:
7.3 torpedo sorties as compared with
24.3 dive-bomber sorties.

Of 340 aerial torpedoes launched 84 hit the target, i.e. 25%. 32 torpedoes were duds, i.e. 9%.

3. Mediterranean

Under cover of his Air Force and for some time practically without restriction, the enemy was able to bring over war material produced in the U.S to North Africa as well as to Europe. This fact seriously affected the German campaign in the Mediterranean.

Whilst the enemy moved a monthly average of

> 640,000 tons of material and
> 160,000 tons of petroleum

Total: 800,000

up to the North African front, the monthly rate of discharge in German-controlled ports in Tunisia amounted to –

> about 65,000 tons during February 1942 and
> about 50,000 tons during March 1942.

For this reason and because German sea transport in the Mediterranean could not be adequately protected, the German bridgehead in North Africa and also Sicily and southern Italy could not be held. In this instance enemy air superiority had a decisive effect. Large warships, especially battleships and aircraft-carriers, could not be sunk.

The situation improved in the autumn of 1942 when K.G. 26 was brought in. Between May 1942 and October 1943 K.G. 26 made 2139 sorties and launched 1653 aerial torpedoes, of which 342 (21.1%) hit the target.

In 18 months the following vessels were sunk by aerial torpedoes:

> 77 merchant vessels totalling about 552,000 GRT
> 1 cruiser,
> 4 destroyers and
> 5 escort vessels.

The following were damaged:

> 165 merchant vessels totalling about 1,100,000 GRT
> 1 aircraft-carrier,
> 12 cruisers and
> 18 destroyers.

August, September and October 1943 were the most successful months. In six major (234 sorties) and 9 minor (82 sorties) attacks

> 64 merchant vessels totalling 423,000 GRT and
> 10 warships

were sunk or damaged. In the course of these operations 55 aircraft and 31 aircrew were lost. In all K.G. 26 lost 141 aircrews in 18 months.

In August 1943 1140 bomber sorties were carried out:

33,000 GRT were sunk and

506,000 GRT damaged.

Compared with this the following losses were caused by only 65 aerial torpedo sorties:

88,000 GRT sunk and

106,000 GRT damaged.

The year 1943 shows a marked change in the air war at sea as the situation again permitted an intensified employment of well-trained formations at full strength. Successes achieved in air operations during this year are mounting again. It is expected that the situation will develop favourably in future.

On the other hand the enemy has brought about a radical change in the situation by reinforcing his air force, so that successes will certainly not be achieved easily.

However, in face of the continual reinforcement of the Luftwaffe, the opportunities which the enemy has used to achieve successes will no longer exist.

Note

According to K.G. 26 reports 999/44 of 4 March 1944 and 1238 of 18 March 1944 the following were sunk or damaged between 1 March 1943 and 29 February 1944.

167 merchant vessels totalling 1,106,000 tons and

27 warships including

5 cruisers,

17 destroyers

5 escorts

Results of Fliegerfuehrer Atlantic's anti-shipping operations in 1942 and 1943:

1942

Merchant Shipping:

Sunk:	13	vessels	totalling	43,000	GRT
Probably sunk:	6	”	”	17,000	”
Damaged:	19	”	”	92,000	”

Warships:

Sunk:	Damaged
1 auxiliary cruiser	2 destroyers
1 destroyer	2 trawlers
2 M.T.B.s	
3 trawlers	

1943

Merchant Shipping:

Sunk:	13	vessels	totalling	98,000	GRT
Probably sunk:	7	"	"	34,000	GRT
Damaged:	16	"	"	106,000	GRT

Warships:

Sunk	Damaged
2 destroyers	2 light cruisers
	2 destroyers
	1 mine-layer

Part 2

I. Survey of supply to Great Britain in 1943

The importance of convoys to the whole economy of the British Isles as well as to Anglo-American strategy can be ascertained from the following figures.

In 1938 British importation amounted to 71 million GRT. This figure fell to 35 million GRT in 1942, a rate which the enemy had to maintain to guarantee a minimum standard of existence.

These 35 million tons comprised:

10 million GRT of raw materials,
9 " " " food,
9 " " " mineral oils,
and 7 " " " ready made goods.

In addition there were 1,800,000 GRT for military supplies required for the British war effort. A monthly average of 5 million GRT was used on the North Atlantic route from the U.S.A. to Britain alone. Of this an average per month of more than two million GRT crossed the Atlantic, while the remainder was in port at either end of the route.

From July to October 1943 three convoy routes were apparent in the

Atlantic, these being from the U.S. to Gibraltar, from Britain to Gibraltar and from the U.S. to Britain and back.

Troop convoys usually consisted of 5 to 20 large passenger vessels or large freighters suitable for use as troop-transports.

Supply convoys generally comprised 20 to 25 freighters. Both types of convoy, and tankers in particular, are extremely important objectives and their destruction has a lasting effect on the enemy war effort.

The strength of the escorting force varies widely and is provided according to the value and importance of the convoy. A temporary shortage of warships has also probably enforced restricted employment of escort vessels. For example, a convoy of 14 troop transports was escorted by:

1 auxiliary cruiser
1 aircraft depot ship
3 auxiliary aircraft carriers
2 destroyers and
6 small escort vessels.

The composition of escorts for freighter convoys varies a great deal, ranging between 5 and 18 warships for every 45 freighters. So far no aircraft carriers have been reported acting as escorts and even a cruiser is rarely seen.

The U.S.–Britain convoys move from the large ports of the American east coast along the great circle to the northern entrance of the Irish Sea. If submarines attack, or even if they are only located, the convoys take evasive action by moving below the coast of Greenland and Ireland. According to statistical data, which extends over a sufficiently long period, one troop-transport convoy runs at the same time interval on this double route every sixth or seventh day and one freighter convoy every thirteenth day.

Convoys from U.S. to Britain generally comprise 35 vessels escorted by a varying number of destroyers and corvettes and frequently by cruisers as well, according to the value of the cargo.

In March 1943 the following vessels arrived at ports on the Irish Sea through the northern channel:

from Iceland:	25 vessels = 100,000 GRT
from U.S.A.	150 vessels = 900,000 GRT
from Central and South America and S. Africa	35 vessels = 200,000 GRT
from Gibraltar and North Africa	110 vessels = 600,000 GRT

The material which had been brought in was distributed amongst the ports on the southern and eastern coasts of the British Isles by coastal shipping moving round Lands End to Southampton and south of the Orkney Islands to Dundee and Edinburgh. In addition there was heavy coastal traffic – 300 vessels totalling 750,000 GRT – from Edinburgh southwards to the Thames and it is probable that a large part of the goods unloaded on the western coast were moved by railway across the narrowest part of the British Isles from Glasgow to Edinburgh and thence by sea to London under cover of the coast.

On the south coast of England 110 vessels totalling 275,000 tons passed through the St. Georges Channel to Southampton during the same period.

II. The strategic air situation in the Atlantic, 1943/44

A fundamental change has occurred recently in the political and military situation in the Atlantic. Conditions for the conduct of air and sea warfare have also changed accordingly.

The construction of bases in the Atlantic was urged primarily by the British.

The Americans were more inclined to protect routes across the Pacific, but as they had invested considerable capital in African undertakings, they turned their attention to acquisition of operational bases in the Atlantic.

In autumn 1940 Britain gave permission for the construction of naval and air bases on Newfoundland, on the Bermuda and Bahama Islands, on Jamaica, Antigua and St. Lucia. After Curacao, Aruba and Dutch Guiana were occupied and American bases established in Brazil, the defence belt extended far into South America. In 1941 the United States occupied Greenland, Iceland and Jan Mayen. Spitzbergen was included in cooperation with the British. A base was also set up in northern Ireland and American troops landed in Scotland. In Africa they acquired the use of ports in French West and Equatorial Africa and in the Belgian Congo area. Even Monrovia, the capital of Liberia, came under their influence. In addition, Dakar, Casablanca and other ports on the west coast of Africa were claimed by the Americans. In 1943 the Portugese were forced to make the Azores available for the establishment of bases. Pressure was maintained to achieve the same result on Madeira and the Cape Verde Islands.

Gibraltar is Britain's most important base for operations in the Atlantic and Mediterranean. In addition, she possesses a number of ports on the western coast of Africa as well as several islands in the southern Atlantic. In the near north British control extends to the Faroes.

There is no longer a gap in the Atlantic. The enemy can cover the whole of the north Atlantic from the Bermudas, Newfoundland, Iceland, the

British Isles, Gibraltar and the Azores. Enemy radar posts may be set up in Spain and Portugal.

However, Germany has also broken out from Heligoland Bay to the open sea. Her operational coastal bases in the west extend from Norway to Biarritz. The Channel Islands (Guernsey and Jersey) are in German hands. The British Isles are now within striking distance of the German-held coast. German submarines from French and Norwegian bases have created a serious threat to enemy sea routes. The Luftwaffe is also advancing further and further into the Atlantic.

It is an essential condition for the Luftwaffe that units can be transferred rapidly between the north Atlantic and the Mediterranean to provide a concentration of forces suitable for the strategic situation and the weather.

However, owing to the weather, it will not always be possible to transfer formations from France to Norway and back without delays.

The standard of training of aircrews and the equipment of aircraft will, however, enable long-range bombers to take off in bad weather. Rainfall, low clouds and even light ground mist do not present insuperable obstacles to aircrews trained in blind flying. The bad weather areas occurring near the coast usually diminish further out to sea, so that even if the aircraft of a formation are compelled to take off singly and fly blind for a short time owing to the weather, they can soon re-assemble. However, aircraft returning from an operation must be directed to a home base where the prevailing weather conditions will permit a landing.

A glance at the map will show that there are ample supply lines from any direction at the enemy's disposal to encounter air attacks at sea. There is only a slight threat to his ocean bases owing to the weakness of German naval surface forces and the range of the bombers available at present. Thus there is no doubt that the enemy can concentrate his defence forces in any area of operation which may be selected by the Luftwaffe and U-boats.

Very great strength will therefore be necessary if successful operations are to be carried out far over the Atlantic.

This leads to the question whether air superiority over Atlantic shipping routes must be gained as a preliminary condition for the conduct of anti-shipping operations.

Whereas the conquest and occupation of a country must be preceded by a battle on land, vital sea communications can be cut without "occupying" the sea area. This is possible as the range of U-boats and aircraft has reached an unprecedented extent and is constantly increasing. Thus, in spite of their superiority at sea, that is according to former conceptions, the Anglo-Americans cannot deprive their enemy of every opportunity of carrying out of operations.

Constant air superiority as regards time and space cannot be achieved. Even Britain and America could not supply the forces required for this purpose. However, air superiority can certainly be achieved temporarily by concentrating all available forces. The degree of effect varies according to the geographical location of air bases which offer the best possibilities. It is much more difficult to achieve air superiority over convoy routes far out in the Atlantic where even the enemy cannot at present maintain continuous air cover.

An enemy air force can be destroyed only under exceptional circumstances. In the Polish Campaign this was brought about by a surprise air attack with greatly superior forces. In the war against France an adequate measure of success was achieved, the preliminary conditions still being favourable. However, the prolongation of the war for several years led not only to parity of forces but later to enemy superiority both in defence and attack. The enemy has acquired a knowledge of tactics and has reached our standard. At present he has surpassed us in the technical field and his total production capacity exceeds ours. In addition to the question of operational strength, it is vital that the available bases should be used to best advantage. The struggle for air superiority will be confined to areas in which targets of economic importance, in this case convoys, must be protected or destroyed. Although the enemy may be stronger, even in fighters, locally limited air superiority is not absolute, as no barriers are possible in infinite space.

If these theories prove correct, German air operations in the Atlantic have great prospects of success in spite of present inferiority.

III. Possible courses of action open to enemy

After the main effort of the Luftwaffe has been transferred to the Atlantic it will not be long before enemy counter-measures become evident. Preparations are already being made to meet this situation. At the moment the enemy appears to be rather negligent as he feels he has the advantage over the Germans. Knox, the U.S. Navy Minister regards the present situation in the Atlantic as such an improvement that he has cancelled plans for building 427 submarine chasers. However, a reduction in the forces engaged in air defence over the Atlantic must not be expected.

Faced by the success of the German submarine offensive, the enemy considered building a large number of transport aircraft. Indeed, such plans may to a certain extent have been put into practice. Nevertheless, the transportation of merchandise will still be carried on largely by merchant ships, for even the American 70-ton Mars transport aircraft with a carrying capacity of about 25 tons have a normal operational load capacity of only 15 to 20 tons. This shows the maximum operational load one aircraft is able to carry. How many aircraft would be required to carry American freight alone may be deduced from the statement of President Roosevelt that in the period between May and August 1943 no fewer than 4,000 American ships had been convoyed across the Atlantic by the U.S. Navy.

The German air and submarine menace is being met rather in other ways:

The simplest solution would be to move the shipping routes beyond the range of German bombers. It is scarcely to be expected, however, that the enemy will stop using the eastern part of the middle Atlantic as long as he can provide his convoys with adequate protection. Besides this, he must expect German attacks to occur very soon also in the northern part of the Atlantic, as modern naval strategy can plan operations on a scale hitherto unknown, on account of the constant increase of efficiency of the Luftwaffe and the U-boats. Whilst the British could afford to vacate the North Sea in the years from 1914 to 1918 because they had nothing to defend there, they are obliged now, in the Atlantic to call upon all their forces, in order to safeguard their economy. For that purpose it is also necessary to bring the convoys by the shortest possible routes to their destinations. The enemy will therefore combat the threat to his supply lines principally by offensive action. Consequently an increasing number of small and medium aircraft-carriers will be used to protect convoys. The Azores will assume great importance as a new base for operations. The inshore escorts on the English coast will receive appropriate reinforcements.

The enemy High Command will also endeavour to put the ground organisation of the German formations operating in the Atlantic out of action by bombing raids. Such bombing operations can be carried out without difficulty from the air bases in Britain, Gibraltar and Africa. Moreover the enemy's forces are sufficient to meet German defence.

Another measure must be taken into account, namely the establishment of air bases in Spain and Portugal, though this would necessitate at least, partial occupation of those countries. This step would have the advantage of considerably shortening the shipping routes. Convoys could then sail close to the Iberian coast under the protection of strong fighter cover. This would severely restrict operations of the Luftwaffe and U-boats.

In the final analysis it is the task of the enemy to capture the German bases. This is possible only by the establishment of a second front in the occupied areas of Western Europe. The enemy might also land in Jutland and south of Norway and then attack north Germany across the Baltic. Moreover, threat remains of a flanking attack through the Balkans.

Other remaining possibilities of attacking supply shipping must be viewed in the light of these considerations. It must be admitted that the enemy is able to put up powerful resistance to the measures introduced by the Germans.

On the other hand it is clear that to cripple Anglo-American merchant shipping would hit the enemy where he is most vulnerable.

This aim can be achieved by operations on a scale which is both practical and justified for a campaign, the probable success of which will considerably improve the general situation.

The great efforts the enemy is making to develop his air force are intended primarily to establish numerical and technical superiority. The German aircraft industry, for its part, will do all it can to keep the air power of the Reich on a par with the enemy air force. In view of the significant productive capacity of Britain and America, this task will not be an easy one. However, skillful leadership and superior technical resources will to great extent counteract the numerical ascendency of the enemy.

IV. Conclusions

Basically, the anti-shipping campaign can be waged in three ways, namely

by the surface craft and submarines of the Navy,
by long-range reconnaissance aircraft and bombers of the Luftwaffe,
by the combined operations of both services.

At the present time the operations of U-boats are being hampered because they can be spotted promptly and fairly accurately by aircraft and warships equipped with D/F apparatus and forced to submerge by air attacks and naval artillery.

The use of reconnaissance aircraft to serve as "eyes" for submarines is certainly not the only way in which this situation can be overcome. The consideration must be to succeed in effectively jamming the enemy's D/F apparatus at the moment an attack is being launched, or to disarm individual ships by torpedo and bombing attacks carried out by the Luftwaffe.

The Luftwaffe has a great advantage over U-boats in operations against enemy convoys. The special character of aerial warfare over the sea at the present time derives from the immense areas involved.

In the first World War U-boats were by themselves the main weapon of economic warfare. The scene of their operations was the North Sea. Even at that time aircraft gave tactical support to U-boats, but only to a limited extent owing to the short range of aircraft.

After the Luftwaffe had been reformed, its unique quality, its effectiveness as an instrument of war and hence its significance, led to its being responsible only to Supreme Command. This fact has a bearing on the special position of the Luftwaffe in the organisation of the Supreme Command. The independence of the Luftwaffe will again become evident after its main effort is transferred to the Atlantic, as it has already proved that it can carry an independent air warfare also at sea.

This applies as much to operations with purely military objectives as to those concerned with economic warfare. For example, it was the Luftwaffe alone that made the capture of Crete possible. The Luftwaffe was also able to hamper the transportation of supplies by sea from Africa to such an extent that the enemy had to forgo the shipment of essential reinforcements. As the first German troops with equipment were on the whole transported to the island by air, interference by enemy naval forces was accordingly ruled out.

It has been proved that in economic warfare the percentage of enemy shipping sunk as a result of the independent use of the Luftwaffe in sufficient force is so high, that a decisive reduction in the delivery of supplies to Britain can be achieved by this means alone.

In 1942 the principle hunting-ground of the Luftwaffe was over the area where Atlantic traffic was picked up by inshore escort forces. In these waters convoys were concentrated in a small area. Convoys could be located by navigational aids. The disadvantage of strong defence could be overcome by attacking at dusk and during the night. Holland offered excellent opportunities as a base for these attacks. Flying from darkness towards a bright horizon assured excellent possibilities for offensive action. For this reason the number of ships sunk off the south-west coast of Britain was high.

Convoys were assembled also on the west coast. In particular, the area between Land's End and the Bristol Channel and also the sea area off Pembroke offered opportunities for successful operations. In this case, however, it was disadvantageous to fly in from the light towards a darkening horizon. Attacks in the Irish Sea could be made successfully only at night, as otherwise the German formations flying in to attack by day could be intercepted by British fighters.

Conditions have changed to the disadvantage of the German attackers since the enemy has reinforced his defence forces more and more. Attacks therefore are undertaken only where defence is weakest. This means that the formations must fly far out over the Atlantic, that is to those areas as remote as possible from enemy air bases in the Azores, Gibraltar and the British Isles. But this increases the difficulties under which the Germans operate, especially as fighter protection must be reckoned with even in these sea areas. Another situation would be created if the enemy could give protection to his convoys from Spanish and Portuguese bases.

The following conclusions may be drawn from a study of these factors.

1. Aircraft and submarines are engaged in the anti-shipping war as equal partners.

   This is the conclusion to which one must necessarily come in considering the possibilities of combined operations by the Luftwaffe and U-boats.

   The Luftwaffe is particularly mobile. It is the Luftwaffe that as a rule locates the convoy and directs U-boats to it. It is the Luftwaffe that seeks out aircraft carriers in order to sink them first. It is the Luftwaffe that fights the U-boats' worst enemy, the fighter and destroys enemy shipping unaided. But the engagements of the Luftwaffe are only of short duration. If an attack is unsuccessful, then the submarines are at an advantage, because they can lurk along the convoy route for a long period and make another attack later. The submarine can also summon the Luftwaffe to make surprise attacks. If contact with the enemy is lost it can again call on the Luftwaffe to carry out reconnaissance so that this may be restored. Both services accordingly help each other as well as possible. From this it is understood that the Commands of the Luftwaffe and the U-boats must be closely connected.

   The ideal solution lies in a combined order of battle for the Luftwaffe and Navy, where the Luftwaffe would have the following tasks:

   a) to locate convoys by long-range reconnaissance,
   b) to attack with torpedoes and put out of action the aircraft carriers which no doubt will in future accompany all convoys,
   c) to jam the D/F apparatus and hence the AA artillery of convoys,
   d) to sink a large number of ships immediately by bombing and torpedo attacks or eliminate them from further action.

   It would then be the task of the U-boats to attack and completely destroy the scattered and defenceless convoy.

2. From an organisational standpoint, the proceedure adopted hitherto appears to be the most effective: the command authorities of the Luftwaffe (Luftflotte) are responsible for the strategy employed in the battle of the Atlantic and have at their disposal the Norwegian bases and close co-operation from others nearby.

   If two subordinate H.Q.s are set up to direct the battle of the Atlantic – if the increase in the size of forces engaged warrant this, – it may be consider desirable to entrust this function to a General H.Q., as a sort of Fernkampffuehrer Atlantik (Long Range Atlantic Command), with unified control along lines laid down by the Luftflottenkommando.

3. Considered from a strategical point of view one can deduce from the possibilities open to the enemy that air warfare carried out for any length of time at sea can only be successful if strong forces are employed.

Really substantial successes can be recorded only if the formations summoned by shadowing aircraft to attack convoys can deal the enemy crippling blows in a combined attack.

The services of twin-engined fighters will also be used in this connection so as to provide cover for formations operating far out over the Atlantic.

Fighters will be able to keep the enemy out of the Bay of Biscay area and also protect German bases from enemy air attacks.

In order to intensify the campaign it would be necessary to provide formations of long range bombers and reconnaissance aircraft and twin and single engine fighters in sufficient numbers, which would, however, depend on the requirements of the war as a whole. Even if only a limited amount of fighter cover can be counted on in the distant areas of the Atlantic, at least it is possible with the latest long-range fighters to make persistent attacks on the enemy air force in the approaches between the Scilly Isles and the Irish coast.

Under the above conditions there would be a decisive increase in the number of vessels sunk.

If the enemy should succeed in establishing air bases in Spain or Portugal, the war against shipping could be continued only after further development of a strong day- and night-fighter organisation. The advantages of supporting air operations from bases on the Iberian peninsula and in southern England would be on the enemy's side, only as long as German forces were inadequate for their task.

In this connection the question of the vulnerability of the German ground organisation assumes a special significance. As long as the long-range bomber formations with their special equipment remain to a great extent dependent on technical facilities of their operational bases, it will be impossible to avoid building bombproof hangars. If this is not possible for technical reasons, other methods of protecting German bases will have to be found.

4. With the whole of the Luftwaffe being turned over to meet the needs of the war at sea, the question of the training of personnel assumes foremost importance.

Study of documents salvaged from British and American aircraft shows that entries are made in log-book fashion and so meticulously that fractions of a second are taken into consideration. Apart from this, an exceedingly high standard of navigational skill can be discerned which can be acquired only after much practice. Of the German formations, the crews that have been most successful are those whose proficiency has been maintained by constant practice in the use of navigational aids in long-range operations. In contrast to this, the formations that have been employed for years in support of the army not only lack professional dexterity but often also the right temperamental approach for carrying out the precise manoeuvres of navigation that are needed in locating targets on the sea. The crews are not to blame for this as they are usually concerned with terrestrial navigation. They seldom have opportunities for enlarging the knowledge of general navigation they acquired during training.

For these reasons there is an all-round shortage of qualified personnel.

The basic reason for the shortage referred to is the fact that the Luftwaffe had to be utilised primarily for supporting the army. Indeed, in the course of the land fighting the concept of the Luftwaffe as a means of overall strategy receded further and further into the background. It will not be easy to recreate a proper strategic air force.

It is obvious that air crews engaged in operations over land need additional training for air warfare at sea. The junior officers of the Luftwaffe should have been familiarized from the beginning with the ideas of warfare over vast areas not only of land but also of sea. We cannot give our officers a one-sided training, confined to either Army, Navy or Luftwaffe operations; they must be schooled in the operations of all three services so that they can play their part successfully in achieving the aims of the general war strategy and later be able to take their places as real leaders of the Wehrmacht.

The question of the training of subordinates also arises in this connection, as the war at sea is governed from the point of view of strategy and tactics by special laws which must be made absolutely clear to them. It is incumbent on all instructors at Luftwaffe training centres to relate their teaching to the intercontinental character of the war strategy as a whole. When Lord Salisbury said "Study large maps!" he epitomized a lesson which we have still to learn after centuries of thinking in terms of single continents.

In the training given to air crews the emphasis must be placed on the teaching of navigation (including astronomical navigation). In addition, the rudiments of naval tactics must also be taught, and a special study made of the use of naval forces, in order to be able to recognise the tactical situation and the most favourable position for attack. This requires the cooperation of the training, surface and submarine forces of the Navy. The combined effort of the services participating, Luftwaffe (bombing, lateral, dive-bombing, long-range and torpedo attacks) and the Navy (especially submarines) will be demonstrated by practical exercises.

5. From a technical standpoint the efficiency of aircraft employed in the battle of the Atlantic is dependent upon great range, high speed, and adequate armament and bomb load.

The fact that the Liberator has proved superior to the Ju-290 serves as another reminder of the enormous strides German aircraft development must make to enable the Luftwaffe to achieve tactical successes in spite of numerical inferiority.

Medium-fast bombers must have a tactical radius of 3,000 km. and a bomb-load of 4,000 kg. Aircraft should be capable of rapid conversion for carrying bombs, torpedoes or Kehlgeraet (apparatus for controlling the trajectory of bombs).

The interior arrangements of aircraft could undergo examination when new developments occur. Operations carried out far out over the Atlantic call for constant navigation. It therefore seems expedient not to burden the members of the crew responsible for this with other duties. The observer and the wireless operator would then be concerned solely with navigation, while the rear gunners would be responsible exclusively for observing and rear defence. Such an arrangement and the provision of the necessary accommodation would guarantee perfect identification of targets and effective use of armaments.

A long-range fighter having a high top speed and carrying full armament would have an operational radius of about 1,000 km. Such aircraft have the double task of covering German bombers during attacks on enemy shipping in the Bay of Biscay and of protecting the arrival and departure of submarines. As already stated, British aircraft used for hunting submarines are equipped with ship locating apparatus of such outstanding quality that they are able to find U-boats through dense cloud and on dark nights, so that generally the submarines do not have time to submerge before being bombed. The enemy is using Beaufighters, Whitleys, Hudsons, Wellingtons, Sunderlands and Liberators. Their performance serves as a guide of what must be accomplished in the development of new long-range fighters.

Long-range twin-engined fighters used for operations far out over the Atlantic must have an operational radius of 3,000 km in addition to improved dependability and performance after air engagements.

Medium-fast reconnaissance aircraft should have an operational radius of 5,000 km. To operate successfully they must have the heaviest armament.

The Kehlgeraet opens new possibilities in the way of weapons. According to the London press, the enemy believes that the battleship *Roma* was destroyed by a remote-controlled rocket-bomb. It is regarded as conclusive proof that the new bomb has its own propelling unit and guiding fins which can be controlled by radio.

Insofar as the controlled flight of this bomb cannot be interfered with, it is a menace to enemy shipping. Tactical manoeuvrability will be improved when it can be released at any altitude and be certain to strike the target with accuracy.

When the development of long-range bombers make it possible for heavier loads to be carried, it will also be possible to increase the effectiveness of torpedoes. This could certainly be achieved if their weight could be increased.

In addition to the question of weight, the following developments might be made with regard to torpedoes:

Increase in range and bombing altitude.

Raising the speed of torpedoes and increasing the distance they can travel;

enlarging the war-head.

Introducing new methods of fusing.

Using an appratus that will give a torpedo a zig-zag course on the convoy route.

Using an apparatus which would enable a torpedo to guide itself to a target.

Eliminating the effect of high seas and cross winds.

In considering the relative values of the bomb and the torpedo the conclusion was reached that the bomb, including the remote-controlled bomb, could not take the place of the torpedo and that the torpedo could not be used to the exclusion of other weapons. Thus, torpedoes, Kehlgeraet and bombs can all be used effectively, the actual weapon chosen for a given operation depending upon the situation and other factors.

As regards radio, the chances of success will be increased by the development of panoramic search and D/F radar to enable torpedoes, bombs and remote-controlled bombs to be launched through cloud and at night.

The need for the development of apparatus for observing and giving warning of radar search signals of enemy origin is indicated, for the use of German reconnaissance aircraft. The range and performance of radar generally needs to be improved. In regard to navigation, it is necessary to evolve a radio system unaffected by altitude and the time of day.

It is not within the scope of this study to go into technical details, but they must always be kept well in the foreground.

Prospects

In considering all the possibilities, one comes to the conclusion that the Luftwaffe can raise not only the diminishing number of ships sunk by U-boats, but can first of all operate independently and strike a decisive blow against British sea power, by paralysing her supplies. The Luftwaffe would fulfil its true purpose if so used. The struggle against British supply shipping is not a matter of applied tactics, but of applied strategy. The situation brought about by the course of the war confirms the intercontinental character of air warfare.

The theories put forward by Alexander de Seversky in his book *Victory through Air Power*, which has been widely read in enemy countries, are of interest in this connection. Seversky is of the opinion that the Germans estimated the effectiveness of the Luftwaffe incorrectly. Mainly short-range aircraft for Army co-operation were produced and the Reich was therefore compelled to carry out the majority of its campaigns on land. These, it is true, resulted in the capture of air bases for operations against Britain, but at that time there were no long-range aircraft available.

Seversky's theory does not make allowance for the circumstances. At the beginning of the war it was correct to use the Luftwaffe against the most important enemy of the moment, the enemy Army and Air Force. Destruction of supply bases would have had little influence on events at that time, as motorised operations against inferior enemy forces came to an end too quickly.

After the attempt to defeat the enemy quickly failed, the Luftwaffe had to concentrate on sources of economic strength. The enemy also appeared to be taking the same course. The Anglo-Americans did not open the full-scale strategic air offensive with terror attacks until last year. So far Russia has not made any such attempt, as her forces are at present fully committed in the struggle against the German Army. However, long-range bomber operations from Russia must be expected, at least by Anglo-American bombers with Russian or foreign crews.

The Germans made allowance for these facts by transferring the main

Luftwaffe effort to operations at sea at the present stage of the war. It is now only a matter of assembling the necessary forces to produce the desired result.

The following statements illustrate the importance of full-strength, concentrated Luftwaffe operations against British supply shipping.

A report by Fliegerfuehrer Atlantic shows, for example, that during the period from 1 March to 22 April 1943 a total of 3,772,000 GRT sailed within effective range of our long-range bombers. If it is correct to assume that the total merchant shipping tonnage at the enemy's disposal amounts to approximately 22 million tons, then this comprises almost one seventh of enemy supply shipping. Thus the methodical and concentrated employment of all available forces under a unified command could not fail to be effective. During the above mentioned period 25 convoys comprising 617 merchant vessels were escorted by 12 cruisers, 38 destroyers, 118 escort vessels and 3 aircraft-carriers. Apart from the aircraft from the carriers, air cover from Gibraltar, the Azores and the British Isles would not present any great difficulty, as until now this has been provided only by long-range bombers or flying-boats. In view of the limited number of aircraft-carriers, fighter cover would not at present be fully effective. However, it is expected that the enemy may use long-range fighters in future also.

Even if one can believe statements made by Knox the U.S. Navy Minister to the effect that ship construction in 1942 exceeded sinkings by more than 1½ million tons, the gap between sinkings and construction could be widened again considerably in favour of the former.

This would result in Luftwaffe operations in the Atlantic striking a heavy blow against British industries without actually attacking them.

There have never yet been any miracles in a war.

New weapons, revolutionary both in number and effect, new ideas of command etc, which would give the weaker side immediate and complete superiority, have never made a sudden appearance.

Military miracles arise only from intense preparation and the use of adequate first rate forces at a favourable moment, at the same time having nullified possible enemy counter-measures.

The air war over the Atlantic, which may be further intensified in the future, must also be considered in this light.

However, a sudden change in the supply battle against Britain and America cannot be expected immediately. Success will rather be achieved only after a lengthy period of operations by numerically and technically adequate forces.

This must be clearly understood.

The number of ships sunk will certainly not rise as quickly as might be hoped, as it will not be possible to release the number of aircraft required and raise technical standards in a short time. The general war situation also makes this impossible, in so far as it precludes a permanent and effective concentration of forces due to difficulties which can scarcely be surmounted even with the closest cooperation between commands.

However, it is all the more necessary to adhere to the primary strategy in the West, namely the widest possible employment of the Luftwaffe in co-operation with U-boats against Anglo-American supply lines. Plans should be made and put into operation on a long-term basis irrespective of any theories and obstacles which can only weaken in every possible way any decision which may be made.

Chapter 5

GERMAN ARMY AND AIR FORCE INFLUENCE ON THE GERMAN NAVY DURING WORLD WAR II

by the Naval Historical Team

With the beginning of the war, there began a period of attrition which whittled German Naval Aviation practically out of existence by September 1944.

Prior to the War Goering had been able to gain administrative control of all Naval Air units. Now he began a campaign to gain tactical control as well, in contravention of the existing directive and agreements. The tactic he employed was twofold: (1) reduce allocations for air units under Navy control, and (2) build up the Air Force's own air units for sea operations, under "X Air Corps."

On 31 October 1939 the Naval Staff had to inform naval group commanders that due to the current lack of sufficient aircraft, naval air operations were to be limited to reconnaissance, while offensive operations against enemy naval units were to be carried out "at present" by the Air Force X Air Corps.

A Naval memorandum dated 15 January 1940 stated that while Naval group commands in the early months of the war were requesting additional air support, for example for duty with destroyers operating in the North Sea, Goering was trying to reduce the number of Naval air units. This memorandum pointed up another manner in which the Navy's aviation was being handicapped, namely, through inferior equipment. The memorandum stated that Goering notified the Naval Staff that no planes of type Do-217 could be granted the Navy "due to the need for transferring all offensive air operations at sea to the X Air Corps." Instead, the Navy would receive type He-115. Raeder protested that the He-115 was obsolete.

This memorandum shows that by December 1939 Naval air reconnaissance operations had come to a standstill. It stated that on 21 December 1939 "it became evident that no responsible command could assign planes of type He-111J any longer to operations over the sea due to technical

A close-up of an He 115C-1 of 3./Kü.Fl.Gr.106, with its offset 20mm MG 151 cannon. By January 1940 the navy was complaining that this seaplane was obsolete.

shortcomings of this type. To overcome this sudden emergency, a temporary agreement was reached between the Air Force General Staff and the Naval Staff whereby the X Air Corps was directed to carry out reconnaissance operations for Naval Group Command West "within the limitations of what is possible."

The memorandum concluded: "The Naval Staff is conscious of the shortcomings in quality and quantity, but must give way to the material situation."

Conferences on this situation continued all through the spring of 1940, but the general picture remained the same. Goering further cut the strength of Naval air units on 4 April 1940 in a revised armament program which reduced the number of planes per squadron from the original twelve to nine in some squadrons, to eleven in others.

The pre-war Navy–Air Force Agreement provided a full strength force of 27 coastal air squadrons and 14 carrier and shipboard squadrons. The greatest strength ever achieved by German Naval Aviation fell considerably short of these figures. On 15 January 1940, there were 18 instead of 27 coastal squadrons. This number shrank rapidly after that date.

Expanding Requirements

Germany's early victories in Norway and France placed further operational burdens on both Naval Aviation and the Air Force which in turn intensified the controversy. The Navy needed more planes to cover the greatly lengthened coast line which fell within its operational jurisdiction. The Air Force needed all the strength it could muster for the "Blitz" against England preparatory to the anticipated invasion. At the time that Raeder was requesting more squadrons from the Air Force, Goering was diverting, over Raeder's protest, Navy Air units to Air Force duties.

German Naval files give the impression that by summer 1940 such an atmosphere of animosity had been generated between the Naval and Air Force commands that a clash of opinion occurred on almost every issue jointly dealt with. Two of such issues were mining operations and the Navy's request, rejected by the Air Force, that air bases be established at Lorient and St. Nazaire to support U-boat operations.

Dispute over Naval Air Group 606

The course of the controversy thus far led inevitably to the bitter, head-on clash over Naval Air Group 606. This case is a classic example of the impossibility of the situation created by divided command over German Naval aviation.

According to a memorandum in the Naval Staff files, dated 8 September 1940, the dispute developed as follows:

The Commander of Air Group 606 approached the Air Force with a request to take part in the air attacks on England, saying that the Group's Naval duties at the time were not heavy. They participated in a number of attacks, but finally the Naval Staff forbade such operations, in order that the Group's operational readiness could be maintained.

During the night of 6–7 September, the Air Force Liaison Officer of Naval Group, West, a Colonel Metzner, telephoned the Naval Staff that Goering had ordered that Coastal Air Group 606 was to take part in operation "Loge" – the attack on London. The Navy Staff stood on its previous refusal to permit Naval units to participate in Air Force operations. The Air Force insisted, Goering requesting the Naval Staff to agree in order to avoid unpleasant friction. The Navy was adamant on the grounds that Goering was not entitled to give operational orders to other Services. The Operations Officer in the Air Force Command Staff took the position that the Group Commander 606 was an Air Force Officer who was bound to carry out the orders of his most superior officer.

After several sharp exchanges on a lower echelon during the day of 7

September, the question was taken to the Armed Forces High Command. General Jodl decided that Coastal Air Group 606 should participate in the attack on London. That ended that dispute. The Navy capitulated.

Hitler's Directives

Finally, at this point Hitler took a hand in the Navy–Air Force controversy, issuing three successive directives. The first dealt principally with immediate matters. On 13 September 1940 Hitler issued an order to Naval Staff on the subject of "Reconnaissance Forces of the Navy." The order apportioned several air squadrons between Air Force and Naval Command, formally stating that Hitler reserved to himself the right to make transfers between the Forces to better meet the needs of both Services with limited equipment.

A second order issued by Hitler, dated 6 January 1941, followed a Fuehrer Conference attended by Raeder on 27 December 1940. The order emphasized the importance of air reconnaissance to U-boat warfare against Britain's shipping, and directed the transfer of a squadron of FW-200 planes, with a minimum strength of 12, to the operational command of Commanding Admiral, U-boats. The order also returned another Coastal Air Group from Naval to Air Force Command.

*A classic German propaganda photograph of the Focke–Wulf Fw 200
Condor, the most feared of Germany's Atlantic anti-shipping aircraft.*

Hitler's third order, dated 28 February 1941, marked the beginning of the end of Naval Aviation under command of the Naval Staff. It revised the coastal and sea areas for the reconnaissance of which the Navy and the Air Force each were to be responsible. It gave to the Air Force the responsibility of reconnaissance over the Atlantic, for which purpose a special command was to be set up: Commander Air, Atlantic (Fliegerfuehrer, Atlantik). He was charged with:

1. Reconnaissance for U-boats;
2. Reconnaissance and patrol during operations of naval surface forces in the Atlantic or for protection of convoys;
3. Meteorological patrol;
4. Such offensive air operations against sea targets and in such areas as were to be agreed upon between the Air Force and the Navy.

This point reversed the decision in Hitler's previous directive placing reconnaissance for U-boats under Navy control.

Hitler's directive went on to state that "an arrangement whereby each branch of the Armed Forces has at all times full command over those units which are required to carry out specific duties, is wasteful and uneconomical."

The organization of air units for coastal and sea duties was reorganized on the basis of this last Hitler directive, in an order issued 8 March 1941 by Commander-in-Chief, Air. In April, Goering further depleted air strength available for Atlantic and North Sea operations by a series of transfers. Some of the planes, under Navy command, were transferred without previous consultation with the Naval Staff. The Navy protested, but the order stood.

On 13 November 1941, the Navy informed the Air Force that it was compelled to recall for U-boat duty 80 to 100 naval officers who previously had been transferred to the Air Force for Naval Air Service.

By the autumn of 1941, the Naval air forces under the Commander, Naval Air had been cut down to one Coastal Air Group, one depleted air squadron and one squadron of ship planes (in contrast to the 41 squadrons promised to the Navy for 1942).

End of Naval Aviation

Early in November 1941, Goering requested that the last full Coastal Air Group under Naval Command be transferred to the 3d Air Force. Raeder consented. Admiral Carls, who was operating this Naval Group in support of naval operations against the Murmansk convoy route, immediately wired a protest that "this would proclaim the verdict of death over the Naval Air Arm."

Raeder wrote Carls a personal letter in reply:

". . . I fully respect all the considerations which you have pointed out and I underline that in principle our views are in full accord. . . . I most sincerely regret this development. . . . Now as always I believe that the needs of naval operations will be served best by a Naval Air Force which has developed out of the ranks of the Navy and which is working in closest cooperation."

The Commander, Naval Air, with his staff of sixteen officers and about 100 enlisted men, now found itself in charge of only two squadrons. The question arose whether further existence of the Command was justified. On 1 December 1941, the General of the Air Force with the Commander-in-Chief, Navy, proposed to Raeder that he suggest to Goering that Commander, Naval Air be transferred to the Air Force as Commander, Air, North Sea (Fliegerfuehrer Nordsee) to take over all air operations in the North Sea. Raeder rejected the proposal, saying:

> "In this affair, I can only see a continuation of the past policy of plundering of naval aviation (Auspluenderung der Marineluftwaffe), regardless of all serious consequences for Naval operation. If the necessary number and types of planes were made available to the Commander, Naval Air, he could carry out all the assignments you describe just as well without having to be separated from the Navy . . . I fully realize that in the end I probably shall again be forced by the Commander-in-Chief, Air to agree to this solution. . ."

Goering did not let the matter rest. The Air Force Command Staff demanded that the staff of Commander, Naval Air be reduced to the strength of an Air Group Command. Faced with this prospect, Raeder was forced to reverse himself and propose to Goering on 18 February 1942 substantially the action which he had previously rejected: namely, "setting up a new Command, Air (Fliegerfuehrer) for the Baltic Coast and the North Sea. I ask that the staff of Commander, Naval Air be assigned to this command. . ."

No answer to this proposal has been found in the German Naval files. However, on 7 April 1942, the Air Force transmitted an order saying: "In accord with the Naval High Command, Commander, Naval Air is transferred immediately to the command of the 3d Air force in every respect." The order listed some of the duties to be undertaken by Commander, Naval Air under his new command, including co-operation with Naval forces.

This order of 7 April 1942 marked the end of the German Naval Air Arm.

Raeder did not give up hope. On 13 March 1942 Hitler had ordered that the aircraft carrier *Graf Zeppelin* be completed "in the shortest possible time in view of the vital importance of such a unit." A memorandum in the fall of 1942 clearly showed Raeder's hope that carriers might provide the Navy with a new air arm of its own. But in January 1943 Hitler ordered all carrier construction halted.

Doenitz and Air Co-operation with U-boats

Raeder resigned as Commander-in-Chief of the Navy in January 1943. He was succeeded by Grandadmiral Doenitz, theretofore Commander, U-boats. With the turn-over in command came an improvement of relations between the Air Force and the Navy.

Doenitz was more interested in getting air support than in the question of who would command such planes. The Navy stated its operational requirements. Satisfactory action was requested. The rest was left to the Air Force. Differences of opinion arose, but for the most part co-operation was not lacking. On the most decisive point full agreement was reached in the summer of 1943. In view of the general war situation all available air strength was to be concentrated on operations against the enemy's sea power. The strength available for such assignment was to be increased as speedily as possible.

The agreement held promise but it never was put to the test. By the summer of 1943 Allied pressure on land, sea and air had begun to increase. The German Air Force found greater and greater difficulty in meeting its commitments. As a result relations between the Air and Naval Commands again became strained. A message from the Air representative on the Naval Staff on 29 June 1944 to the naval representation at Hitler's Field Headquarters stated that "the present figure of 15 to 11 Ju-290 does not permit any systematic reconnaissance over the Atlantic in support of U-boat operations but only occasional reconnaissance in support of (air) combat units."

A final reorganization affecting Naval Aviation was ordered on 26 September 1944 by the Air Force General Staff. It had little practical importance as German Air and Sea forces were becoming more and more restricted in their operations. The reorganization abolished the posts of General of the Air Force with the Commander-in-Chief, Navy. Their functions were distributed among other offices. The reorganization created a new post, General of Sea Affairs of the Air Force (General des Seewesens der Luftwaffe) with the rank of a divisional commander. Administratively he was under the Air Force Command, Reich. By the time the order went into effect German air operations at sea had practically ceased.

Training, Type of Duty, Equipment

Crews and Training

Pilots for planes on naval duty were drawn from the Air Force. Observers for sea reconnaissance usually were Naval Officers. Special training was given both flying and non-flying personnel, with special emphasis on Naval subjects. In 1942 there were at least eight sea-airplane pilot schools operating.

Type of Duty

Aircraft used for Naval purposes fell roughly into these categories of duty:

1. Ship borne.
2. Reconnaissance, anti-shipping operations and submarine escort.
3. Air-Sea Rescue Service.

Ship-Borne Aircraft

All German battleships and cruisers except two had from two to four aircraft for catapulting with one or two catapults. The battleship *Bismarck*, for example, had four aircraft, four Air Force pilots (all sergeants), two Air Force officer-observers, and two Naval officer-observers. The "ground crew" comprised seven Air Force non-commissioned officers as mechanics under a technical sergeant, and six Naval ratings under a petty officer to operate the catapults. The Air Force personnel was under the charge of one of the Air Force officer-observers. The Captain of the ship controlled the planes and personnel aboard his ship.

Germany had several catapult ships, which carried up to three aircraft. German Raiders (camouflaged armed merchantmen) during the war also carried catapult planes.

Germany never completed her aircraft carriers, the *Graf Zeppelin* and "B". Admiral Doenitz told Allied interrogators after the War that had the *Graf Zeppelin*, on which work was far advanced, been completed, the Navy would have controlled her navigation and strategic employment, but the Air Force would have controlled the planes.

Coastal Reconnaissance

The first Coastal Flight Group for naval duties (Kustenfliegergruppe) was formed in 1935. It comprised three squadrons:

The pocket battleship Lutzow *in 1939-40, with an Arado Ar 95 biplane on its midships catapult. Such aircraft were seen as an important adjunct in the commerce-raiding mission.*

1. N-Squadron, for short-range shipping reconnaissance (Kustennahauf-klarungsstaffel).
2. F-Squadron, for long-range reconnaissance (Kustenfernaufklarunge-staffel).
3. K-Mz Squadron for miscellaneous duties (Kustenmehrzweckstaffel).

By 1938 a few other similar groups had been formed to operate princi-pally over the North Sea. It would be said that the entire purpose of these Coastal units was reconnaissance.

By 1940, the major portion of the N and K-Mz Squadrons (short-range and miscellaneous) had been re-equipped with land aircraft. As this occurred, the squadrons were detached from the Coastal Air Force, which thus continually decreased in size.

At the time of Germany's surrender, the crews in the Coastal Reconnaissance squadrons were experienced and well-trained. The ground personnel had been greatly reduced owing to continual with-drawals. Women workers were drawn in to fill the gaps.

A major in the Luftwaffe who had been associated with the Sea-Air Forces from their inception in 1935, stated, after his surrender, that "the fact that the Coastal Air Force throughout the war was only supplied with obsolescent aircraft created an impression in the minds of all operational personnel that the higher authorities had little or no interest in this branch of the Luftwaffe." He said that the Sea-Air Force, "standing as it did between the Luftwaffe and the Navy, received really effective support from neither." (It is interesting in this connection to recall the neglect from which the British Coastal Command suffered.)

Air-Sea Rescue Service (Seenotdienst)

This service was under the general control of the Air Ministry Inspectorate 16 in Berlin, but operationally came directly under the respective Air Fleets. Each Air Fleet operating in a coastal area had a chief of Air-Sea Rescue who in turn controlled one or more Regional commands. In addition to their normal duties, Sea Rescue Staffs also engaged in shipping reconnaissance, convoy escort, anti-submarine patrols and weather-reporting.

Equipment

The following planes were used by the Coastal Flight Groups on sea tasks:

Arado Ar-196

Two place, single-engine, low-wing, twin-float seaplane for observation and reconnaissance. For catapulting from warship.

Heinkel He-115

Five place, twin-engine, mid-wing, twin-float seaplane for long range reconnaissance and mine laying. Originally, a torpedo bomber.

Heinkel He-60 (Training)

Two place, single-engine, bi-plane, twin-float seaplane for instruction and dummy bomb practice.

Dornier Do-18 (Sea Reconnaissance)

Five-six place, tractor-pusher two-engine flying boat employed as a reconnaissance bomber.

Blohm and Voss BV-138

A three-engine, high-wing monoplane flying boat used for reconnaissance and bombing.

Blohm and Voss BV-222

A six-engine high-wing monoplane flying boat used for transport purposes, and possibly for long range reconnaissance.

When it became too outdated to serve as a frontline shipborne reconnaissance seaplane, the Heinkel He 60 was used by coastal flight groups for instruction and dummy bomb practice.

Long-range maritime reconnaissance and bombing were the roles performed by the twin-boom, three-engine Blohm und Voss Bv 138 flying boat. This is the pre-production Bv 138A-0 after conversion into the first, strengthened, Bv 138B-0.

The massive Blohm und Voss Bv 222 Wiking transport and reconnaissance flying boat was powered by six 1,200hp Bramo Fafnir 323R-2 nine-cylinder radial engines. This is the Bv 222 V3, the first of the type to be officially taken on strength by the Luftwaffe, on 9 December 1941.

Heinkel He-59

A twin engine, twin-float biplane. Originally designed as a torpedo bomber, was used for reconnaissance and mine-laying.

The Coastal Flight Groups, up to 1939, flew He-60's with an endurance of about five hours; Do-18 (which replaced the Do-Wal) with an endurance of up to 18 hours, and the He-59 with about 10 hours endurance. All had a speed of about 180 kms. per hour and a ceiling of 3,000–4,000 meters.

At the beginning of the War the Arado 196 was brought out, with a performance greater than that of the He-60. A switch was made from the He-59 to the He-115.

It was realized at an early date that a special plane would be required for sea reconnaissance. In 1935 a Blohm & Voss flying boat, the BV-138 was decided on. They were put into duty in 1941, already an obsolescent plane.

A few large flying boats, the BV-222, were later put into service for long-range Atlantic reconnaissance.

The Arado 196, a seaplane scout, was used on warships and raiders.

Designed as a torpedo bomber and also used for reconnaissance and minelaying, in addition the Heinkel He 59 served as an air-sea rescue aircraft, as seen here.

PART III

1939–40

This section contains three sequential narratives of German naval air operation in their three key campaigns of 1939: the North Sea campaign of the "Phoney War" period of the first six months of the war; the Norwegian campaign, and the Battle of Britain. This last, as it became apparent that Britain would not surrender, nor would it be invaded, led into the Battle of the Atlantic, as the severing of British lifelines became more important.

From the start, in the absence of either an effective naval air arm or a specialist air force arm on the model of RAF Coastal Command, Germany's air war at sea would be one of improvisation. It started in the "Phoney War", when the seaplanes committed to combat over the North Sea proved vulnerable to British land-based aircraft. The lack of understanding of naval requirements by the Luftwaffe implementing naval operations led to piecemeal initial use of the magnetic and acoustic mines that Germany had placed such great weight on pre-war. This, in turn, allowed the British to develop countermeasures. The Luftwaffe also used over a third of available mines as demolition bombs against British cities in 1940–41, contributing to the destruction of the Blitz, but undercutting the naval campaign, even after Hitler's directive number 23 of February 1941 ordered the Luftwaffe to concentrate on cutting off Britain's supplies.

These battles demonstrated the difficulties in cooperation, the near-total lack of communication, losses in friendly-fire incidents, and the difficulty of both aircraft and U-boats knowing their own positions.

Chapter 6

GERMAN NAVAL AIR OPERATIONS IN THE FIRST SIX MONTHS OF THE WAR

by Oberst (i.G) Walter Gaul

(1)

In the autumn of 1939, the outbreak of war found the German Navy insufficiently prepared to meet the immediate strategic tasks, as the fleet was still in its initial stage of reconstruction. It had to protect home waters from enemy incursions, safeguard the outward and inward passage of its own units to and from the Atlantic and intercept and capture enemy merchant shipping.

As a first measure, in order to ensure freedom of movement for their own forces in the Heligoland Bight and to lessen the threat on the flank, extensive minefields were laid in the southern North Sea, stretching from Holland as far north as the Skagerrak. This system of mine defense was known as the "West Wall".

As a further measure, as soon as the battleships were ready for service they were to make sorties into the northern North Sea and through the Bergen–Shetlands Strait into the northern Atlantic. These operations had the object of partially immobilizing the British fleet and thus hampering its anti-submarine activities and, at the same time, relieving the pressure on the pocket battleships attacking merchant shipping in the Atlantic. In the meantime, destroyers and torpedo boats were to operate against enemy shipping in the Kattegat and Skagerrak.

All these operations required the support and co-operation of the Air Force, as the naval forces had to be safeguarded from surprise attacks; the necessary information and background had to be provided for the planning of naval operations, and the fighting strength of the enemy fleet had to be gradually sapped in order to compensate for the weakness of the German Navy. The Naval War Staff had at their immediate disposal the naval air units already trained for naval air warfare; they also hoped that they might call upon the fighting potential of Fliegerdivision X during operations by their light forces. It was the duty of C-in-C Air Force, however, to reconnoiter enemy naval bases and to attack their fleet in port or at sea.

It was therefore essential to co-ordinate German Air Force activity over the sea with the aims of naval strategy. It was also essential, in the performance of operations to lessen the difficulties inherent in a dual command. Consequently, the Air Staffs had to be thoroughly briefed on the general situation prevailing throughout the same operational area and had to be constantly informed of the Navy's intentions and movements of units.

The Staff work was greatly helped by the understanding and co-operation of the Commander of Fliegerdivision X and his Chief of Staff and by the excellent system of communications between the two Headquarters.

All the necessary factors for successful co-operation were there, and furthermore, the Memorandum of 27 January, 1939 clearly defined the spheres of action for the Air Force and the Navy.

(2) *1. The engagement of 26 September, 1939*

In preparation for destroyer operations in the Skagerrak area against enemy merchant shipping, an extensive reconnaissance was flown over the North Sea by the German naval air units on 26 September. During this reconnaissance, ships of the Home Fleet were sighted northwest of the Great Fisher Bank at 1115. These were identified as two battleships, two battle cruisers, one aircraft carrier and a group of light forces; the Fleet was formed in three groups. The German planes maintained contact with the capital ships and directed Fliegerdivision X to the attack. Owing to the very favorable weather conditions, Luftflotte 2 sanctioned the attack which would serve as valuable fighting experience for the air crews. Only a small number of aircraft were available and, soon after midday, four Ju-88 and nine He-111 took off and carried out the attacks between 1405 and 1435.

From German Air Force reports the German Supreme Command estimated that the aircraft carrier *Ark Royal* had been heavily damaged and two battleships hit by bombs.*

Certain conclusions drawn from this engagement definitely affected the naval and air force outlook on the conduct of the war.

It was established in the first place that co-operation between the two services was flawless; the naval air units had located the enemy during their reconnaissance and had directed the bombers of Fliegerdivision X to a successful attack. The organization built up for combined conduct of air/sea warfare had stood the test and proved its worth.

---

* Kriegstagebuch Skl. Teil C, Heft V, Luftkriegfuehrung Sept. 39.

The Air Force came to the following conclusions:

(1) The aircraft carrier must have been sunk*
(2) In a rough sea, anti-aircraft fire from the ships could not effectively stop the attacks, especially dive-bombing as carried out by Ju-88.
(3) A small number of aircraft (13 in this case) were capable of causing severe damage to heavy naval units.

Although somewhat skeptical in regard to the sinking of the carrier, the Naval War Staff was nevertheless deeply impressed. They maintained that this first air attack, carried out without loss over 300 miles from the take-off fields, would be a clear indication to the British fleet of the danger of approaching the German coast and of the fighting efficiency of the German Air Force. They also believed that, in future, recognition of these facts would probably influence the enemy's decisions.**

2. The engagement of 7 October, 1939

The German Navy's confidence in the Air Force had been greatly strengthened. But this confidence, shared by the two services, was soon to receive a severe setback. The massed attack carried out by 127 He-111 and 21 Ju-88 on the Home Fleet off Utsire on 7 October, 1939 was unsuccessful. This attack occurred during operations by one German battleship, one cruiser and several destroyers against enemy shipping and bad weather conditions proved, for the first time, that air attacks at sea had definite limitations. The smooth and flawless interplay between reconnaissance, shadowing, leading-in and attack collapsed owing to low cloud, poor visibility and strong wind.

Fliegerkorps X*** had to admit that their aircrews were not yet sufficiently trained to overcome these difficulties. In spite of this failure, the Naval War Staff conceded a high operational value to the intervention of the Air Force in the northern North Sea and were inclined to overestimate its striking power.****

In the operations of 21 and 26 November, 1939, and during the sortie against the enemy convoy intercepted on 18 February, 1940 between the coast of Norway and the Shetlands, the German Air Force scored no successes, nor did their presence prevent enemy naval forces from giving the necessary support to their own shipping.

* *The War at Sea* Vol. 1, page 13, states that ". . . A bomb struck the *Hood* a glancing blow on the armor but did no damage, the *Ark Royal* was attacked thrice without being hit . . ."
** Kriegstagebuch, Skl. Teil A, Heft 1 pages 178-179.
*** On 8 Oct. 39, Fliegerdivision X was reformed and renamed Fliegerkorps X.
**** Kriegstagebuch Skl. Teil A, Heft Oktober, 1939, page 82.

(3) *1. Minelaying offensive with surface craft*

In order to maintain the initiative in naval operations and to intensify naval activity while the heavier units were out of action, the Naval War Staff decided to carry out minelaying operations with destroyers off the east coast of England.

These operations entailed considerable risk, as there was always the danger of a flank attack by units of the Home Fleet based on Scapa Flow or other points of the east coast.

Differences of opinion arose between Naval Group West and C-in-C Fleet as to the support and covering force which should be supplied to the destroyers. Naval Group West maintained that the Air Force could supply the necessary covering force and that aircraft could replace surface craft for this purpose. The Naval War Staff decided to adopt these views and to depart from the operational methods of the First World War.* Nine destroyer minelaying operation were carried out successfully throughout this offensive, concentrating on the Thames and Humber areas. The air units under Naval Air Commander West paved the way for this work by making a detailed survey of convoy routes and of the lights, lightships and buoys used to mark them. The close fighter escort provided for the destroyers and the long-range cover to be given by bombers in the event of an emergency, functioned satisfactorily.

2. Developments in the general political situation and their effect on the Navy's minelaying policy

In the meantime, it had become evident, from the development of the general political situation after the collapse of Poland that the Western Powers would continue to fight. The Supreme Command, therefore, became convinced that a German victory could only be secured by completely crushing Great Britain. The Fuehrer's directive No. 9 of 29 November, 1939 decreed that all military and civil measures were to be directed towards this objective**. A large-scale offensive in the West and the occupation of parts of the Channel coast would produce a strategically favorable position for the invasion of England and the German Air Force and Navy together could then complete the conquest of Great Britain.

The measures to be undertaken by the armed forces were as follows:

Offensive against the principal British turn-round ports, shipping and fleet; interruption of troop and supply transport to France; destruction

---

* Kriegstagebuch, Skl., Teil A, October, page 101.
** Weisungen O.K.W. (Fuehrer) Akte IV, 1 from 3.9.39 to 10.11.41, Vol. I.

of war industries and their plant, especially those engaged in aircraft production; disruption of public services such as gas, water and electricity supplies.

However, as the western offensive was subject to continual delay and German Air Force attacks on Britain were temporarily postponed, the responsibility for carrying on offensive actions during the last three months of 1939 rested with the Navy alone.

The three minelaying operations performed up till then had proved very effective and the Naval War Staff came to the conclusion that the enemy had not yet discovered a successful means of defense against this weapon. They saw a favorable opportunity of pressing home this temporary advantage and decided to exploit it with every means at their disposal. As trade off the east coast of England was of great importance to the British war effort, it was to be the German Navy's next objective. All east coast ports were therefore to be blocked and all shipping movements stopped by ground mines along this coast. In this new phase of the minelaying offensive it was decided that besides surface craft and U-boats, aircraft were to be employed as soon as it was possible.*

3. The aerial minelaying policy and its development (a) by the Navy and, (b) by the German Air Force

(a) On 18 November, 1939 the Chief of the Naval War Staff gave permission for aerial mines to be laid by units of the Naval Air Force.

In taking this step, the Naval War Staff abandoned their previous attitude. At the outbreak of war the Staff had decided not to start aerial minelaying operations until there were sufficient aircraft and mines to carry out an intensive program. Thus, it was hoped, the enemy would be denied an early opportunity of building up an organization to counter this new weapon, as they might be able to do if it were used sparingly. C-in-C Air Force was in complete agreement with this policy. Both services favored an all-out and continuous minelaying program which would close all estuaries and trade routes to traffic. The Naval War Staff altered their policy, however, on reviewing the situation, and their action was based on the consideration that an early and continuous minelaying program, making full use of temporary favorable circumstances, would outweigh any attendant disadvantages and be more decisive in the long run.

The naval program for the construction of aerial mines provided for completion of about 2,500 LMA and LMB mines, of which 150 LMA and 100 LMB were to be ready by 1 November, 1939. From November until

* Kriegstagebuch Skl. Teil A, November, 1939, pages 137–138 & page 162.

April there was to be a monthly supply of 50 LMA and 50 LMB mines; from April onwards, a monthly delivery of 100 mines of each type. The probable stock of mines by 1 July, 1940 would then be about 700 LMA and 800 LMB mines.

The Naval War Staff had hoped to carry out continuous minelaying operations until the Air Force was in a position to take over the task. On 17 December, 1939 however, all aerial minelaying operations were stopped owing to the icing-up of the seaplane bases and the consequent grounding of the aircraft.

Up to this time, five operations had been carried out and altogether 46 LMA and 22 LMB mines were laid along the enemy coast and in river mouths.

It was now up to the Air Force to continue the operation with land-planes. The chances appeared to be good, for on 17 January, 1940 in accordance with a directive from the Fuehrer, C-in-C Air Force instructed Major General Coeler to take all necessary steps for the furtherance and development of the aerial minelaying campaign.

(b) The German Air Force High Command viewed the naval development of minelaying warfare with misgiving and consented grudgingly to the use of the naval aviation for these operations. They only did so, because the Naval High Command contended that aerial minelaying operations formed an essential part of the general naval plan and required the navigational skill of the naval airmen for their execution. The Air Force High Command had always regarded aerial minelaying, and especially large scale employment of aerial mines, as their prerogative. Arrangements for lavish expenditure had been made and in accordance with a first estimate of Air Force requirements, plans were made for the construction of 50,000 mines, to include 30,000 LMB and 20,000 LMA. The delivery of the mines was to start on 1 April, 1940 and by planning production on a rising scale it was expected that the following target figures would be reached:

By 1 July	1940	800	LMA	and	LMB
" 1 August	"	1,600	"	"	"
" 1 September	"	2,800	"	"	"
" 1 October	"	4,800	"	"	"

These targets were to represent the minimim number of mines completed on these dates.

Concurrently with the delivery of mines, the aircraft production program was to be stepped up. On 1 March, 1940 the first Gruppe of He-111 – He 4, carrying 2 LMA or LMB was to be ready; on 1 April, 1940 the second Gruppe and on 15 June, 1940 the third Gruppe.

Aircraft proposed for the role of minelaying included the Dornier Do 217 (top), represented here by a Do 217E-2, the Focke-Wulf Fw 200 (middle), represented here by an Fw 200C-1, and the Heinkel He 177 (bottom), this example, an He 177A-5/R2, having a ventral fuselage rack and Kehlgerat underwing mountings for weapons including the Fritz X controlled-trajectory bomb and Hs 293 air-to-surface guided missile.

It was also planned to use as mine-carrying aircraft, the projected Do-217, carrying either 2 LMA or LMB; the Ju-88 (from the 400th aircraft onwards, which it was estimated would be completed about March, 1940) carrying 2 LMA; the FW-200, carrying 2 LMA and the He-177, carrying 6 LMA or 4 LMB.

A corresponding expansion in the organization and training of aircrews for minelaying was planned to parallel the construction program and, finally, the selection of a suitable Commander to carry out the Air Force policy was necessary. On 7 January, 1940 C-in-C Air Force appointed Major General Coeler to this task. On 1 February, 1940 the formation of Fliegerdivision IX was decreed. This division was to consist of the following units:

Bomber Geschwader 4,
Gruppe III/Bomber Geschwader 26, (when formed)
Staffel VII/Bomber Geschwader 26,
Gruppe I/Bomber Geschwader 30,
Gruppe I/Bomber Geschwader 40,

The appointment of Major General Coeler, Naval Air Commander West, as Ninth Division Commander placed this officer administratively under the command of Luftflotte 2 and, operationally, directly under C-in-C Air Force.*

The Naval High Command found this appointment and the proposed organization incompatible and fought the Air Force High Command with varying success during the next few months in an attempt to improve the Navy's position in respect to aviation.

On 24 February, 1940 the Chiefs of the Air and Naval War Staffs held a conference at which the Chief of the Air Staff announced the future intentions of the Air Force. These were:

1. Rapid expansion of Fliegerdivision IX and, as a first step in this direction, transfer of the mine-carrying Gruppe 106 from the Naval Air Force to Fliegerdivision IX.
2. Fliegerdivision IX was to be entrusted with the direction of all future aerial minelaying operations.**

Although these proposals meant a weakening of the prestige of the Naval Air Force, the Naval War Staff decided to agree, as it was in their

* Kriegsakten 1/Skl., 1 L-1, page 286. Akten 1/Skl., 1 La 7-1, page 206.
** Akten 1/Skl., 1 La 7-1, page 208.

interest that an efficient organization should come into existence as soon as possible to deal with the mass employment of the aerial mine. At the same time they considered that an early resumption of aerial minelaying operations with the remaining Staffeln of the Naval Air Command was essential. C-in-C German Air Force however, prevailed on the Fuehrer to agree that all aerial minelaying operations should be stopped until Fliegerdivision IX was ready.

A Fuehrer Conference took place on 23 February and on 26 February Naval War Staff was informed by the Supreme Command of the Armed Forces that the Fuehrer, after carefully considering all facts, had decided that the proposals of C-in-C Air Force were to be carried out and all aerial minelaying by naval air units was to cease until further orders.

On 8 March, 1940 a startling announcement in the London press, confirmed by foreign reports, brought about a complete change in the situation. This announcement stated that the British Admiralty had found a counter-measure for the German magnetic mine and that a great number of British ships were being equipped with anti-magnetic contrivances. This had been achieved by the salvaging and dismantling of a mine dropped in November, 1939.*

It was evident, therefore, that the enemy was in possession of all the technical details of the mine and of the firing mechanism and that he had had several valuable months to develop and produce efficient counter-measures. Another Fuehrer Conference took place on 26 March, at which C-in-C Navy stated his case for an immediate resumption of aerial minelaying operations. These reasons can be summarized as follows:

1. The present stock of mines and the expected rate of production made it possible to resume aerial minelaying operations at once on a gradually increasing scale.
2. The intended aerial minelaying operations in Scapa and in the Channel would draw the enemy's attention to the imminence of danger to other ports and he would obviously strengthen his anti-aircraft defenses.
3. Swift action was therefore necessary since the enemy had already devised a possible counter-measure.
4. Operations by mine-carrying Staffeln of the Naval Air Force, carrying naval mines only, would not upset the Air Force plans. At this juncture these operations would be of great importance, as all other naval measures were being held back in preparation for the invasion of Norway.**

* Kriegstagebuch Skl. Teil A, March, 1940, pages 57–58.
** Akte, Ob.d.M. (persönlich) Heft 11.

On 2 April the Fuehrer gave permission for minelaying to be resumed by naval aircraft.

From this date until the opening of the western offensive, six aerial minelaying operations were performed off the south-eastern coast of England and outside the French Channel ports. These operations came under the direction of the Ninth Fliegerdivision Commander and were flown by Naval Air Staffeln in conjunction with serviceable aircraft of Ninth Division. A total of 188 aerial mines were laid.

On 25 April, 1940 Major General Coeler was replaced by Major General Bruch as Naval Air Commander West. General Bruch had, up till then, been Naval Air Commander East. This change was necessitated by the ambiguous situation created by General Coeler's appointment to command of Fliegerdivision IX.

The struggle between the High Commands, and between their respective staffs, was largely due to questions of prestige as well as to difference in outlook and policy. Whether the policy of the Air Force or that of the Navy was the right one is still a moot question, since, in the later course of the war, the aerial mine was never used with the mass concentration contemplated and therefore did not achieve the expected results. One fact is certain that, owing to the early discovery of the secret of this weapon, its effectiveness was already reduced during the minelaying operations in preparation for and in the actual course of the Western offensive. The studied opinion of the author is that the Naval High Command's method was wrong because the operations were started too soon and carried out on too small a scale. The temporary success achieved by dropping about 70 parachuted mines was lastingly cancelled by the limitations at once imposed on the weapon.

(4) *1. Loss of four He-115 during an attack off Cromer*

The differences between C-in-C Navy and C-in-C Air Force were reflected in the opposite points of view taken by their respective operational staffs. This led to friction and faulty staff work which, in two instances, resulted not only in material loss, but, for the Navy, in loss of prestige and a loosening of its grip on the Naval Air Force with a consequent reduction of its influence in naval air warfare.

The first instance showed a lack of co-ordination in timing. It occurred during an engagement off Cromer, on 21 October, 1939, between R.A.F. fighters and a formation of He-115 which had been ordered to attack a convoy by Naval War Staff. At that time the German Air Force had not completed their rearmament or training and were therefore reluctant to commit themselves prematurely to operations with weak forces and run the risk of a setback without achieving any noteworthy success. Also at that time, attacks were not permitted on convoys but only on the armed escort.

The Naval War Staff, on the other hand, believed in action at any price and in seizing the initiative as early as possible with daring operations carried out successively with small forces.

In this case, the Naval War Staff gave Naval Air Commander West permission to attack a southbound convoy reported by air reconnaissance.

The Air Force, after a certain amount of wavering, decided to attack the convoy's armed escort with Ju-88 aircraft. They arrived at the scene of action long before the slow and cumbersome seaplane formation, which, therefore, had to bear the brunt of the fully developed R.A.F. fighter counter-action.* In this action four He-115 were lost. This revealed not only faults in timing, but also a lack of tactical co-ordination.

It caused C-in-C Air Force to inform C-in-C Navy that he considered it necessary to reduce the strength of the Naval Air Force and at the same time to ask him to withhold the slow and unwieldy seaplanes from actions off the enemy coast in the future. He also pointed out that he was the only authority responsible for air actions at sea when no fleet operations were in progress and that, so far, his bomber forces had been usefully and successfully employed in naval warfare.

On 15 November, 1939, C-in-C Air Force ordered the reduction of the naval air coastal units to nine long-range reconnaissance Staffeln and nine multi-purpose Staffeln. It was also established that in future the reconnaissance of the 25-mile wide strip along the east coast of England would be the responsibility of C-in-C Air Force.

2. Loss of the destroyers Maass and Schultz during operation "Wickinger"

The second instance occurred during the execution of operation "Wickinger". This operation was planned to round up British fishing vessels reported by reconnaissance planes to be frequenting the fishing grounds off the Dogger Bank in large numbers.

At 1200 on 22 February, 1940, Captain (D) proceeded to sea with six destroyers from the Jade. Between 1740 and 1818 of the same day, eight aircraft of Bomber Geschwader 26 under orders of Fliegerkorps X, took off from Neumünster to operate against merchant shipping between the Thames and the Firth of Forth. Between 1945 and 2000 one of these aircraft sighted an unlighted armed vessel 20 miles north of Tershelling Lightship, proceeded to attack and reported having sunk the vessel. At 2030 Captain (D) reported that destroyers *Maass* and *Schultz* had been

---

* Kriegstagebuch F.d.L. West, 16 October – 31 October, 1939.

sunk and received permission to abandon the operation. A Commission of Inquiry was set up which established the following:

(a) The two destroyers had been sunk by the action of a German aircraft.
(b) Fliegerkorps X had informed Naval Group West at noon on 22 February of the intended aircraft operations; on the other hand, Fliegerkorps X had not been informed of the imminent destroyer operations in time to brief the first wave of bombers, before their take-off.
(c) Fliegerkorps X had not used radio to warn the first wave that they might encounter their own destroyers, in case, amongst other reasons, the signals should imperil the operations.

All these errors which, as shown, brought about serious material losses, originated primarily in the basic organizational defect which provided for two services with independent commands operating in the same area with equal responsibility.

For a practical solution of this problem the only alternatives were:

(a) That all the naval air forces should come under the operational direction of C-in-C German Air Force through Fliegerkorps X.
(b) That Fliegerkorps X should come under the operational direction of C-in-C Navy through Naval Group West.

The first alternative, however, would not satisfy all the conditions required for the successful conduct of naval warfare and would only increase existing difficulties.

The second alternative broke down because C-in-C Air Force maintained that his forces must be independent and must stand on an equal footing with the Navy at sea.

(5)

Up to November 1939, air offensive activity was limited to attacks on the fleet at sea and when at anchor in its bases at Scapa and in the Firth of Forth. The first air attacks on the Firth of Forth and on Scapa, on 16 and 17 October respectively, were carried out with weak forces and achieved only minor successes.

Taken in conjunction, however, with the forcing of the entrances to Scapa by *U-47* and the sinking of the *Royal Oak*, they were successful in making these bases unsafe for the Home Fleet.*

---

* With reference to the attack on Scapa, the British Admiralty states: "The attack missed its main objective, for the C-in-C Home Fleet, with about 16 units was at sea off Iceland covering the Northern Patrol but in conjunction with the sinking of the *Royal Oak* only 3 days before, it still further discounted the value of Scapa and led to proposals for establishing the Home Fleet in the Clyde."

The Air Force was not able to launch an attack on the Home Fleet assembled in Scapa until 16 March, 1940. At dusk on that day an attack was made by strong bomber forces of Fliegerkorps X. The Naval War Staff was particularly anxious for this attack to be carried out in view of reports from the radio intercept service indicating that there was a strong concentration of naval forces at Scapa. This was confirmed by air reconnaissance.

From this information, the Naval War Staff decided that the defense measures against U-boat penetration and aircraft attacks had been completed, that the enemy no longer considered the cruiser escort adequate support for his Norwegian convoys and that he expected German naval forces to attempt to break through to the Atlantic during the new moon period. Moreover, this concentration of forces was of special importance in view of the developments of the Russo-Finnish conflict. From the available information, the Naval War Staff assumed that a further reason for the assembly of this heavy naval striking force might be in preparation for landing operations on the Norwegian coast in support of Finland.

It was therefore vitally important that the German Air Force should attack with strong forces in order to cause effective damage to the enemy's heavy naval units.

Apart from the obvious advantages of causing severe damage and putting units at Scapa out of action, the operation might have a decisive effect on future enemy plans for the occupation of Norway or for dispatching strong contingents of troops to intervene in Finland.[*]

At 1600 on 16 March, 18 Ju-88 and 16 He-111 from Fliegerkorps X took off for the attack and the Air Force reported the following results:

Five heavy units and one cruiser hit with 1,000 kg. bombs.[**]

These results exceeded all expectations. The Naval War Staff made the following entries in the War Staff diary of that date: "Fliegerkorps X, with its successful attack on Scapa, has achieved a remarkable feat. Details of the results cannot be confirmed at once but from available reports there is no doubt that a number of battleships and cruisers have been fairly heavily damaged and it is estimated that one ship hit by two 1,000 kg. bombs will be out of action for a considerable time. . . . It is still too early to be certain whether, in view of this new evidence of the vulnerability of Scapa to air raids, the Home Fleet will give it up as a permanent base and will transfer to ports and inlets of the west coast. . . . In view of the fact that German naval forces will be sent to the Atlantic in the near future, every effort must be made to prevent British naval forces remaining in the Orkney base,

---

[*] Kriegstagebuch Skl. Teil A, Heft March, 1940, pages 56–60.
[**] Kriegstagebuch Skl. Teil C, Heft V, 1940, page 54.

where they will be in a position to intercept ships proceeding through the Shetlands-Norway sea area."*

Radio intercept reports of 19 March indicated that the entire Home Fleet had sailed from Scapa. This information cast grave doubts on the accuracy of the Air Force reports of results. Even if the sailing of the Home Fleet from Scapa did not disprove actual hits on battleships, it was obvious that no ship had been put out of action.**

(6)

1. The attitude of the Air Force High Command (Operational Staff) to the question of war on merchant shipping

The war on merchant shipping offered a further opportunity for aircraft to prove their effectiveness in operations over the sea.

At the outbreak of war, in September, 1939 however, during discussions which had taken place between the Naval War Staff and the operational staff of the Air Force High Command, the Chief of the Air Staff had declared that, for political reasons, aircraft could not be used in the war on shipping. The Staff regarded direct attack on and destruction of the shipping as the only possible bomber tactics in this kind of warfare and therefore they could not conform with international procedure as laid down by the Prize Laws. Furthermore, the Air Force had to keep their principal objectives in view and their main effort was soon to be directed against the British aircraft industry with the aim of crippling British air power at its source.

Not until the end of 1940 or the beginning of 1941, would the Air Force possess a sufficient number of suitable aircraft (He-177), with sufficient endurance, to participate effectively in the blockade of the British Isles even to areas west of Ireland.

Until then, they regarded the blockade of the English North Sea coast as a subsidiary assignment, which could be met by occasional attacks on the principal trading ports and fleet bases.

At first, therefore, the Navy could only count on the support of the Air Force in the event of an engagement with enemy surface craft during destroyer operations against shipping. Aircraft of the Naval Air Commands were, however, available to work with the destroyers. These aircraft reported the routes used by shipping and, on sighting merchant vessels, directed them by flag signals or signal floats to rendezvous with destroyers which searched them or brought them into harbor as the situation demanded.

---

* Kriegstagebuch Skl. Teil A, March 1940, page 124.
** Kriegstagebuch Skl. Teil A, March 1940, page 142.

2. Operations of Fliegerkorps X against merchant shipping in the North Sea

On 1 November, 1939 the Air Force was finally directed to attack enemy convoys, permission being granted to attack the merchant vessels themselves, as well as the escorts. It was still forbidden to attack unconvoyed vessels, unless their enemy identification could be definitely established.

Fliegerkorps X was given the task of attacking shipping in the North Sea area. At first, these operations were based on the reconnaissance reports of naval aircraft, which also shadowed and directed the bombers to the targets. Operations ranged from the Norwegian Coast to north of the Orkneys and along the east coast of England.

Soon however, Fliegerkorps X took over reconnaissance of the trade routes and proceeded to attack at varying times in different places with strong forces. These operations took the form of sweeps over the sea areas and were termed armed reconnaissance.

The sweeps began on 1 December, 1939, were repeated on 18 and 19 December and continued successfully during January. Attacks on shipping carried out on 29 and 30 January caused the sinking and damaging of a considerable number of merchant vessels. Only a few operations were possible during February and March owing to unfavorable weather conditions. On 3 February about 12,000 tons of shipping were either sunk or damaged off the East coast. On 20 March attacks were made on fourteen ships of an eastbound convoy 60 miles southeast of the Shetlands; the convoy scattered and six to eight merchant vessels were so heavily damaged that it was assumed that they had been destroyed.*

With these sweeps the Air Force intensified the war on sea-borne trade and carried it on during the winter months when ice and weather conditions had handicapped the movements of the warships.

The Naval War Staff expected that this action would prevent neutral and enemy shipping from putting to sea in the danger area and hoped that certain aims of naval warfare were being achieved, such as:

the tying down of enemy light naval craft and personnel to escort duties and patrols; destruction of war material and personnel; disorganization of the import trade; congestion and slowing up of the turn-round of ships and transport services. Lastly, this Air Force action, if continued, would supplement the tonnage sunk by U-boats so that a marked increase in the total of enemy shipping losses was to be expected.**

---

* See Appendix.
** Kriegstagebuch Skl. Teil A, Heft October, 1940, page 25.

3. Naval Air Force activities in the Baltic and the control of shipping

After the Polish resistance at Gdynia and Hela had been overcome with the assistance of the Naval Air and carrier-borne Staffeln under the orders of Naval Air Commander East, the main war effort was centered on the land front. From that time, therefore, the activities of the Naval Air Force in the Baltic were directed to anti-submarine patrols and control of shipping in the Gulf of Danzig and the Baltic approaches.

The Naval War Staff regarded a strict control of sea-borne trade in the Baltic as an effective way of attacking British trade, for it was public knowledge that an intensive traffic in lumber and agricultural produce passed from Sweden, through the Swedish and Norwegian territorial waters to England.

The Naval War Staff therefore ordered C-in-C Group East to institute the control and search of all shipping for contraband using the naval auxiliaries *Grille* and *Bremse* and later the minelayers *Tannenberg, Kaiser, Hansestadt Danzig, Konigin Luise*, in accordance with the Prize Laws. The control area at first comprised the Hanö Bight, East Coast of Sweden, Gotland and Oland. At the end of October this area was extended to include the eastern Baltic north of latitude 56 degrees N., up to the Aaland Sea and the Gulf of Finland up to the longitude of Reval (Tallin). The neutrality of the areas round the Aaland Islands and in the Moon Sound and Irben straits was to be respected. At Russia's request, the Gulf of Finland was excluded from the control area, and the eastern boundary was fixed at first at longitude 20 degrees 30 minutes E. on the 27th October, 1939, and later was moved to 20 degrees E as a result of further Russian representations.*

It was decided to use all available naval aircraft for the control of shipping.

After the transfer of the long-range and multipurpose Staffeln from the Baltic to the North Sea, Naval Air Commander East, whose headquarters were at Dievenow, had at his disposal three short-range reconnaissance Staffeln consisting of He-60 and He-115, based on the naval air bases of Bug auf Rügen, Dievenow and Pillau.

The control of shipping by seaplanes was carried out in two ways:

(a) The seaplane stopped the ship to be searched and after landing alongside, put a search party aboard.

(b) The seaplane stopped the ship and then directed her by signaling from the air, to proceed to the vessels making the search.

---

* Kriegstagebuch Skl. Teil A, Heft 2, page 251.

On 2 October, 1939, forces under Naval Air Commander East and Flag Officer Commanding Baltic Defenses began a combined naval and air shipping control. The area chosen was the Hanö Bight and Hammer Straits. Patrol vessels took up station at four different positions to carry out the examination of the merchant vessels. Forty planes made four successive sweeps of the sea area as far as the Oland Sound during two days. These planes included two Ju-52 on floats carrying prize crews who could be transferred to the captured ships by rubber dinghy. During this first operation 126 ships were sighted and fourteen of them, between 1,000 and 3,000 tons, were examined.

Valuable experience was gained during these operations. It was found that, owing to the prevailing wind and state of the sea, seaplanes could make water landings only in very exceptional instances, and that the safest and most effective method was to direct the merchant ships with signal floats. In the meantime, five He-59 aircraft were added to Naval Air Commander East's forces and the seaplane base of Schwarzort, near Memel, was equipped for operational use.

Designed as a two-seat reconnaissance, patrol and light-attack seaplane, the Arado Ar 95 was not ordered by the Luftwaffe, but some originally intended for export found their way into German service. This Ar 95A-1 was serving in the Baltic with 3./SAGr.125 in 1941.

The next sweep on 8 November produced no results. Further undertakings of this kind showed that all shipping kept within the Swedish and Finnish territorial waters and that vessels could only be caught by surprise, where they had to leave territorial waters for navigational reasons.

In the eastern Baltic, shipping kept to uncontrolled waters east of 20 degrees E. until it reached the Finnish and Swedish territorial areas in the north. As shipping between the Baltic States and Sweden avoided the open seas and as the long flight to the operational areas obliged the seaplanes working from the coast to remain only for a short period in these areas, this system became ineffective. C-in-C Group East therefore suggested that all the minelayers employed on shipping control should be supplied with two He-60 seaplanes. The Naval War Staff passed on this proposal to the Air Staff as they considered this measure would make it possible to use seaplanes after the bases had become icebound. On 2 February, 1941 the freezing of the Baltic brought the war on sea trade in that area to an end.

(7)

The aerial torpedo was the only weapon left to the Naval Air Force which C-in-C Air Force had not attempted to adopt or acquire for the Air Force.

A prototype of the F 5 aerial torpedo had been bought in Norway and, in the early stages, developed secretly, as at that time Germany was not allowed under the Treaty of Versailles to construct modern weapons. By the beginning of 1938, although Germany's rearmament had been in full swing for some time, the performance of the F 5 torpedo did not yet come up to the required specifications. In February of that year, the Navy therefore decided to buy an aerial torpedo from the Italian Whitehead Torpedo Factory at Fiume; but, in accordance with the contract, the first batch of a hundred torpedoes was not to be delivered before 1942, so the Navy meanwhile continued to improve and construct the F 5 type. In January, 1939, the stock of run-in torpedoes was 152 and, by completing ten torpedoes per month, it was intended to bring this stock up to 362 torpedoes by autumn, 1940.

At the outbreak of war, the multi-purpose Staffeln were being converted from the He-59 to the He-115 type of seaplane. This type had too great a speed for the F 5 and further experiments were carried out releasing the torpedo fitted with air rudders which reduced its air speed.

While this experiment was going on the F 5 torpedo had to be used with the He-59.

The lessons learnt in peace-time exercises showed that in order to attain any degree of success, the He-59 as a torpedo-carrying aircraft required the weather conditions which are essential for surprise attack, such as low visibility, light wind and calm sea. Also it was found that the best time to make torpedo attacks was during the twilight hours.

A great disadvantage of the F 5 aerial torpedo was that, owing to its initial dip, it required a minimum depth of water of 23 meters (about 75 feet) for its release. In view of the shallow waters along the east coast of England, in the Downs and off the German coast, its employment was very restricted.

The first attacks were tried out during the course of armed reconnaissance flights on single ships or weakly escorted convoys.

On 7 November, 1939, at about 0800, a torpedo-carrying kette sighted two enemy destroyers east of Lowestoft and at 0845 the first F 5 of the war was fired at one of the destroyers.* The destroyer took evasive action and the torpedo missed astern.

In the spring of 1940, when the seaplane bases were once more free from ice, Naval Air Commander West took every opportunity of using the F 5 aerial torpedo as he especially wanted to test this weapon under service conditions with He-115.

Operations carried out during March on evening reconnaissance sorties resulted in no sinkings of ships but showed, nevertheless, that the F 5 torpedo was, at its present stage, technically ready for service.

This was especially important, as the Naval War Staff had been informed by C-in-C Air Force Operations Staff on 4 December, 1939, that following an interview with C-in-C German Air Force, the Fuehrer had decided to stop the construction of F 5 torpedoes.** An exchange of views between the Chiefs of the Naval and Air Force Operations Staffs defined the relative position of the two services in this matter. It was ascertained that the Air Force retained their interest in the aerial torpedo, but did not intend to supply this type of torpedo to their bomber units until its performance, especially with regard to speed of release and initial dive, was substantially improved. This did not in any way affect the requirements of the Naval Air Force.

(8)

Anti-submarine warfare was carried out by the Naval Air Force under the Naval Air Commanders during armed reconnaissance sweeps, by both specially planned submarine hunts and in the course of close escort duties. In the first case, aircraft on armed reconnaissance were allowed to attack all

* The Admiralty reported as follows: "The first torpedo attack by aircraft in the war took place on November 7th when the Polish destroyer *Blyskawica*, 70 miles east of Lowestoft, was fired at by a torpedo from an enemy seaplane. . . ."
** Kriegstagebuch Skl. Teil A, January 1940, pages 258, 249.

submarines sighted within certain well-defined sea areas, and constant aircraft patrols were maintained from dawn to dusk over small sections of such areas. All naval units and transports which put to sea were escorted by two to three aircraft as close cover against submarine attack.

1. Anti-submarine measures in the North Sea and Heligoland Bight

Increased submarine activity in the Heligoland Bight, which had led to the damaging of the cruisers *Leipzig* and *Nürenberg* and to the loss of an escort vessel on 13 December, necessitated continuous patrol offshore by naval air units. Patrols and submarine hunts were frequently interrupted, however, by requests from C-in-C U-boats for suspension of anti-submarine measures during movements of his own U-boats. For this reason, and because planes on reconnaissance were often in doubt as to the identity of U-boats sighted, Naval Air Commander West advised C-in-C Group West that the Naval Air Force's anti-submarine measures were being rendered ineffective. These representations met with no response from C-in-C U-boats, and it was only when the German U-boat forces were concentrated round Scapa and off the Norwegian coast, in preparation for and after the start of the Norwegian campaign, that the Naval Air Force was able to operate successfully against submarines.

On 7 April, 1940, an He-111 flying at 100 meters, succeeded in hitting a submarine of the *Grampus* class in the act of submerging with 250 kg. bombs. Oil and large air bubbles rose for a long time at the point of sinking.* On 6 May, one of the aircraft providing close cover to northbound transports, sighted a submarine at about 2040 at 58 degrees 07 minutes N. and 7 degrees 15 minutes E, and attacked it with two high explosive 250 kg. bombs. The submarine surfaced twice and was engaged with machine guns. This submarine was thought to be heavily damaged.**

On 8 May, in position 56 degrees 45 minutes N. and 06 degrees 12 minutes E., two aircraft which were escorting a northward bound group of steamers, sighted the tracks of a salvo of four torpedoes. One plane immediately took up firing position and, from a height of 200 meters, attacked the submarine, which was showing its conning tower, with three 250 kg. bombs. All bombs were well placed. A large patch of oil spread from the place of the explosion and wreckage was seen floating amongst the oil. For an hour after the attack, air bubbles continued to rise. This submarine was thought to have been destroyed.***

On 5 July at 2325 at 58 degrees 51 minutes N. and 4 degrees 15 minutes

---

* Kriegstagebuch F.d.Luft. West, April 1940.
** Kriegstagebuch F.d.Luft. West, May 1940.
*** Kriegstagebuch F.d.Luft. West, May and July 1940.

A German wartime propaganda illustration depicting a fictional sinking of a large British submarine by an Arado Ar 196, probably inspired by the role of these aircraft in successes against such vessels during 1939-40. (US National Archives)

E., an Arado 196 attacked a surfacing submarine with bombs and scored two hits. The submarine capsized after the explosion and sank after 12 minutes, after being subjected to cannon fire.*

In the same waters, in position 58 degrees 51 minutes N. and 04 degrees 25 minutes E., on 6 July, another submarine was hit by bombs and, being unable to dive, surrendered to an Arado 196 and a Do-18. The Captain and First Lieutenant were taken prisoner by the Do-18, but the submarine sank while in tow.**

2. Anti-submarine activities of the Baltic Naval Air Forces

Towards the end of March, 1940, when the thaw had set in in the Baltic, the forces under the Naval Air Commander East were detailed to carry out submarine hunts and provide close cover to transports in the Kattegat and Skagerrak. This was in preparation for and in support of the invasion of Norway. After being suitably reinforced, the units available for this purpose were:

* Kriegstagebuch F.d.Luft. West, May and July 1940.
** Kriegstagebuch F.d.L West, May and July 1940.

The Dornier Do 17Z was used for anti-shipping and submarine hunting operations.

3 Staffeln Do-17,
1 Staffel He-111,
3 He-115 planes and 1 Staffel of Arado 196 consisting of 6 ship-borne
   planes.

Anti-submarine patrols and hunts were carried out, even during darkness when the aircrews were sufficiently trained in night flying.

On 13 April, the possible destruction of two submarines in the Kattegat was reported, one by a dive-bomber and the other by an aircraft of Bomber Geschwader 100, although no direct evidence was available.*

On 29 April, at 57 degrees 57 minutes N. and 10 degrees 28 minutes E., about 15 miles NNW of Skagen, an Arado 196 carried out a successful attack. From a height of 230 meters, two 50 kg. bombs were dropped on a submerging submarine. The second bomb struck the hull 3 or 4 meters in front of the conning tower. The explosion was so violent that the plane itself was damaged and was forced to make an emergency landing. Wreckage was sighted by an He-115 sent to aid the distressed plane.**

* Kriegstagebuch F.d.L Ost 16-30 April, 1940, pages 77, 86, 87.
** Kriegstagebuch F.d.L Ost 16-30 April, 1940 pages 77, 86, 87.

Even if no further sinkings of submarines could be directly attributed to aircraft, the many hours flown in day and night patrols and the many sightings reported by these patrols were of considerable assistance to anti-submarine campaign of the naval vessels.

An instance of the valuable help given by aircraft was the interception and capture of H.M. Submarine *Seal* on 5 May, 1940. The submarine had sustained damage in the deep minefield and could not dive. An Arado 196 of Naval Air Commander East succeeded in intercepting the submarine before it reached Swedish Territorial waters, taking the captain prisoner and enabling naval patrol vessels to escort the submarine into harbor.*

(9)

The aircraft carrier *Graf Zeppelin* and her sister ship "B" were laid down on 1 January, 1936 and 1 April, 1936 respectively. Their design and construction were chiefly based on the experience of foreign countries and influenced by information received from Japan.

Their displacement was 20,000 tons; their speed was to exceed 30 knots; armament was to consist of medium-sized guns, with special provision for a strong anti-aircraft defense. The carriers were designed to have two hangar decks, three elevators, and two catapults. The complement of aircraft was as follows:

20 multi-purpose aircraft Fi-167
13 dive-bomber   "   Ju-87T } with folding wings.
10 fighter   "   Bf-109T.

The date of completion for the *Graf Zeppelin* was expected to be 1 June, 1940.

On 9 October, 1939, the Air Force was informed by the Navy that the *Graf Zeppelin* could not be completed before 1 October, 1940 and the building of Carrier "B" had been cancelled. This change in program was due to the priority given to construction of other ships and U-boats considered to be more important to the general conduct of naval warfare. Owing to the deterioration of the armament situation in the later course of the war however, the *Graf Zeppelin* was never commissioned.

(10)

During the first six months of the war, the German Air Force prepared and built up its forces for future offensives and at the same time established its ascendancy over the Navy in the field of naval air warfare. This was not

* F.d.L. Ost. Gefechtsbericht Aufbringung Eng. U.B. Seal 5 May, 1940.

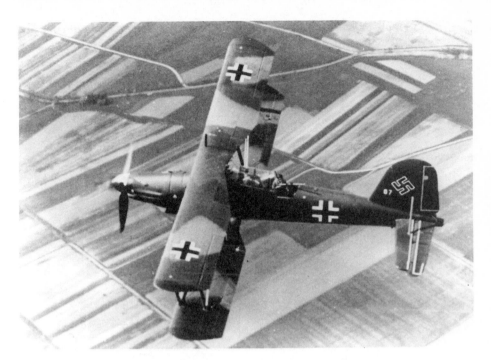

Each of the two uncompleted German aircraft carriers were to have twenty Fieseler Fi 167s included in their complement of aircraft.

only due to the influence of air power and to the course of events during this period but, in a great measure, to the forceful personalities of Reichsmarschall Göring and his entourage who aimed at establishing the independence of Air Force action over land and sea and enhancing its prestige. The Navy feared, however, that its needs would not be fully met and struggled to obtain possession of the air weapon; it succeeded in gaining it only for defensive tasks such as reconnaissance and anti-submarine patrols.

In this internal conflict, which eventually became public knowledge, the Navy always kept its objective in view and had to induce the Air Force to intervene as effectively as possible, even at the cost of personnel and equipment, for the promotion of the war at sea.

Fully conscious of the consequences, the Naval War Staff consented to C-in-C Air Force taking over tasks in naval air warfare and thus sealed the fate of the Naval Air Force, precluding any further expansion of this arm and leading to further reductions.

As the independence of the Air Force in sea operations increased, the disadvantages due to absence of a single command in the operational field made themselves felt proportionately. However willing the Air Force was to support naval aims, this fundamental defect could not be eliminated and the Navy had, for the future, to rely completely on the goodwill of C-in-C Air Force. In the opinion of Grand Admiral Raeder, the Navy, in itself highly efficient, would have achieved a far greater measure of success had it possessed its own Naval Air Force.

Sources

1. Files of the Naval War Staff, First Division I, Air Files for the years 1935 to 1939.
2. Reorganization of the Naval Air Forces – PG/33046/NID.
3. War Diaries of Naval War Staff, Parts A and C – from September, 1939 to March, 1940.
4. War Files of Naval War Staff, First Division Air.
5. Files of C-in-C Navy. (Personal) Vol. II.
6. War Diary of Naval Air Commander West, 16 October – 31 October, 1939.
7. Supreme Command of the Armed Forces, Fuehrer Directives. Vol. I.
8. Preliminary Narrative, The War at Sea, Vol. I.

List of ships sunk or damaged by the German Air Force
November 1939 – April 1940. From German Documents

| | | | Type of Ship | |
Date	Area	Sunk	Damaged	Displacement
17.12.	East Coast of England	Patrol Vessel "Pearl" Motor Ship "Serenity" Patrol Vessels "New Choice" "Eilead Wray" "Evelina"		
18.12.	East Coast of England	Fishing Vessels "Granton" "Zealus" Patrol Vessels "Sedgefly" "Trinity"		
			1 Steamer	1,000 tons
19.12.	East Coast of England	Patrol Vessels "Active" "Ocean" "Astras"		
			1 Steamer	1,500 tons

Date	Area	Sunk	Type of Ship Damaged	Displacement
9.1.40	East Coast of England	Steam Ships "Oakgrove"		1,985 tons
		"Upminster		1,013 tons
		"Cowrie"		689 tons
		2 Patrol Vessels		Together 1,600 tons
			Danish Steam Ships "Ivan Kandreys"	1,368 tons
			"Feddy"	955 tons
			British Steam Ship "Tavington Court"	4,544 tons
11.1.40	Off Peterhead		2 Patrol Vessels	Together 1,600 tons
	Off Humber		1 Steamer	3,000 tons
12.1.40	East Coast of England	1 Patrol Vessel		300 tons
			1 Patrol Vessel	–
			1 Steamer	400 tons
			1 Steamer	600 tons
29.1.40	Off Newcastle	1 Steamer		5,000 tons
	Off Scarborough	1 Steamer		4,000 tons
	Southeast of Lowestoft	1 Steamer		2,000 tons
	Off Wash	1 Patrol Vessel		300 tons
	Northeast of Hartlepool		1 Steamer	1,200 tons
	East of Scarborough		1 Steamer	1,100 tons
	North of Humber		1 Steamer	3,000 tons
	East of Harwich		1 Steamer	–
	Off Flamborough Head		1 Patrol Vessel	400 tons
30.1.40	Off Orkney Islands	1 Steamer		3,000 tons
	Off Coppinsay Island	1 Steamer		3,000 tons
	Northeast of Cromer	1 Steamer		4–5,000 tons

Date	Area	Sunk	Type of Ship Damaged	Displacement
	Southeast of Lowestoft	1 Steamer		–
	East of Cromer	1 Steamer (Royal Crown)		4,360 tons
	Off Flamborough Head	2 Patrol Vessels		–
	South of Peterhead		1 Steamer	1,000 tons
	Off Lowestoft		1 Steamer	2,000 tons
	Off Thames Estuary		1 Steamer	3,000 tons
	Off Thames Estuary		2 Patrol Vessels	–
3.2.40	Off East Coast of England	Minesweeper "Sphinx"		
	Off Flamborough Head	2 Patrol Vessels		
	Off Holy Island	1 Steamer		2,000 tons
	Off Hartlepool	1 Steamer		2,000 tons
	Off Whitby	1 Steamer		2,000 tons
	Off Humber	1 Swedish Steamer		3–4,000 tons
	Southeast of Orkneys		1 Patrol Vessel	–
	Off Sunderland		1 Patrol Vessel	–
	In Stromsay Firth		1 Steamer	–
	Off Sunderland		1 Steamer	
	Off Flamborough Head		1 Steamer	–
	Northeast of Wash		1 Steamer	–
	Off Lowestoft		1 Steamer	–
9.2.	Off Peterhead	2 Patrol Vessels		
	Northeast of Cromer	1 Steamer		500 tons
	Off Peterhead		1 Tanker	3–7,000 tons
	Off Dundee		1 Steamer	3,000 tons
	Off Crail		1 Steamer	4,000 tons
	Off Newcastle		1 Steamer	–
	Off Bridlington		1 Steamer	–

Date	Area	Sunk	Type of Ship Damaged	Displacement
10.2.	Off East Coast of England	1 Patrol Vessel		–
20.2.	Off Kinnaird Head	1 Steamer		1,000 tons
	Off Yarmouth		1 Steamer	1,000 tons
	Off Yarmouth		1 Steamer	1,000 tons
27.2	Firth of Moray		1 Patrol Vessel	–
1.3.	Off Hartlepool		1 Steamer	2–3,000 tons
	Off Scarborough		1 Steamer	1,500 tons
	Off Scarborough		1 Steamer	1,500 tons
	North of Kirkwall	1 Steamer		2,000 tons
2.3	East Coast of England		1 Steamer	3,000 tons
	Between Kinnaird Head and Newcastle		1 Steamer	–
	" "	1 Steamer		2,000 tons
	In the Channel		1 Steamer	–
	" " "	1 Steamer		2,000 tons
3.3.	East of Whitby		1 Steamer	3,000 tons
6.3.	Off Middlesbrough		1 Steamer	3,000 tons
	Off North Sunderland		1 Steamer	3–4,000 tons
7.3	East Coast		1 Steamer	3,000 tons
	" "		1 Steamer	1,500 tons
	" "		1 Steamer	3–4,000 tons
	" "	1 Steamer		2,000 tons
	" "		1 Steamer	6,000 tons
14.3	On the Dogger Bank	1 Danish Fishing Vessel		
17.3.	Northeast of Peterhead		1 Patrol Vessel	
20.3.	60 miles N.E. of Kinnaird Head		1 Steamer	5–6,000 tons

			Type of Ship	
Date	Area	Sunk	Damaged	Displacement
	60 miles N.W. of Kinnaird Head		1 Steamer	12,000 tons
	60 miles N.E. of Kinnaird Head		1 Steamer	4–5,000 tons
	Off Kinnaird Head		1 Minelayer	–
	" " "		1 Steamer	2,000 tons
	60 miles Northeast of Kinnaird Head		1 Steamer	4–5,000 tons
	North of Great Fisher Bank	1 French Supply Ship		1,500 tons
	East of Southern end of Shetlands		1 Steamer	3,000 tons
	East of Southern end of Shetlands		1 Steamer	10,000 tons
	South of Brighton		S.S. "Barshell"	–
28.3	60 miles S.E. of Shetlands	1 Patrol Vessel		
	60 miles S.E. of Shetlands	1 Steamer		2–3,000 tons
	N.E. of Kinnaird Head		1 Steamer	1,000 tons
	North of Whitby	1 Steamer		4,000 tons
3.4.	East Coast of England	2 Patrol Vessels		
	N.E. of Shetlands	2 Patrol Vessels		
	East Coast of England	1 Steamer		2,000 tons
	" " "	1 Steamer		4–5, 000 tons
	" " "		1 Destroyer 1 Patrol Vessel	
	" " "		1 Steamer	1,000 tons
	N.E. of Shetlands		1 Steamer	4–6,000 tons

Chapter 7

THE ROLE OF THE LUFTWAFFE AND THE CAMPAIGN IN NORWAY

by General der Flieger Ulrich O.E. Kessler

A. The Campaign in Southern and Central Norway

I. General outlook on the prospects of the campaign

Nothing, in the early stages of World War II, is more illustrative of air power and its revolution of the traditional concept of warfare than the invasion of Norway. In prewar times the very idea would have been considered preposterous that a country of about 2000 miles coastline with its principle harbours within 24 hrs. reach of the British Navy could be conquered by a nation lacking in sea power. It would have been argued that even if an initial surprise landing were successfully accomplished such an invasion were doomed to final failure. In a country where the sea is the ordinary line of communication and the ship the customary and mostly the only means of transport, where hundreds of fjords give easy access and shelter to any amount of ships the supplying of the invaded troops seemed impossible with the British Navy as an opponent.

The campaign in Norway, however, has proved that sea power alone is no match to air power whereas air power under certain conditions might establish control of the sea and make up for the lack in sea power. It is worth notice that the repellent effect on the British Navy was produced by Air Forces which were numerically feeble and, owing to the "landmindedness" of the High Command of the Luftwaffe, had neither the training nor the appropriate weapons to fight the British Navy. Moreover, the Air Forces were committed to support the ground troops tactically rather than to concentrate on keeping away the British Sea Power and its prerequisite – the Royal Air Force.

II. Planning and organization of the campaign

For the planning of the campaign in Norway a special staff comprising officers of the Army, Navy, and Luftwaffe was formed within the OKW.

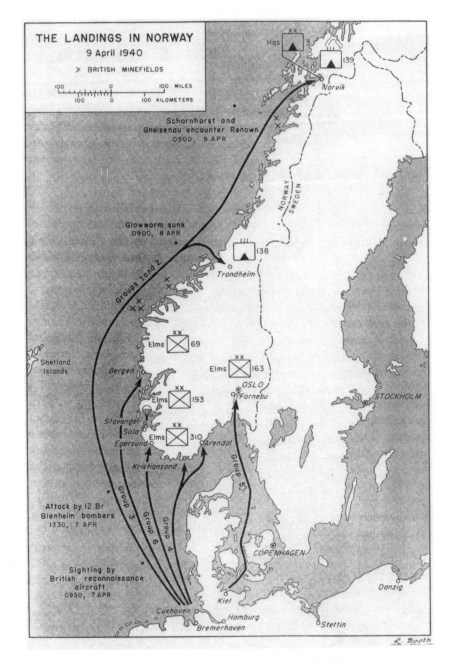

The 1940 Norwegian campaign is often described as a duel between airpower and seapower, with the less deficient German command system playing a key role. (E.F. Ziemke, The German Northern Theater of Operations, *US Government Printing Office, Washington D.C., 1959)*

Besides from co-ordinating the major problems of the operation the staff did much spadework for the way in which the surprise attack should be carried out. All this preparatory work was done in complete secrecy.

a.) *General Ruediger von Falkenhorst as Commander in Chief of the campaign in Norway.* The execution of the plan was entrusted to General Ruediger von Falkenhorst. De jure, von Falkenhorst was in command of all land, air and naval forces used in the occupation of Norway. De facto, nothing resembling a Supreme Command of the United Services came into existence. The idea of a Supreme Command of the United Services had always been disliked by the Army as well as by the Navy and Luftwaffe because each service was afraid of losing in influence and self-consistancy; with von Blomberg's release the idea of a Supreme Command of the United Services had died. Falkenhorst had no training in a universal conception of warfare nor was he the personality to live up to the task of a Commander in Chief of the Army, Navy and Air Forces. He remained an Army commander and with respect to strategy confined to ground operations. As to the Air Forces he was wedded to the old concept that Air Power was restricted to support these operations. The Navy didn't interest him at all. Thus, the "Supreme Command" was executed in matters of territorial supremacy only – (until, this too, got lost to the Reichskommissar Terboven). Otherwise, instead of a combined staff of Army, Navy and Air Force officers each service had its own headquarters. Tactically the co-operation was close and efficient at least between Army and Air Forces.

b.) *Flieger Korps X in Command of the Air Forces.* The command of the air-operations in the campaign of Norway was given to Fliegerkorps X with Generalleutnant Geisler in Command. During the months of "phony war" on the landfront Fliegerkorps X had won much credit and publicity by raids on the British fleet at Scapa Flow and Edinburgh. These attacks originated from Hitler's and Goering's tendency to show off. With respect to air strategy I consider them fundamentally mistaken. Psychologically, however, these raids might have impressed the British Navy. Practically they resulted in that the Air Forces of Fliegerkorps X gained some practice over sea and some idea of sea warfare which had been criminally neglected within the Luftwaffe.

c.) *Strength and composition of the Air Forces used originally in the campaign in Norway.* As to the Air Forces subordinated to Fliegerkorps X for the campaign in Norway I have to rely on my memory and the little of details I was able to gather. The respective units were:

1.) *1 squadron (Ju-88) long distance reconnaissance planes* (Fernau aerungsstaffel)

2.) *4 Bombardment wings* (Kampfgeschwader K.G.)

K.G.26	3 groups He-111	} cadre units of
K.G.30	1 group He-111	Fliegerkorps X
	1 group Ju-88	
(* L.G. 1	3 groups He-111)	Additionally sub-
		ordinated for
K.G. 4	1 group He-111)	the campaign

(* L.G.1 = Lehrgeschwader 1 = bombardment instructing wing.

3.) *1 Twin engine fighter wing* (Zerstoerergeschwader Z.G.)
Z.G.26 resp. Z.G.77   2 groups Me-110

4.) *1 Fighter group* (Jagdgeschwader J.G.)
J.G. 1   1 group Me-109

5.) *1 Coast reconnaissance and naval support group* (Kuesten-fliegergruppe)
1 group He-115

6.) *4 special purpose transport wings* (K.G.z.b.V.)
K.G.z.b.V. 101, 102, 106, 107 (each wing was in fact only a group of 3 squadrons, each squadron of 20 planes, type Ju-52; 1 squadron of K.G.z.b.V. 107 was mixed of 4 engine FW-200's and Ju-90's. The greater part of the pilots came from the "Deutsche Lufthansa".)

7.) *1 Seaplane transport group*
Do-24, 26, 18; Ju-52 (on floats)

d.) *Composition of the Staff of Flieger Korps X.* To take care of the special purpose transport wings the late Oberst d.R. Freiherr von Gablenz, Director of the "Deutsche Lufthansa", was attached to Flieger Korps X. Furthermore, to make sure that the operations were carried out according to schedule the Staff of Flieger Korps X was increased by several officers of the OKL who had worked in the preparatory secret planning of the campaign. These officers took over the duties of Ia and Ic of the cadre staff officers of Flieger Korps X.

III. The initial stage of the campaign

a.) *The moment of surprise.* The prearranged schedule, however, was wrecked considerably by that the German expedition forces ran into a concentration of British submarines off the Norwegian coast. Whether this concentration of submarines was the initial stage of the British "Stratford-Plan" for the occupation of Norway as the OKW

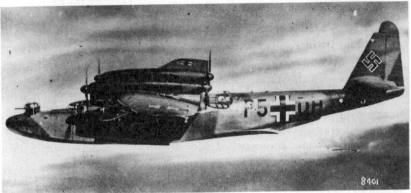

The TransozeanStaffel seaplane transport group of Fliegerkorps X in Norway was equipped with the Dornier Do 24 trimotor flying boat (top), the four-engine Dornier Do 26 (middle), which had tilting rear pusher propellers, and the seaplane variant of the Junkers Ju 52/3m (bottom), designated Ju 52/3m g5e by the Luftwaffe.

and the OKM believed or whether it was meant to make the blockade of the western (Narvik) route of the iron ore supply more effective the fact remains that several freighters with fuel (e.g. for the destroyers at Narvik) equipment and troops were sunk before 9 April, the day fixed for the invasion of Norway. Quite a lot of soldiers who had been hidden aboard the torpedoed ships were shipwrecked and came ashore in Norway in uniform. By that the Norwegian coastal defence was given some premonition of the imminent attack and the moment of surprise got partly lost; therefore the German naval forces met with some unforeseen resistance.

b.) *The initial landings of air-borne units.* The air forces, on the other side, which were to inaugurate the occupation of Norway by parachuting troops at Forneboe, the commercial airfield of Oslo, at dawn, 9 April, were frustrated, at first, by bad weather and returned to Germany. (K.G.z.b.V.101).

K.G.z.b.V.102 and 107, however, accomplished their tasks at schedule 0830 hours 9 April by landing about 3000 infantry men within two hours, at first under the fire of the defence at Forneboe. The defence caused some casualties, inter alia a group captain was killed and the landing was accomplished only at the cost of 31 crashes.

Stavanger and Kristiansand, too, were occupied by air-borne units (K.G.z.b.V.106) which met with next to no resistance.

With the transport of reinforcements to Drontheim (11 April) the initial landing operations were successfully ended. (At Drontheim, the landing took place on a frozen lake about 4 miles south of Drontheim as the airfield at Varnaes was unserviceable). I am of the opinion that the display of air power as shown during the landings of troops and material with hundred of planes roaring over Southern Norway helped much to facilitate the occupation of the first objects.

c.) *The supply situation.* In the early days of the invasion a very critical situation arose with respect to supplies. Out of the supply ships so many were sunk that sea transport was stopped for more than a week. By combined effort of the German Navy and the Luftwaffe the Kattegat and Skagerrak were cleared so efficiently within a short time that no further losses occurred for years. Nevertheless for some time a great many supplies had to be transported by plane. Day by day hundreds of Ju-52's, W-34's and "Weihen's", all of them are unarmed, rotated on the way from Skagen and Aalborg to Oslo without being interfered, though there was only 1 fighter group with squadrons at Aalborg and Kristiansand resp. to protect the whole area. The British, of course, did venture some attacks on the airfields of Aalborg and Stavanger but, then, the agressors were nearly annihilated.

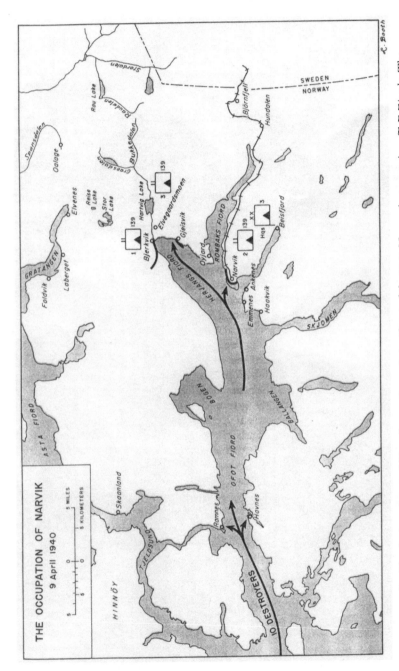

The air-sea-land battles in and around Narvik were the most significant of the 1940 Norwegian campaign. (E.F. Ziemke, The German Northern Theater of Operations, US Government Printing Office, Washington D.C., 1959)

Unarmed Junkers W 34s (top) and Focke-Wulf Fw 58 Weihes (above) played a vital role as supply transports during the invasion of Norway, when supply ships failed to get through.

IV. The second phase of the campaign; the Allied landings at Andalsnaes at Namsos. Air power the decisive factor

a.) *New headquarters are formed.* Of all the airfields in Norway none was equal to the needs of modern air forces. Even at Stavanger Sola where the airfield was comparatively up to date, the runways had to be lengthened and some hindrances of approach blown off. Thus, the improvement of base services became of paramount importance lest the British would win air superiority by making use of their aircraft carriers. To see to it that the appropriate airfields were built as soon as possible a "Luftgaukommando Norwegen" (air force administration command Headquarters Norway) was formed with Generalmajor Suessmann, later Generalleutnant Kitzinger in Command. It had to take care of the supply services also.

The "Luftgaukommando Norwegen" was subordinated to Luftflotte 5 at Oslo which after the initial operations had been carried through successfully was established to gratify Secretary of Aviation Milch rather than meet actual needs. In fact, with only 1 Flieg.Korps, 1 Luftgaukommando and next to no anti-aircraft defence units Luftflotte 5 was the first major instance of overorganization which was to become so characteristic of the Luftwaffe, especially in the last years of war when, practically, air forces had ceased to exist.

b.) *Flieger Korps X sticks to headquarters at Hamburg.* Nominally Flieger Korps X which, hitherto, had been directly under the OKL was subordinated to Luftflotte 5; in fact, Flieger Korps X for some weeks to come received its orders same as before immediately from the High Command of the Air Forces. With the bulk of the Air Forces operating from bases in Germany (Schleswig, Westerland, Fuhlsbuettel, Uetersen) and Denmark (Aalborg, Kopenhagen, Okagen), with the very poor signal communications in Norway Oslo was hardly the appropriate place to commit the Air Forces. Hamburg, on the other side, had excellent signal communications to Oslo and Stavanger as well as to the respective airfields in Germany and Denmark and to the OKL. Then, at Hamburg was a very efficient radio intelligence service. (As far as I remember most of the British radio messages were deciphered within a short time until the Allied landing in Sicily). Above all it was evident that if there was any danger of a failure this danger would originate not from the Armed Forces of Norway but from England. That is why Flieger Korps X stuck to headquarters at Hamburg keeping an eye on England as well as on the operations in Norway. In the early days of the invasion the British made an attempt either to check the German invasion of Norway precipetatedly or – as the German Supreme Command had reason to believe – to execute the

213

"Stratford-Plan" according to preconceived schedule. This attempt was smashed off Stavanger by the bombs of the Air Forces. I do not know what losses the British Navy actually suffered. In any case they must have been impressive enough to keep away the British Navy from every Norwegian port except Narvik.

c.) *The Allied landings at Andalsnaes and Namsos; Air Power the decisive factor.* Air Power was the decisive factor. As the British durst not contend for air supremacy within the first critical days of the invasion by rigorously committing their aircraft carriers German air control was established automatically in Southern and Central Norway when the Norwegian airfields had been occupied. Now, the German Air Forces were free to give whatever support the Army wanted.

The Allied landings at Andalsnaes and Namsos, on the other side, were doomed to fail as they were left without any assistance both from the British Navy and the British Royal Air Force. Moreover, these forces had next to no antiaircraft artillery. To be sure, the German Air Forces were handicapped too by that they had to fly their missions from airfields in Germany and Denmark; only one bomber group of K.G.26 was at Stavanger. Thus, each mission took about 8 hours; then, the weather conditions were bad with clouds hanging deep into the valleys. Therefore, the Allies were able to advance quickly from Andalsnaes to Dombas and farther south to Ringebu.

To get hold of the important railway junction of Dombas Generalmajor Suessmann, Commanding General of Luftgaukommando Norwegen, had ordered a detachment of about 200 parachutists to be parachuted at Dombas. Due to bad weather the concentrated landing of these troops failed. Widely scattered in small units, some of them far away from Dombas, they were unable to rally. Thus, they were annihilated by the combined Allied and Norwegian forces. Generalmajor Suessmann was court-martialled but acquitted. Nevertheless he was released from his command and replaced by Generalleutnant Kitzinger.

d.) *Fight in Southern and Central Norway comes to an end; Air Forces are withdrawn to prepare for the campaign in France.* When weather improved the position of the Allied Forces became untenable. Bombed continually by the German Air Forces, threatened in the flank by the German ground troops the Allied units from Andalsnaes were forced to retreat and evacuated on May 2. At the same time the Allied units from Namsos gave up and re-embarked. The re-embarkment of the Allies was, to my knowledge, not realized at first. Therefore, in preference to ships leaving Norway for England which were considered in ballast the ships coming from England were bombed.

The Norwegian divisions in southern and central Norway surrendered under the psychological stress of complete impotence especially with respect to air rather than because of actual losses suffered from aerial bombardment or in action.

Thereafter, about 5 May, the air forces additionally subordinated to Fliegerkorps X were withdrawn and even the cadre bombardment wing K.G. 30 was ordered to Germany to prepare for the campaign in France.

B. Fight in Northern Norway

I. Point of main effort is shifted to the North

Important as the successes in Southern and Central Norway were the ultimate goal and the actual object of the whole campaign – Narvik and the iron ore – were still at stake and about 500 miles away. With the fight in Southern and Central Norway ended the point of main effort was shifted to Northern Norway. As, in the mean time, thousands of Norwegians had been busy to improve the airfields all the air forces of Fliegerkorps X could be stationed in Norway. Fliegerkorps X transferred headquarters first to Oslo, then to Drontheim where von Falkenhorst had his headquarters.

a.)   *Location of the air forces from 10 May 1940.*

(rough estimate from memory; minor errors are likely.)

Drontheim:	K.G. 26	two groups
	Stukas	one group
	Me-110	one squadron
	Coast reconnaiss.	two squadrons
	Seaplane Transport	one group
Stavanger:	K.G. 26	one group
	Coast reconnaiss.	one squadron
	Me-110	two squadrons
	(*Ju-88	one squadron

(* Long distance reconnaissance

| *Kristiansand:* | Fighter | two squadrons |

Oslo (Kjeller and Forneboe) All the transport groups of Ju-52's and FW-200's. These transport groups were no longer subordinated to Fliegerkorps X but to a special "Chief of air supply services" under the Luftflotte 5 or the Luftgaukommando Norwegen.

215

At Drontheim the supply situation was difficult at first. The railway did not yet operate and transportation by car was restricted because some bridges had been blasted and the emergency bridges did not allow trucks. Sea transport was rightly considered too risky as speed-boats and armed freebooters waylaid single steamers and a convoy system was not yet established. Thus, bombs and fuel had to be flown from Oslo to Drontheim, a system which besides from being uneco-nomic did not amount to much. Therefore, even submarines were used to equip the air forces at Drontheim with bombs and fuel.

b.) *First meeting with von Falkenhorst elucidates discrepancies of conceptions concerning the use of air power.* About May 15, as acting Chief of Staff of Fliegerkorps X I reported at von Falkenhorst's headquarters at Drontheim at the Hotel "Britannia", where I was given accommoda-tion together with my small operations staff. (The Commanding General of Fliegerkorps X had remained at Oslo with the rest of the staff.) General von Falkenhorst asked me how I thought the air forces could give maximum support to Dietl at Narvik. I answered, by keeping away the British Navy and, most of all, British aircraft car-riers. This statement was interpreted by von Falkenhorst that I refused to help the Army at all. His idea was that the air forces should give close support only, though, at that time, neither Dietl nor the detachment advancing northward from Drontheim to relieve Dietl – a reinforced battalion of the division Feuerstein – did need any support besides from supplies by transport planes which, of course, they got.

c.) *Supplying Dietl.* At first, the supplying of Dietl – at least with food – had been effectuated by railway via Sweden to Narvik under the cover of "Red Cross Relief", whereas ammunition, weapons, equipment were parachuted by transport planes. This method worked well for some time. One day, however, this supply was stopped because the Allies had protested and the supplying fell to the transport planes alone. The very sight of these planes which made their appearance from the first days of the invasion whenever weather conditions allowed helped much to keep the troops at Narvik in good morale. By seaplane which landed in the Rombaksfjord east of Narvik personal contact was estab-lished; by these planes even mountain guns were transported to Narvik. At first, these planes, met with no resistance worth speaking of. Later on they were endangered by murderous antiaircraft fire from the British naval force near Narvik and from the Swedes who would strafe the slightest violation of their territory. (The drop point in the last stages of the campaign was so close to the border that it was dif-ficult not to touch Swedish territory.) Moreover British fighters made

A Dornier Do 24 in a calm anchorage. The successful use of the prototype in an operational role during the 1940 Narvik campaign persuaded the Germans to adopt the design, which was originally produced to a Netherlands specification. (US National Archives)

their appearance and British interceptor planes waylaid on the route to Narvik and downed several unarmed Ju-52's.

d.) *Supplying of the Feuerstein Detachment.* In a similar way the reinforced battalion advancing northward from Drontheim was supplied by parachute delivery as well as by seaplanes. It is significant of the extreme lack in sea power that the German Navy strictly declined to risk any vessel in supplying this battalion as, indeed, some craft which had started on the responsibility of the Army had been captured or sunk by Norwegian freebooters, Nor did the German Navy venture to give any assistance by minesweepers or destroyers. Although the sea was closely watched by the coast reconnaissance and naval support group the patrol was not deep enough to allow the feeble German naval forces to withdraw in time to Drontheim when superior naval forces were scouted. Nor did the number of planes allow to survey all the inland waters which provided innumberable hiding places. It happened that British destroyers interfered with the supplying of the battalion which worked its way northward to Mo, Bodoe, as the only road leading north run often along the fjords; sometimes the road would discontinue and all the traffic would go by ferry to the other side of the fjord. Those raids, however, were a nuisance rather than an actual danger for the battalion.

II. Fight against the British sea forces off Narvik

a.) *Sinking of an aircraft carrier stimulated by Goering.* With respect to Narvik the situation was different. Until beginning of May the landing operations at Namsos and Andalsnaes had won priority over Narvik, but even then ships had been the main target of the air forces. Thereafter, with Major Harlinghausen in command of the air forces at Drontheim and von Falkenhorst still at Oslo the only effort of the air forces was to fight ships, especially in the waters off Narvik. This fight was stimulated by Goering personally who, in the meantime had realized that the British aircraft carrier *Ark Royal* which the OKW had claimed to be sunk by a bomb hit did still exist. (It is, by the way, significant of the mentality and the methods of the OKL that neither the air crew nor the Fliegerkorps had ever claimed that the *Ark Royal* were sunk. The report submitted by the Fliegerkorps was to the meaning that the tail gunner of the Ju-88 which had bombed the *Ark Royal* had observed a burst of flames at the stern of the aircraft carrier; that the other members of the crew had not seen anything; that the sea patrol ordered to check upon the result of the attack had not found the *Ark Royal* nor the conveying destroyers. The "sinking" of the *Ark Royal* was done in the OKL.) To sink an aircraft carrier had become something like a fixed idea with Goering. Therefore, he promised to award the Knight's Cross and – in contradiction to pre-Hitler German military traditions – a premium of RM. 100,000. – for the sinking of an aircraft carrier. The prospect of this reward brought about odd results.

b.) *Shortcomings of the air forces in the fighting of naval forces.* That British aircraft carriers were in the Northern region became obvious when British fighter planes of the Gloucester type were encountered. Because of unsufficient speed and armament these planes could not accomplish much against the He-111's raiding the Ofot-Fjord and the Vest-Fjord for naval forces and the waters off the Lofoten and Westeraalen for aircraft carriers.

The committment of the bombers was handicapped by several snags: First, there was no previous reconnaissance work as the seaplanes had no sufficient range to survey the waters off Narvik and the long-distance Ju-88's were scarce; moreover their crews had no training in reconnaissance work over sea. Then, the bomber crews had no adequate training in precision bombing nor, at that time, a bomb sight which would have guaranteed precision bombing. The crews had not been trained nor educated in mass bombing, at least not above group's strength to make up for the deficiency in precision bombing. Development and production of torpedos had been cancelled by Hitler personally when suggested by Goering and Milch who, both of them, had hardly ever seen a torpedo. Finally, when opposed by modern fighters, our bombers were handicapped by inadequate armament; this had been censured and opposed by the flying officers from the very beginning but was maintained by the technicians who alone had the say within the Technical Office and who stressed that speed was the real Simon Pure.

Because of lack in reconnaissance the bombers were committed in armed patrols searching – in flight's or squadrons strength – for naval forces. This method had the disadvantage that, as far as I know, a concentrated attack of all the bombers available was never accomplished. True, there were concentrated attacks by two and more bomber groups on the enemy ground troops or on naval forces previously reported by Dietl. But then, too, the approach flight was made independently by the squadrons, or, at group's strength at the utmost.

From personal experience and from 20 years of service in the German Navy (-1933) I had become rather sceptical with respect to the reports of the air forces concerning naval forces. I knew that the German Navy disbelieved in the successes claimed by the Luftwaffe for the raids of Scapa Flow and Edinburgh. I knew of the story of the *Ark Royal*; then, during the landings at Namsos and Andalsnaes or somewhat later a British super-dreadnought had been claimed to be sunk by a single 500 lbs. bomb hit from a Stuka. Though the sinking of the ship and the fact that the ship was a modern super-dreadnought had been checked by the convoying seaplane crews the success appeared too unbelievable, especially as the description of the type applied only to the *Hood* or, maybe, to a battleship of the *George V* type. The day I came to Drontheim a British aircraft carrier had been reported "deadly hit" and another "badly damaged". The "deadly one" when last seen by the successful bomber had been nearly capsizing from heavy list. Goering, personally, urged by phone to give her the knock-out. The next day all the bombers were an armed patrol in search for the sinking aircraft carrier and the badly damaged one. They were not found. Instead, three or four new aircraft carriers were reported to be seen, bombed or hit at different places. Fortunately, from Stavanger the long-distance reconnaissance squadron had been ordered which, at the time of the armed patrol, had covered the whole area by aerial mapping cameras. The aerial mosaic proved that not a single aircraft carrier had

been within the fjords and that the spotted, bombed or hit aircraft carriers were either merchant ships or destroyers or just phantoms.
Goering was very indignant when instead of the final sinking of the
aircraft carrier he learned that I was sceptical about the success of the
previous day because of the nature of the new "successes".

III. British fighters are growing more dangerous at Narvik

When evaluated more intensively the aerial mosaic disclosed another very
interesting fact which, under the spell of aircraft carrier hunting, had been
left unnoticed: the old airfield of Bardufoss, 60 miles northeast of Narvik
which had been destroyed in the early days of the invasion and, since then,
had not been watched closely, was operated by British fighters. Moreover,
at Skaanland, about 40 miles northeast of Narvik, at the waterway con-
necting Ofot-Fjord and Vaags-fjord a new airdrome of one or two runways
had come into existence. This airfield, too, harboured British fighters.

This discovery accounted for the appearance of Hurricanes and Spitfires
which since about a fortnight had replaced the comparatively harmless
Gloucester fighters and were responsible for the increasing rate of downed
He-111's and Ju-88's. (One group of K.G. 30 had been re-attached to
Fliegerkorps X end of May.) For this reason the twin engine fighter group
of Me-110's had been ordered to Drontheim to convoy the inadequately
armed bombers. The Me-110's, however, were no match for the Spitfires
and Hurricaines. Apart from being inferior to fighter planes anyhow they
were additionally handicapped by their "Dackelbauch" (Dachshund's belly)
which enabled them to cover the 500 miles to Narvik and have some 20–30
minutes left for action there. For this reason it had been our concern to get
our fighter planes within the range of Narvik. At Hatfjedall (112 miles
northnortheast of Namsos, 5 miles south of Roes-Vand) a terrain was
found which with some major effort was converted into an airfield for
Stukas and fighters. Until the end of the campaign in Norway only Stukas
were able to make use of it.

a.) *More headquarters at Drontheim; discrepancies in the concept of air power.*
Fliegerkorps X had always emphasized that the main effort of the air
forces was to keep away the British naval forces and by doing so enable
Dietl at Narvik to resist until relieved by the ground troops of
Falkenhorst. Now, Fliegerkorps X stressed that to give efficient
support to Dietl and cut down the rate of losses in bombers air
supremacy must be re-established first thing.

These basic conceptions were in no way approved of by General von
Falkenhorst nor by General Stumpff who about 10 May, had succeeded
Secretary of Aviation Milch as Chief of Luftflotte 5. Unfortunately,

Stumpff with his Chief of General Staff had come to Drontheim, as I imagine on the request of Falkenhorst who because of my divergent conception of air power as pronounced at my debut considered me noncooperative.

There was no lack in headquarters for the little air forces at Drontheim.

1.) General v. Falkenhorst, C.I.C. of all land, air and naval forces in Norway with Oberst i. G. Buschenhagen as Chief of Gen. Staff.

2.) Gen. d. Flieg. Stumpff, Chief of Luftflotte 5, with Generalleutnant Foerster as Chief of Gen. Staff.

3.) Generalleutnant Geisler, Commanding General of Flieg. Korps X, with Generalmajor Kessler as Chief of Staff.

4.) Generalmajor Kessler, General in Command of the air forces at Drontheim (in personal union with 3.)

With General Stumpff fawning von Falkenhorst who in the times of the Reichswehr had been his superior the main effort of the air forces was shifted more and more to close support of the ground troops, both, at Narvik and advancing northward from Drontheim. At a distance of 500 miles the bombers were committed to bomb machine gun nests and the twin engine fighters to strafing attacks against enemy infantry men they could hardly recognize. Bodo was bombed because the only remaining British battalion there was supposed to build up a strong resistence or a possible bridgehead for another Allied landing. Fight against the British naval forces fell short.

b.) *Dietl's situation becomes untenable.* Because of the mistaken use of air power Dietl's position had become more and more critical. Already twice Dietl had been reinforced by air. At first, by the 1. company of parachute regiment 1. The parachutists, however, did not satisfy Dietl. Dietl maintained – as General der Fallschirmtruppen Meindl implies from professional jealousy – that the parachutists same as the sailors from the sunk destroyers were more nuisance than actual help; only mountain infantry men would do in the Narvik terrain. Thereupon, a detachment of mountain infantry men trained for a fortnight in parachuting bailed out at Narvik. It was a drop in the bucket. On May 28, the British landed 2 miles east of Narvik and, within a few hours, the town was captured. Dietl retreated along the railroad to the East and SOS-ed for reinforcements and close support by air. Otherwise he would have to cross the Swedish border to be interned. On June 3, the 2. company of parachute regiment 1 started in about 24 planes for Narvik. Out of these planes only 2 had the good luck to spot the

A Heinkel He 60 of KG z.b.v., Tromso, Norway, about 1941, grounded to prevent it sinking because of leaking pontoons.

railway to Narvik through a rift in the clouds hanging deep into the valley. The other planes failed and had to return.

c.) *Clash between Luftflotte and Fliegerkorps X.* Until then, because of bad weather the bombing of Skaanland and Bardufoss airfields which, for some time, had been fixed up by the Fliegerkorps and duly reported to the Luftflotte had fallen short. Now, at last, weather had improved and according to program Skaanland and Bardufoss airfields were in for it. The air forces were more than half way to Narvik when they were ordered back by the Luftflotte which wanted all the air forces give close support to Dietl. As before landing the planes had to release their bombs unarmed and reloading and refuelling at Varnaes took about 8 hours because of the restricted facilities much time and material was wasted. I answered this affront by resigning on the spot. (The day before Gen. d. Flieg. Kuehl to get some service at the front – and the Iron Cross – had taken over command of Fliegerkorps X for about 4 weeks from Generalleutnant Geisler who, otherwise, would have resigned too.)

The "Contreordre" of the Luftflotte was of demoralizing effect on the air crews; "ordre, contreordre, desordre." All of them had been looking forward to the bombing of Skaanland and Bardufoss. Now, they were enraged because instead of getting even with the British fighters they had again suffered heavy losses by those fighters. Then, the discrepancy among their superiors had become evident and the air forces had to pay for it.

IV. The end of the Campaign in Norway – a result of the bombardment?

From the fact that the British evacuated immediately after the bombardment it might be deduced that, after all, the bombardment of the ground troops was instrumental in bringing about the evacuation of the British and the ensuing surrender of the last Norwegian division. General der Fallschirmtruppen Meindl who, then a colonel of the mountain infantry had parachuted on June 3 and witnessed this and other bombardments at Narvik maintains that besides from being psychologically impressive the bombardments did not do much damage and, because of the terrain could not cause much harm to the ground troops. But then General Meindl is of the opinion that he personally has influenced Dietl to renounce any idea of crossing the Swedish border whereas I know for certain that Dietl had sent a radio message and a report by telephone that his position was untenable and that he had prepared for crossing the Swedish border on June 10; this report dated from June 8, 12 hours before the Allies evacuated. As the evacuation was camouflaged by terrific bombardment from the naval forces it was considered the final attack. Therefore, the surrender of the Norwegians came as a complete surprise and a sort of miracle. Personally, I am of the opinion that Dunkirk was responsible for the end of the Campaign in Norway. But for Dunkirk it would have ended differently.

In the early days of the invasion air-supremacy had fallen automatically to the Germans; it had been left undisputed during the landings at Andalsnaes and Namsos. In the last decisive stage of the campaign, however, the Germans were about to lose air-supremacy. The committment of the air forces at Narvik was – in my opinion – symptomatic for the "landmindedness" of the German leadership. In fall 1940 this concept resulted in the failure of the "Blitz" and thereby in the ruin of Germany. In June 1940 but for Dunkirk it would have ended in the loss of Narvik and thereby in the failure of the Campaign in Norway waged for the iron ore supply.

Chapter 8

GERMAN NAVAL AIR OPERATIONS
APRIL – DECEMBER 1940

by Oberst (i.G.) Walter Gaul

The following is a survey of German Air Force operations from the beginning of the French campaign until the end of 1940.

The author has purposely omitted a detailed analysis of the position of the Naval Air Force, as at this period all operations were directed towards the defeat of Britain, a task in which the bomber formations of the German Air Force played the main part. At first, even the Navy welcomed this exclusive concentration and lost no chance of pointing out to C-in-C German Air Force how important it was to attack naval forces and to lay aerial mines to ensure the blockade of the British Isles. Furthermore, up to the fall of France the Navy approved the allocation to Fliegerkorps IX of the Staffeln of Naval Air Commander West which had been trained for aerial minelaying operations.

After the fall of France, however, the Navy thought it should stress the need of naval flying units in support of naval operations, particularly for reconnaissance and air cover off the recently captured Atlantic coast, off the Channel coast and in the western part of the North Sea. However, as is shown in Para. 14, C-in-C Navy was unable to regain his naval air Staffeln. The German Air Force had sustained great losses over Britain, and therefore refused to surrender any aircraft able to carry bombs or mines; thus, until further notice, C-in-C Navy was deprived of a mine-carrying Gruppe, a Gruppe of Ju-88 and a Gruppe of Do-17 belonging to the Naval Air Force.

In vain did Naval War Staff point out that future naval operations had been planned, which required the support of a well-trained naval air force. The Supreme Command was exclusively concerned with the immediate target, Britain. The author has endeavored to show the extent of the German Air Force contribution with reference only to their campaign against shipping and minelaying operations from the air. This narrative is compiled from German sources and tables of operations may be found in the appendices.

Minelaying from the air during April, 1940

1) In April, 1940, the plans of Naval High Command were chiefly centered round the invasion of Norway.

   The critical situation at Narvik demanded urgent concentration of
   all available forces against the enemy's supply lines. In addition to
   plans for intensifying U-boat warfare and for battleship operations,
   Naval War Staff considered that increased aerial minelaying in Scapa
   Flow, Kirkwall Bay and the Clyde (Glasgow) would effectively hamper
   British action in Norway.

   All such proposals were however rejected by the Führer and C-in-
   C German Air Force, since Fliegerdivision IX felt that both training and strength were inadequate for this purpose. In fact only
   the first Staffeln of Bomber Geschwader 26 were about to complete
   their training.

2) Minelaying operations which were finally resumed in the middle of
   April were really only a continuation of previous activity off the southeast coast of England, interrupted in January, 1940. Fliegerdivision IX
   carried out the offensive at the orders of Naval Group West, who had
   put at their disposal for the purpose 3 multi-purpose Staffeln of Naval
   Air Commander West.

   Up to the time of the German western offensive this combined formation made six sorties in all against the area off the southeast coast
   of England and off the north French Channel ports. From the reports
   of the air crews and the radio intercept service it was evident that the
   enemy had considerably strengthened their defenses.

   Concentrated use of air mines with the new type of firing which had
   been released, was more than ever a necessity (magnetic firing with
   reverse polarity).

Air Offensive over the Sea during Operation "Gelb" (Western Offensive)

3) On receipt of the code-word ordering Operation "Gelb", the focal point
   of the war was switched to the west.

   The German Air Force had two main tasks:
   a) Support of the army by direct participation in the land battles and
      by defeat of the enemy air force, and
   b) severing of Dutch, Belgian and French rear communications with
      Britain by attacking ports and ships in the operational area.

   Two Luftflotten were detailed for these tasks: Luftflotte 2 on the
   right wing in support of Army Group B, Luftflotte 3 to the south in

support of Army Group A, each consisting of 2 Fliegerkorps with the necessary reconnaissance, bomber, dive-bomber and fighter forma- tions. For this purpose Fliegerdivision VII (parachute units), the transport Geschwader of Fliegerdivision XXII (army airborne units) and Fliegerdivision IX (aerial minelaying division) were placed directly under the command of C-in-C German Air Force.

4) Sections of Luftflotte 2 (Bomber Geschwader 30 and Greifswald Training Geschwader) and Fliegerdivision IX, enlarged to Fliegerkorps IX later in the campaign and, at the same time, subordi- nated to Luftflotte 2, undertook operations in support of the Navy. These operations were dictated by the extent of the army's advance and the requirements of the naval offensive.

The Navy had been allotted the task of opening the western offen- sive by prompt mining of the ports along the Dutch, Belgian and French coast. As early as 27 April, however, Naval Group West had pointed out that owing to repeated postponement of the offensive they could no longer guarantee a campaign of unobtrusive minelaying by these light forces in view of the short nights. Group West proposed to entrust this task to Fliegerdivision IX which, together with the forces of Naval Air Commander West, possessed a sufficient number of air- craft. Naval War Staff agreed to this proposal, more particularly since they felt that in this way units so urgently needed for future escort assignments might be spared inevitable losses.

5) According to Group West's calculations, the first wave would require approximately 30 aircraft carrying 50 aerial mines. C-in-C German Air Force approved commitment of this operation to Fliegerdivision IX.

About 0345 on 10 April, 1940, and during the evening of the same day, 48 He-115 and 15 He-111 took off on two operations, mining the harbors and approaches of the Dutch-Belgian coast, concentrating on den Helder, Ijmuiden, Rotterdam, Flushing, Zeebrugge and Ostend.

The object of this opening phase of the air offensive, as far as the naval front was concerned, was to deny the enemy the use of sea- power in support of his land forces, whether for the landing or evacuation of troops, and to prevent intervention of surface forces in the land fighting.

Guided by the reconnaissance planes of the Luftflotten and of C-in-C German Air Force and assisted by information from the radio inter- cept service, the aircraft attacked merchant shipping and transport, warships and harbor installations. The attacks took place by day and

Heinkel He 111s, in company with He 115 seaplanes, mined the harbours and approaches of the Dutch-Belgian coast in April 1940. This is an He 111H-4.

night in the form of armed reconnaissance and in operations by close formations. Fliegerdivision IX supplemented this strategy by continuous minelaying operations.

6) After the defeat of the Belgian and French air forces, air operations were concentrated on the coast. Units not required for direct support of the land fighting were brought up for attacks on shipping and ports. Fliegerdivision IX received reinforcements from Geschwader 26 and a Gruppe of Bomber Geschwader 4, and now turned to simultaneous mining operations and bombing of harbor installations, thus diverting the enemy's attention from the minelaying. The operational areas gradually moved as the Army advanced. Having made the shipping routes off den Helder impassable, the approaches to Amsterdam were blocked, after which the mouth of the Scheldt became the center of operations.

7) The operations yielded considerable success, although allied defenses, disorganized at the outset but now slowly consolidated, accurate flak

from ships' guns and fortified areas by day and increased R.A.F. fighter defenses, had all to be overcome. The Eleventh French Destroyer Division suffered particularly heavy losses, when attempting to participate in the land fighting from the Scheldt estuary. On 19 April it was compelled to withdraw to Dunkirk and Cherbourg after every unit had been damaged.

The radio intercept service revealed allied difficulties due to the necessary commitment of large numbers of ships along the coast for escort and transport duties. Aerial minelaying operations forced the allies constantly to shift their assembly points and anchorages for shipping, slowing down the process of embarkation and disembarkation and thus achieving great tactical significance. Radio and press reports during this period showed that the mines laid by aircraft had sunk a great number of ships, and indicated that the allied defenses off the Belgian-French Channel coast had been inadequate in face of surprise and continuous minelaying from the air.

On 22 May, German armored divisions thrust along the coast to prevent large-scale withdrawal of allied forces from the Channel ports, thus bringing the Calais-Dunkirk area into prominence. On 26 May air reconnaissance reported strong concentration of shipping off Dunkirk.

The Battle of Dunkirk

8) German Air Force reports on 29 May indicated that allied evacuation of troops from the Flanders pocket had reached its climax. In addition to small steamers and minor vessels, brought up in force, destroyers, M.T.B.s and trawlers also took part.

The Naval War Staff had only a few E-boats available to prevent this allied operation. Despite the occasional success of these boats in repeated sorties, there was no doubt that the German Air Force was the principal weapon against allied evacuation. German Command, therefore, looked primarily to the bomber units of the Luftflotte. Could they hold up the evacuation; could they for a short time over a relatively limited area override naval supremacy and gain mastery from the air?

9) On that day successive waves from fourteen Bomber Gruppen of both Luftflotten attacked the troops evacuating. All aircraft which could be spared from the direct support of the Army were employed on this task to which, until the first days of June, they were primarily committed.

German Air Force reports of successes obtained, frequently verifiable by the radio intercept service, were astonishingly high.

10) Nevertheless the major part of the British Expeditionary Force was successfully withdrawn to England. Despite favorable conditions, short approach flights and a confined operational area, the German Air Force had not succeeded in overriding naval supremacy. The lessons learned at Andalsnes and Namsos during the Norwegian campaign were repeated here: the striking power of a fleet in the disputed area was a permanent asset which could not be replaced by bombers alone.

Moreover the knowledge that mines laid by aircraft could be swept relatively quickly was particularly disconcerting. Now it was that the enemy's knowledge of the method of firing the aircraft mine, acquired in the winter of 1939, was felt to be a serious disadvantage. Hence, on 24 May, the Naval War Staff was forced to release the additional apparatus for magnetic firing (period delay mechanism) in order to complicate the enemy's task of mine-clearance. At the same time the Naval Armament Department was requested to devise a completely new firing mechanism as quickly as possible, in order that enemy countermeasures might be rendered extremely difficult and the German mining offensive decisively effective.

By the night of 3/4 June the allies had completed the evacuation of Dunkirk.

German Air Force operations up to the capitulation of France

11) After conclusion of the contest at Dunkirk the air offensive was again focussed on objectives in support of the Army in the direction of the Somme and with a view to penetration of the Maginot line, nevertheless the German Air Force was still committed to the task of preventing further allied attempts at evacuation from the French ports. The attacks were directed against withdrawal of the British 51st Division from the St. Valery, Le Havre and Cherbourg area and against evacuation of British Expeditionary Forces and allied troops from the other French ports on the Atlantic coast, including Bordeaux. Apart from occasional raids by dive-bomber formations, the brunt of the attacks on shipping was borne by Luftflotte 2 and Fliegerkorps IX. Particularly successful were the raids in the area around the Loire estuary and off St. Nazaire carried out on 17 June, 1940.

Campaign against shipping until the start of the Battle of Britain

12) The "all-out" offensive for the defeat of Britain had once again been forced into the background. The Naval War Staff therefore felt it to be their duty at this time to impress on C-in-C German Air Force the necessity of future bombing operations over Britain. They based their interpretation on Führer Directive No. 13 (Armed Forces Decree/Air Section No. 33028/40) of 24 May and the "Supplement to Directive No. 9", in which the Supreme Command, Armed Forces, laid down a revised policy with regard to the campaign against British economy. The Supreme Command's Directive fully accorded with Naval War Staff principles, authorizing the G.A.F. to conduct a large-scale air offensive against Britain as soon as forces were available and hoping for close cooperation between their two services in the coming campaign to be waged with bombs and mines against Britain.

The Naval War Staff still regarded Britain's sea-borne trade as the most vulnerable spot. They were only interested in attacks on British naval bases, on the south coast for example, if these operations in no way detracted from the attacks on import centers. The great ports of London and Liverpool and those in the Bristol Channel were, in their estimation, the most vital targets.

13) Already in the second half of June, 1940, the German Air Force had begun nuisance raids on industrial targets and airfields in Britain. Air operations after the fall of France did no more, however, than put defenses in the British Isles to the test in an endeavor to maintain pressure on the enemy while replacing losses in material and personnel incurred during the previous campaigns. It could not as yet be termed a concentrated effort for the purpose of bringing Britain to her knees.

Naval War Staff therefore welcomed the resumption of discussions with the German Air Force on combined operations against Britain, the subject of a communication from C-in-C German Air Force dated 25 January, 1940.

14) Details of the above negotiations between C-in-C German Air Force and C-in-C Navy are beyond the scope of this work. Once again the views of C-in-C German Air Force prevailed. The Staffeln of Naval Air Commander West were to remain with Fliegerkorps IX and two more Coastal Air Gruppen, which had meanwhile been converted to Ju-88 and Do-17z, were put under the command of Luftflotte 3.

The German Air Force took over reconnaissance at sea west of

Britain, in the Orkneys and Shetlands area and along the east coast over a strip 30 miles broad, also of the Channel area south of 53° N.

Air reconnaissance of the North Sea, coastal patrol of the Heligoland Bight, protection of the sea routes to Norway and anti-submarine measures were allotted to the remaining naval air units.

Naval Commands in the occupied coastal areas were directed to cooperate closely with Luftflotten 3 and 2.

Patrol of the coast and the Channel area was to be undertaken by units of C-in-C German Air Force.

On these arrangements were based the attacks on Britain's sea-borne trade awaited by Naval War Staff.

15) The findings of the radio intercept service and the many sighting and success reports from E-boats based on Boulogne proved that a considerable stream of import traffic was proceeding along the south coast of England to the Thames, despite German occupation of the Channel coast. The fact that the British were running increased risk in this sea area, even with some of their overseas convoys, emphasized the importance of the Thames as their main commercial thoroughfare. Attacks on this supply route were therefore of vital importance. Naval War Staff therefore urged the Air Force Command to attack Channel convoys, in addition to intensive mining of British ports.

16) After a short respite, Luftflotten 2 and 3 commenced operations in July against shipping in the Channel and along the southeast coast of Britain.

Operations alternated between armed reconnaissance and attacks by fairly strong forces of bombers in close formation according to intelligence received regarding convoys or particular harbor installations. Ju-87 dive-bombers and Ju-88 formations were primarily employed by day, and He-111 Geschwader by night, particularly for raids on port installations or for minelaying.

Quite soon, however, well-organized defenses made their appearance along the south coast of England. Approaching formations were promptly picked up by radar and ran into strong British fighter opposition. The need for German fighter cover rendered attacks very difficult. Luftflotte 3 requested the Naval War Staff to mine the south coast of England in such a way as to force British convoys to proceed nearer to mid-Channel. This request could not, however, be conceded owing to progress of landing preparations. (Operation "Seelöwe" – the invasion of England.)

The German Air Force then altered their tactics, detailing fighter-bombers (Me-109 and Me-110) to bear the main weight of the attacks

A German propaganda photograph of an S-boote (E-boat) motor torpedo boat. The E-boats were unable to make good use of the Luftwaffe for stand-off targetting in their offensive operations against British coastal convoys, which would have further enhanced their effectiveness. (US National Archives)

The Junkers Ju 87 Stuka dive-bomber was used extensively in the anti-shipping campaign that preceded the Battle of Britain, attacking convoys and port installations.

on shipping, since they could carry a load of one or two 500 kg. bombs or 250 kg. bombs. The sudden appearance of these units again considerably raised British losses.

17) Up to the middle of June, the aircraft-minelaying offensive had remained in the background and activity was only resumed after an order from C-in-C German Air Force on 14 July to the effect that Fliegerkorps IX was to be employed exclusively on large-scale minelaying operations.

At that time the stock of mines available stood at about 1,800. Luftflotte 2 was of the opinion that the current production of 800–1,000 mines per month would not suffice for sustained large-scale minelaying operations. In agreement with Naval War Staff, the Luftflotte therefore limited operations to intensified minelaying, with focal point the Thames, in the hope that full-scale operations would coincide with the start of the "all-out" attack against Britain. It had

Britain's western ports, the River Clyde and Belfast were mined by the Focke-Wulf Fw 200s of Fliegerkorps IX. Seen here is an Fw 200C-8 with FuG 200 Hohentwiel radar antennae in its nose. This version could carry a Henschel Hs 293A air-to-surface missile beneath each wing.

been agreed, by means of scattered operations in as many places as possible, to attempt dispersal of the enemy's air and mine defenses. Some mine-carrying FW-200 were incorporated in Fliegerkorps IX for mining of western ports, the Clyde and Belfast.

18) During this period Luftflotte 5 also took part in the campaign against shipping, flying right across the North Sea with bomber and torpedo aircraft (Coastal Air Gruppe 506) in repeated and successful attacks on convoys off the east coast of Scotland.

The period from the end of June up to the middle of August thus ably demonstrates the capacity of an air force efficiently controlled and given one main objective, in this case the destruction of enemy shipping. As a result of the reciprocal use of mines and bombs, of alternation between day and night operations, of the appearance of bombers with torpedoes and bombs at scattered points on the coast and extension of aerial minelaying operations to the west coast of Britain as far as Belfast, the enemy was faced by colossal defense tasks. Approximately 500–600 aerial mines were laid (Bomber Geschwader

126 dropped their 1,000th aerial mine on 26 July) and 50–60 bomber sorties were flown against convoys and shipping targets.

Even if, when assessing German Air Force claims in the campaign against merchant shipping, the Naval War Staff allowed for overestimate in the tonnage of the ships sunk and for duplication of reports from air crews yet, taken all in all, these bombing operations made an effective contribution to the naval objective, namely stoppage of supplies to Britain, and was a promising opening to the coming siege of Britain.

The Effects of the Battle of Britain upon air/sea warfare

19) The Air Force continued to concentrate its attacks in this way until about the middle of August, 1940, when a new phase of aerial warfare set in as a result of Führer Directive No. 17, dated 1 August, 1940.

By 5 August, 1940, intensification of the air offensive against Britain was sanctioned. Its aim was to secure air supremacy over the British Isles by focussing the main attacks on the Royal Air Force and the aircraft production industry, then to destroy all food imports and stocks, to shatter the morale of the British people and so, in effect, to achieve the conditions necessary for the performance of "Operation Seelöwe".

20) On 13 August, therefore, attacks on shipping were relegated to secondary importance. Most of the available bomber forces, including the two Coastal Air Gruppen converted to land-aircraft (Ju-88 and Do-17z) and, sporadically, Fliegerkorps IX (aerial minelaying), were briefed for bombing attacks on land targets, particularly on London. Only minelaying by aircraft was carried on with relative intensity covering wide areas as far as and including Greenock. In connection with the attempt to destroy London from the air, some 450 aerial mines were laid in the Thames estuary alone during this period in an attempt to cut off London's food supplies.

The aims of the Battle of Britain were not achieved. On 17 September the Führer decided to postpone the landing operation in Britain indefinitely and on 15 October it was finally abandoned for 1940.

Resumption of the campaign against merchant shipping

21) Not until the beginning of November did attacks on shipping and convoys come to the forefront again, in addition to the continuous air raids on London. Minelaying by aircraft of Fliegerkorps IX was

particularly successful in November and December. This increased success was very probably due in part to a change in minelaying tactics. Up to that time the practice had been to drop relatively few mines aimed at definite targets over wide areas. This had compelled the enemy to employ a large number of escorts and minesweeping vessels and to direct their shipping along narrow, controlled channels. Such channels could not however be covered by the bombers. Not only had distribution of the patrol vessels to be maintained over the entire coastal area but there must be a guarantee that those channels which had been swept, situated at the entrance to the main ports, were, in fact, mined. The only solution was to drop as many mines as possible on consecutive nights in relatively confined areas along 5 mile strips, their mechanism so timed as to become effective simultaneously. This procedure was used in the Thames estuary in December with particular success. Fliegerkorps IX reported that according to their radio interception the mouth of the Thames had been blocked for 14 days and that on 19 December, 1940, a convoy of 9 steamers had been wiped out while attempting to cross a mined area.

The torpedo-carrying aircraft of Naval Air Commander West and of Coastal Air Gruppe 506 (the latter subordinate to Fliegerkorps X in Norway) also reported successful attacks.

22) Unfortunately however these operations suffered interruption for a space at the beginning of December. On 27 November, 1940, C-in-C German Air Force issued an order to the Air Marshal on the staff of C-in-C Navy, prohibiting the supplying of torpedoes to coastal air units. The reason given was that the Führer desired a special operation with aerial torpedoes in the Mediterranean. Meanwhile the German Air Force had carried out torpedo trials with He-111, and on 27 November, 1940, the first successful attacks had been made with them in the western part of the Channel (Lizard Head). Thus it was established that the aerial torpedo was fit for service with the German Air Force bomber units, and C-in-C German Air Force at once resolved to reserve this weapon for the exclusive use of his bomber forces. On 7 December, 1940, after the intervention of the Supreme Command, Armed Forces and the Führer, C-in-C German Air Force countermanded his order but succeeded in impressing upon the Supreme Command, Armed Forces that the intended establishment of torpedo-carrying units was primarily the concern of the German Air Force and not of the Navy. Thus, just as use of the aircraft mine had passed over to the Air Force, the Navy was now deprived of another offensive weapon for naval/air warfare.

23) Reviewing German Air Force operations during the period concerned, the character of this service as an instrument of the Supreme Command, Armed Forces, is clearly revealed. In accordance with the demands of the overall offensive, the Air Force was called upon at one time to serve the aim of naval warfare and at another to furnish support for the Army. During the first phase of the Battle of Britain, air operations were directed exclusively against the opposing air force and yet, as a weapon of the Supreme Command, this was in order to create favorable conditions for subsequent action by the Armed Forces ("Sealion").

From the point of view of naval strategy this frequent alteration in German Air Force operations was undesirable, since the present organization did not provide adequate air support for naval operations. Again the disadvantages of a separate independent air force were demonstrated. The Navy regretted this all the more since the periods of German Air Force activity against merchant shipping with bombs and mines had shown how effectively the U-boat war on tonnage might have been supplemented.

PART IV

THE BATTLE OF THE ATLANTIC

The Battle of the Atlantic's multi-year scope and the sheer number of critical actions and battles make a narrative recounting less valuable. This section includes two naval views of air cooperation with U-Boats. From the Luftwaffe side, there is a document on what Fliegerfuehrer Atlantik was trying to do and the limitations of the aircraft they had available. The OKL's 8th Abteilung used historical experience, in March 1944, to set out requirements for the Luftwaffe support for the resurgent U-Boat activity that was expected when the schnorkel-equipped submarines were to become operational in large numbers. But, even at that time, the realities of German defeat made the future recommendations a fantasy.

The opening stages of the Battle for the Atlantic saw the Luftwaffe's most spectacular contribution. From August 1940 to February 1941, FW-200 long-range bombers were able to sink 52 allied merchant ships for the loss of only four aircraft. This was at a time when there were only an average of a half-dozen of the "scourge of the Atlantic" operational.

These account also demonstrate the limited maritime training of the Luftwaffe's non-specialist aircrew. The FW-200s could have caused the destruction of many more ships than they bombed had they been used systematically in scouting for U-boats. Their use tended to be undercut by their inability to pass on an accurate location (leading to the development of the Schwan beacon buoy) and the reluctance to put the FW-200s under naval control for more than a brief period. When the U-boat/FW-200 combination succeeded, the results could be devastating, but its effectiveness was undercut by how the Germans operated.

One of the problems was the inability of either U-boats or aircraft to obtain accurate positions. This lead to U-boat wolfpack picket lines, generally intended to run north and south with some overlap between boats' areas of visibility. In reality, boats would be both east and west and north

An Fw 200C-3/U1 Condor of 1./KG40 is refuelled in readiness for another mission. Limited training for maritime operations meant that the non-specialist crews of Fw 200s destroyed far fewer vessels during the Battle of the Atlantic than they might have done had the aircraft been used to scout for prey for U-boats.

and south of their intended positions, creating gaps and making position reports inaccurate. Aircraft reports of convoys tended also to be inaccurate. Much of the evolution of German air-naval cooperation was an attempt to deal with navigational inaccuracy, a factor, in retrospect, often overlooked.

After 1941, the Germans were always short on resources. At its height, Fliegerfuehrer Atlantik did not have more than 50 aircraft operational on any given day. The use of aircraft against shipping in the Battle of the Atlantic was de-emphasized. This was intended to make aircraft available for new campaigns in the Mediterranean, the Baltic and Black Seas and against the Russian convoys. These were often highly effective and sank many Allied ships, but they were not going to defeat Britain.

The events in the German wartime documents reflect reality as then perceived, rather than clearer post-war accounts. To select one example of many, the report (in Part III) that states that Ju-88s dispatched to help the battleship *Bismarck* in its final fight but were deterred from attacking a nearby British cruiser by Gloster Gladiators has to be considered in the light of both actual events (there were no British fighters near the battle, though the Ju-88s may have seen some torpedo-carrying Swordfish) as

Raids against England and shipping tallies are recorded on the fin and rudder of an Fw 200.

well as operational capability (a Gladiator had difficulty catching a Ju-88, even with a full weapons load).

One of the more interesting elements in the German plans for using the Luftwaffe to support the U-boats is the idea of a fighter version of the He-177. This dreadnought of the north Atlantic was to counter the Allied ASW Liberators that made a practice of shooting down German long-range maritime patrol aircraft when they encountered them, as well as Coastal Command Beaufighters and the fighters aboard escort carriers. Of course, the He-177's mechanical problems prevented this idea from being implemented.

The German accounts underline also the importance of the use of guided missiles and bombs for Luftwaffe anti-ship operations in 1943–45. Plans were made for large numbers to be made available throughout occupied Europe to defend against Allied invasion. But while these weapons inflicted some painful losses, the ability of the Allies to respond with a wide range of countermeasures and the limited resources the Germans had available for the naval air war prevented them from being of strategic significance.

Heinkel He 177A-5/R6 bombers of II./KG 40 at Bordeaux-Mérignac in the spring of 1944, after the Gruppe had reverted to the Atlantic reconnaissance role.

Chapter 9

COOPERATION OF U-BOATS AND LUFTWAFFE IN ATTACKS ON CONVOYS

By Korv. Kapt. Otto Mejer

Without the aid of documents it is scarcely possible for me to state whether and in what individual instances U-boats and aircraft were employed in attacking convoys under a universal plan, and to what extent aircraft – regardless of any agreement – failed to restrict themselves to attacking the escort units instead of attacking the ships in the convoys.

It is of course quite possible that specific instances like the above did occur, although I am unable to recall that any such case was recorded in the War Diary of the Chief of Naval Operations (Seekriegsleitung) which I had charge of from Summer 1941 up to the end of 1944. It may sound doubtful but it is nevertheless true that uniformly conducted operations of U-boats and aircraft by the Germans during the war, rarely if ever took place. Such operations could not be undertaken because the Luftwaffe, as an independent Air Force, took special pains to ensure that its independent course of action was not restricted. All agreements involving attacks on the same target by aircraft and naval units, required the decision of the highest Staffs or their subordinate Commanders. But the Luftwaffe, so to say, carried out actual operations just about "on its own". Thus those operations undertaken by the Navy which required the assistance of the Luftwaffe, had to suffer because of this factor. The following remarks will serve to furnish a clear understanding of this situation.

A great part of the work of the Operations Division of Naval Operations (Skl) was devoted to collaboration with the Luftwaffe Operational Staff. A liaison officer was assigned to each other's staff. In Naval Operations (Skl) there was a Staff Officer from the General Staff of the Luftwaffe (Lt.Col. Gaul); to the Luftwaffe there was originally sent a Captain, later Rear Admiral Moessel. Gaul was an ex-naval officer; he was one of the several young naval officers who had been selected for assignment with the German naval air arm, the creation of which had been started but which under the pressure of Goering was turned over to the Luftwaffe in 1937.

Both liaison officers constantly tried to hold down to a minimum the friction that arose as a result of the faulty organization (for the Navy). From a superficial point of view the impression was created, especially from the side of those who championed the stand point that 'everything that flew' should belong to the Luftwaffe, that organization and cooperation were excellent and left nothing to be desired. This argument was strengthened by pointing to the no-better cooperation among the individual Combat Operational Staffs of both the Luftwaffe and the Navy. In these cases as well, the Luftwaffe was, as a rule, represented by officers who like Gaul, had come from the Navy and therefore had a better understanding of naval warfare needs.

With the growing strain on the Luftwaffe the ability of the Luftwaffe Operational Staff to meet the Navy's requirements was restricted to such an extent that obtaining approval of requests required the decision of the highest Operational Staffs, that is, the Naval Operations (Skl) and the Luftwaffe Führungstabe in every individual case. From this it can be seen how wrong it was from the standpoint of the Navy to submit to a condition where every function of naval warfare that required the employment of aircraft, needed the approval of the highest Operational Staffs. In reality this meant that the Navy was forced to rely on the ability, insight and the good will of the Luftwaffe. Even if such an arrangement functioned without friction, in effect such intolerable procedure cannot deceive one of the organization's deficiency.

When in summer of 1941 I was placed in charge of the War Diary of Naval Operations (Skl), to my surprise I gained the impression that the Navy had completely agreed to this condition. Almost daily it was my duty to record the heavy traffic of TWX and correspondence between the Naval Operations and the Luftwaffe Operational Staff. This correspondence included requests made by the Navy on the Luftwaffe for employment of appropriate aircraft (not to be placed at the Navy's disposal) and the replies given by the Luftwaffe. Again and again differences arose between the two Operational Staffs of the two branches of service that had to be smoothed out.

The main side of this problem was not affected since the problem had been created by a "decision of the Fuehrer." The success of the torpedo planes at Pearl Harbor in December 1941 caused the CinC of the Navy, on the occasion of a speech by Hitler, to bring up the question of the basic importance of a Naval Air Arm, but without making any specific requests. Consequently this question was forgotten and the situation remained unchanged so that the Luftwaffe prosecuted its own naval warfare. The only success obtained was that the almost forgotten development and training in use of torpedo planes was resurrected – but not by the Navy: instead by the Luftwaffe.

Another chapter was the laying of sea mines by aircraft. It was obvious that the use of this weapon, by its very nature, was a duty that could best be handled by naval officers. It was known that the German land-mine with magnetic fuse was known to the enemy because the Luftwaffe had dropped these on the beaches of the English Coast which are dry at low tide. This tremendous faux pas did not lead to returning the use of this mine to the Navy, but it did help the Navy in getting the Fuehrer to decree that the use of this weapon would henceforth only be undertaken by the Luftwaffe in cooperation with the Navy. Thus the Navy was at least able to ensure that in mine warfare the Luftwaffe did not interfere with Naval operations or lead to failures like in 1939. However, the Navy was not able to bring about the full use of this promising weapon with its ensuing effects as it would have been possible to do had training therein and actual use thereof been left to it. A systematic examination of the War Diaries will show that the Luftwaffe uselessly wasted a large amount of valuable mine material.

The very-promising mine with a new type fuse which was ready for use in 1944, was the basis of an extensive plan of the Navy and Luftwaffe which was to extend over the operational sectors of the English Coast and which called for the shocklike use of masses of this new mine. Since the Luftwaffe could not meet the necessary requirements for carrying out this operation, it could not be undertaken.

Combined planning for combined operations of both branches of the Wehrmacht within the larger framework occurred but seldom since opportunity for the employment of German Navy surface units in such operations did not frequently arise. But even in those cases where this occurred, the Luftwaffe forces were never placed at the disposal of the Navy, but due to previous acquiescence, were used independently by the Luftwaffe. This was also the case in the break through of the English Channel by the *Scharnhorst, Gneisenau* and *Prinz Eugen,* for which the preparations for the cooperation of Navy and Luftwaffe units was especially carefully planned. An especially capable naval officer was assigned as advisor and Liaison officer to the Staff of General Galland who was in command of the Luftwaffe units. This operation left a good impression as regards cooperation.

It is impossible to give an account and to make critiques of all operations involving cooperation between the Navy and Luftwaffe without the documentary evidence before me. But it is believed that when checking this material carefully, it will be convincingly revealed that the cooperation was unsatisfactory. At least that is true for the majority of the air operations which would normally have been the function of the Naval Air Arm. It is difficult to say where in practice the line between tactical and operational air warfare would have to be drawn. The emphasis on German naval warfare was placed on attacking enemy shipping; surface forces and U-boats used all their weapons for this purpose. The Luftwaffe as well thought it was its main task to destroy as much tonnage as possible. The high-lights of all these combat operations occurred in the Battle of Atlantic and in the Arctic Ocean. In both of these battles the possibilities of German U-boats were not fully utilized because:

a) the operations of the U-boats were restricted in many instances by the independent operational air warfare carried out against the same targets by the Luftwaffe; and

b) the necessary tactical support given by the Luftwaffe was, in general, inadequate.

It was precisely in the attacks carried out against the convoys that cooperation was required between the naval and air force units. Reconnaissance could have been undertaken with incomparably better effect – as far as radius of action permitted – by aircraft than U-boats. The aircraft, of course, had to avoid detection for as long a time as possible. Aircraft attacks against the convoy of the escort units themselves should only have taken place after the U-boats had taken up their attack positions. There is no need to explain that a combined operation of this nature could only succeed if it is directed by a single command, namely a naval commander. This requirement, however, was not met due to the attitude of the Luftwaffe, not to mention that from a material standpoint, the Luftwaffe was not equal to the task. During the first years of the war the Luftwaffe emphasized the development of bombers, while for the conduct of naval air warfare, the development of reconnaissance aircraft with greatest possible range and long distance fighter-planes were of major importance.

From 1943 on, Admiral Doenitz made every effort to make good that which had been neglected. At first he attempted to reason with Goering and when he did not succeed he went directly to the Fuehrer to get him to intercede for all of his requirements. But it was now too late to manufacture and deliver the required aircraft types. For this reason alone the tactical support of the Luftwaffe had to remain inadequate.

U-boats were thus forced to locate convoys by themselves, through slow and burdensome lines of position. Their situation was further aggravated because the enemy reinforced their escorts and added carriers and auxiliary carrier based fighters for convoy protection. Sometimes even the ships in the convoys were equipped with planes. In the end the Battle of the Atlantic was lost due to this increased escort defense. Similar conditions held true with regard to the attacks carried out against convoys from and to the Murmansk Coast and to Archangel in the Arctic. The advantage of restricted area was nullified by extremely difficult weather conditions and poor visibility. Certainly many chances for success were ruined for the U-boats because the convoys were warned by the Luftwaffe attacks carried out against them. They dispersed, turned into the protecting ice, or escaped into the dark of night. This was more or less a direct result of the Luftwaffe's independent course of action against the convoys. Independent action by the Luftwaffe against convoys was only justified when the convoys were in the inshore waters where the employment of U-boats was generally impossible due to enemy air threat. But the Luftwaffe was not capable of carrying out such an assignment because it did not and could not come to know the elements of naval warfare and because it lacked the necessary material (aircraft) and personnel to execute such a task.

An objective evaluation of the files (War Diaries) on this subject will show that the lack of an own naval air arm was accompanied by fatal effects. Whether it would have been possible to make good this mistake in view of the status of German armament in 1943, is a debatable question, Hitler himself had by then realized that it was a huge mistake to have sacrificed a naval air arm for Goering. But he thought it was impossible to effect a change in the situation during the course of the war, especially in view of the existing state of affairs.

Chapter 10

COOPERATION OF THE LUFTWAFFE WITH THE GERMAN NAVY DURING WORLD WAR II

By Kapt. zur See Hans-Jurgen Reinecke

"My statements are based on personal experiences as Staff Operations Officer in the Operations Division of "Skl" from 1938 to 1941, as Staff Operations Officer of the Battlecruiser Force from December 1941 to December 1943, and as Commanding Officer of the cruiser *Prinz Eugen* from December 1943 to the end of hositilities. My opinion can be corroborated by former Admiral Ciliaz, CinC of Battlecruisers from 1941 to 1942, and Admiral Kümmertz, CinC of the Naval Force in North Norway. Although my statements are more or less based on the relation between surface craft and Luftwaffe, they are also applicable to submarine warfare.

Before the war the Navy had a small Naval or Fleet Air Arm, the personnel for which was recruited from the Navy and trained under strong naval influence. Navigation, scouting, recognition of ships types and tactical efficiency were on a very high level in this Force.

The building up of the Luftwaffe put an end to this instrument of Naval warfare, although under Raeder the Navy tried everything in order to retain it. But the influence of Goering was much too strong and even a limited proposal of the Navy in 1939 to have a small air Arm, recruited and supplied from the Luftwaffe, but trained by the Navy, was rejected. Goering's standpoint was that nobody was to take the air except under him, with his training and under his responsibility. So the Navy had to cope with this situation and make the best of it. The few remaining ex-Naval officers, now in the Luftwaffe, were not treated well in that force, although they were mostly men of very high standard. They were not given responsible or good jobs in flying units except when they turned renegades; only a few who did this reached top rank later. The ex-naval airmen were used mostly in the mining branch, which was not very much thought of, or at schools, because even the Luftwaffe could not deny that they were the only ones who understood something about navigation over sea.

With the natural loss of many good officers during the war the very thin sprinkling of ex-navy men in the Luftwaffe became thinner and thinner, and the discriminating personnel policy of the Luftwaffe resulted in the fact that most of the surviving ex-naval officers reverted to the navy from 1943 on in which they made excellent records.

During all these negotiations and struggles with the Luftwaffe a complete misunderstanding of conditions and lack of tactical background in naval warfare were always to be noted. An exception was the Fighter Force, but even in this the young fighter pilots only saw an opportunity to fight in cooperation with the Navy – nothing deeper. The development of aircraft types and weapons, and technical matters, was governed by the "bomb-minded" people in the Luftwaffe. It was generally thought that the Navy's training schemes, sponsored by the Navy and backed up by some brave ex-naval airforce officers, were superflous and therefore were always cancelled or hampered by lack of gasoline, lack of forces and other reasons.

For the reasons mentioned above the Luftwaffe was never "sea-minded". The Luftwaffe Supreme Command thought it could perform the tasks of the Navy alone – sinking enemy fleets, destroying convoys, etc. and to act independently against shipping which was of importance to the Navy.

Without proper training from the start the Luftwaffe bombed anything that moved on the surface, not taking much trouble to distinguish what it was. Even own ships were bombed and it was always a risk to pass an area where own bombers were liable to be operating. Scouting was on a very low level. Through poor navigation and failure to identify any spotted craft, neither the strategical CinC on shore nor the tactical CinC at sea could rely on Luftwaffe reports. Positions 40–60 miles off and reports identifying a destroyer as a battleship were the rule. This caused much concern on bridges and in staff operation rooms.

Cooperation in combined operations, both with submarines and surface units, was hampered by a trend of the Luftwaffe to make headlines. This was due to Goering's influence. Instead of dividing a task between the two, i.e. Navy and Luftwaffe, in a reasonable way to get the best results, the Luftwaffe considered the naval forces only as an appendix. For instance, instead of attacking destroyer escorts and sloops in the convoys on the North Atlantic or Gibraltar route – leaving the cargo vessels to the U-boats – the Luftwaffe attacked the cargo ships, scattering them and leaving the escorts free to attack the U-boats; but they could report sinking an exaggerated amount of tonnage forgetting that in proper teamwork, the two services could have bagged the whole lot. Special Luftwaffe officials, known for their unrelenting "Luftwaffe-First" mindedness, were put in command of squadrons off the Atlantic Coast which were officially declared as "auxiliary" for the subwarfare. And they reached their object, i.e., "headlines for the Luftwaffe".

Cooperation in the dash through the Channel February 1942 was excellent, but this was due to the cooperation of the Fighter Force. Bombers only attacked Southampton in the early morning as diversion.

After activity had been transferred to North Norway the same troubles started again. Results against the Murmansk Run could only be decisive if the covering force was affected or driven off by our Luftwaffe. This concerned both anti-submarine escort and heavy surface escort. The commanding officer (Flieger Fuhrer Lofoten, General Major Roth) was an ex-naval pilot of World War I and an excellent man, full of understanding; but because of this he was a black sheep in the eyes of his superior (General Oberst Stümpf) and carefully watched. All the Navy's problems were aired thoroughly and rehearsed with our own and his forces, but in actual operations he was given *strict* orders not to attack war ships, especially heavy ships and carriers, but to sink tonnage. Then neither the subs could do very much – the convoy being scattered and the escort in full strength – nor could the German Norway task force because a mostly far superior heavy escort with carriers was standing by absolutely unmolested.

I have only part of my diary of the year 1943 but from it I gather the following details:

(a) On 14 April 1943 a conference was held on board the flagship with representatives of the Luftwaffe to arrange cooperation. Results were mostly negative. On May 1st the CinC of the Surface Forces, Admiral Schniewind, (now at Garmisch Camp), talked with Stumpf at Oslo.

(b) On May 1st scouting planes failed to spot an enemy group reported by subs northwest of Drontjem.

(c) Another conference about the matter was held with Cdr. Pruetzmann, naval liaison to Air Fleet 5, emphasizing that in combined operations everybody could not follow his own way, but that teamwork was essential, putting behind the publicity and prestige standpoints.

(d) June 12; Carrier aircraft were reported by subs South of Bear-Island (between North Cape and Spitzbergen), but the Luftwaffe was unable to spot the enemy.

(e) Sept. 4; Information was received from skl about a new training scheme for the Luftwaffe in naval warfare. I remarked in the diary: This sounds to me like our dream of 1939!

(f) In October 1943 several requests for more and more efficient scouting in the sea North of Norway remained unanswered.

(g) More forces for scouting were requested again by Navy group command North (Kiel) for Air Fleets.

(h) The special training group, formed according to plan (see above under (e)) was dissolved in 1944.

From memory I can add the following:

(a) In July 1942 the force from Norway left the bases to attack PQ 17 (convoy to Murmansk). The Luftwaffe was supposed to attack and drive off the heavy escort, about 200 miles west of (behind) the convoy. Instead all aircraft were directed against the convoy, with good but not decisive results, and the surface force and submarines had to be called back because of (a) the menace of the heavy escort and (b) because the convoy had time enough (between the air attacks) to scatter and to seek shelter in the loose ice to the north.

(b) In March 1942 a sortie of the *Tirpitz* with four destroyers was without result although we were very near the target (a convoy) because the Luftwaffe failed to spot it. On March 9 (I think this is right) we approached the heavy escort unaware and were heavily attacked by carrier torpedo planes which the Luftwaffe had failed both to spot previously and to attack after we had deciphered its position by intercepting signals between the enemy aircraft and their carrier. No harm was done to us, but an opportunity was lost.

Goodwill on the lower level of command of the Luftwaffe undoubtedly existed in many cases, but on the higher and highest levels it was entirely lacking, and the Navy in its comparatively weak position against the strong British home fleet, both in submarines against destroyers their heavy opponents, could have done more and better with full and seaminded assistance of the Luftwaffe as an integrating part of all modern warfare at sea."

Chapter 11

EXAMPLES OF LUFTWAFFE COOPERATION WITH U-BOATS FROM WARTIME REPORTS

By Kapitanleutnant Hans-Diedrich Freiherr von Tiesenhausen and others

Communication between U-boats and A/c

Source: NA London, # 1210, June 20, 1941.

Some additional information on this subject has since been obtained from the W/T rating of *U-70*, which was sunk on 7/3/41.

This rating described a form of Fühlungshalter procedure (literally "keeping in touch") but this should not be taken as confirmed. According to his description, an aircraft sighting a convoy would report the grid position and other details to its own ground station. This information would then be passed on to the B.d.U. at Lorient, who acts as W/T control for U-boats. From here the information would be passed on to the nearest U-boat or U-boats with the addition "listen for D/F signals". In the meantime the aircraft would have been instructed to act as "Fühlungshalter" and transmit D/F signals on which the U-boat could take D/F bearings. The reverse of this procedure is also envisaged, the U-boat maintaining contact with the ship and sending D/F signals to guide the aircraft.

It is understood that aircraft crews are as a general rule advised of the presence of U-boats in their patrol areas and it is understood that U-boats are also kept informed of the presence of German A/c in their vicinity.

Co-operation between U-boats and Focke-Wulf Kondor A/c

Source: NA London, # 1088, May 2, 1942

Prisoners emphasised that there was no direct communication between U-Boats and Focke-Wulf Kondor aircraft sent on reconnaissance patrols to locate British convoys.

According to prisoners, when a Kondor sets out, its patrol area and D/F frequency is signalled to U-Boats by the Vice-Admiral U-Boats.

This signal is repeated at definite times, one of which is believed to be 1400 hours.

Upon sighting a convoy the aircraft begins transmitting D/F signals to its base. These signals were stated by prisoners to be either long dashes, or a series of "V's". The D/F frequency of Kondors is between 500 and 600 metres, strength of transmission being between 40 and 70 Watts. Between signals, the aircraft sends short messages in code, which may be either the course the convoy is steering or the distance and compass bearing of the convoy from the A/c.

Any U-Boat picking up these signals transmits their bearing to the Vice-Admiral U-Boats, who, knowing the whereabouts of the U-boats, can calculate the position of the aircraft and convoy by plotting cross bearings.

The positions of the convoy is then transmitted to the U-Boats in the area and the necessary dispositions made. The number of ships in convoys and their escorts is not transmitted by Kondors, presumably because they will return fairly soon to report in full.

Aircraft Reconnaissance

Source: C.B.4051 (38) February 1942. Copy No. 217.

The U-boat command was stated to have five FW a/c, manned by naval pilots, continuously at its disposal. These a/c locate the convoys and signal the position continuously. U-boats are informed if any of the naval recce a/c are shot down.

Source: C.B. 4051 (39) February 1942. Copy No. 217

In *U-574*'s [sunk 19 December 1991] last attack on the convoy, the cooperation between Kondor a/c and U-boats had been excellent. Whenever *U-574* had last contact with the convoy on account of having to submerge, she received messages from the Vice-Admiral U-boats telling her that Kondors would reconnoiter at a certain time and that *U-574* whould wait until then for the information she required. Such information followed with great accuracy and enabled her to re-establish contact with the convoy.

Captain of U-331 on Naval-Air Cooperation

Source: N.A. London No. 1301, 1 April 1943.

The captain of *U-331* [Kapitanleutnant Hans-Diedrich Freiherr von Tiesenhausen] said that originally the German Fleet Air Arm consisted of about 10 a/c. They were completely ignored by Göring and never got more than the smallest percentage of pilots and a/c. Subsequently a few Kondors were put at the disposal of the Navy for Atlantic recce and a few in the Mediterranean, but they worked with the Air Force. He stated that in the Mediterranean all a/c sightings are reported first to the Air Force in Rome, thence to Captain (U-boats) there, and from him to individual commands. He did not think, however, that squadrons reporting direct to the Navy would be an improvement as (sic), recce information is so contradictory that it must be vetted to get positive results. He agreed, however, that it would be a good thing if pilots could have special training for Navy work.

He remarked, that torpedo carrying a/c had also been neglected by Germany.

Airplane Coverage for U-Boats

Source: Chf. P/W Br. G-2, B-440, 27 Sept. 1943

A bomber observer from a Ju-88 describes how they rendezvoused with a U-boat in the Bay of Biscay. They were given the U-boat's course and speed and proceeded to a fixed point, taking D/F bearings on the way. At the appointed spot they checked position with their Sonne Apparatus and a W/T beacon. But P/W says the W/T has a limited range of accuracy. Farther out in the Bay of Biscay they get a discrepancy of 20, 30 or 40 degrees from the W/T beacon. In this connection P/W speaks of being at a good altitude with visibility about 300 km. and land in sight.

Source: Etousa to WAR, L-9986, 3 April 1944

On 2nd April, 2 FW 200s operated from Norway and carried out homing procedure for subs on to Russian-bound convoy.

Air Contact with U-Boats

Source: Chf. P/W Br. G-2, B-584, 8 Feb. 1944

In communicating with the Navy the GAF use a method called "Eagle", and they use both R/T and lamp signalling. The frequency is settled in advance and communication is in code, chiefly using the names of towns and animals. "Tiger" indicates English battleship. Blockade-runners have both English and German names but operate under their English names, being camouflaged to resemble English ships. The frequencies are only given to the chief W/T operators in a private room after the briefing has been completed.

In cloudy weather a contact a/c is not considered necessary and a pilot who has spotted a convoy will make off, informing the U-boat that he is 30 km. west of the convoy. The U-boats take a bearing from this information received through W/T. While Kondor planes also act as contact-keeping a/c, the Ju-290 is preferred because of its more powerful armament.

The Germans want their fighters to keep with the U-boats and the U-boats to proceed on the surface. When the U-boats are D/F'd, and they know when they are, they continue on the surface until the English a/c arrive, and then the German fighters go into action against enemy a/c.

Watchkeeping and Communications Procedures

Source: Chf. P/W Br/G-2, B-586, 9 Feb. 1944

U-boats have a 4-man watch all day long, with each man having a 90° sector to watch. These men are equipped with very strong glasses and the Sub-Lt. claims that they always see everything before the U-boat itself is observed. He further claims that German a/c acting as air escort to subs, when it is known that enemy subs are lying in wait outside the German bases, fly over their U-boats without seeing them, and even when the U-boat has fired to attract the attention of their own a/c the latter have not been aware of it. Hence he emphasizes that the strong point of the U-boat is that the crew always "see everything first".

The sergeant W/T operator who served in an FW-200 with KG-40 states that:

The BdU W/T station listened to a/c W/T traffic. When the a/c transmitted the signal for the day BdU listened in and then called the U-boats, telling them to switch to such-and-such a frequency. Then the U-boats would hear the a/c's D/F signals and make their way towards the convoy. The a/c always knew their position and carried out accurate astro-navigation with the octant. When calling up on the R/T they do not give the a/c's full designation; they have a three-letter-and-figure group with perhaps one figure and two letters and to it they append the last letter of the a/c. The last but one letter is the one denoting the a/c.

Use of D/F to Direct U-Boats

Source: Op-16-Z, U.S.N. No. 110, 12 Feb. 1944

During the attack on the convoy in the course of which U-536 was sunk [20 November 1943], contact had been maintained, and U-boats homed on to the convoy, by a/c. The a/c engaged in this operation were said to be long range He-177 and Ju-290. Prisoners stated that the U-boats received a code signal from Control instructing them to listen in on a certain wavelength, which changed at certain hours during the day. At known intervals the a/c transmitted their positions and bearing from the convoy, as well as details of the convoy itself, such as the number of merchant ships and escorts and their course and speed. These signals were usually sent in plain language. The frequency used was said to be between 250–600 k/cs.

When a U-boat picked up bearing signals from a contact-keeping a/c, she reported her position by short signal to Control, stating that she had the bearing of the a/c. Having noted the positions of all U-boats in the area, Control signalled details of the convoy's course and speed.

It was stated that a/c also dropped contact-keeping flares near the convoy which were said to burn for three to four hours. They said that this practice is not favoured by Control, as only U-boats in the immediate vicinity benefit from the flares. In order that other U-boats may be directed to the scene, the sending of homing signals is considered necessary.

Air Directions to U-Boats

Source: Spot Item No. 232, (Op-16-Z) 4 Mar. 1944

The following information was obtained from a radioman from *U-231*, now a P/W. His statements should not be accepted as facts unless confirmed from other sources.

When *U-231* was on her last patrol [sunk 13 January 1944], operating in the group of U-boats stretched from Cape Finisterre to the Azores, she was instructed by control to listen for a/c beacons for three days, at 0800 and 2000. The transmissions were said to be on a frequency of 385 k/cs. *U-231*'s approximate position was 42N–15W.

It was claimed it is now a practice for U-boat patrol lines operating within range of German a/c to remain submerged continually. The spacing between the U-boats was said to be about 20 miles. A/c search for an expected convoy and upon sighting report to control. U-boats receive transmissions from control every hour, either while at periscope depth or while surfaced, proceeding surfaced to the position given by the a/c.

Since experience has shown that positions given by a/c are known to be unreliable, control will then generally instruct the a/c to transmit a beacon signal. Thereupon each U-boat reports the bearing on which she has heard the a/c beacon, together with her own position. From this information control plots the exact position of the a/c (i.e. the convoy) and issues the necessary orders to the U-boats which are to participate in the attack.

Simultaneous attacks of U-boats and a/c's against convoys have not been heard of by P/W.

U-Boat Cooperation With Aircraft

Source: NID 1/PW US 391/44 17 March 1944.

17 May 1944/1m1, *194__*

1. An NCO from the German Air Force stated that U-boats sometimes have V.H/F. communication with aircraft if enemy forces are in the neighborhood. The normal procedure, however, is for the U-boat to communicate directly to Control. (NID Note: There is no recent evidence from U-boat prisoners of the use of direct communication with aircraft on V.H/F.)

2. He said that at Bordeaux and Cognac, naval liaison officers are serving with the air force.

Office Memorandum · UNITED STATES GOVERNMENT

VH/F

Source: C.B. 04051(92), December 1943, *U-732*.

DATE: 24 March 1944

File *naval aviation*

The Lo. 10 U.K. 39 set fitted in *U-732* [sunk 31 October 1943] was intended for communication with aircraft. A prisoner from *U-136* [sunk 15 July 1943] still under interrogation states that his boat carried a Fu. G. 17 for the same purpose but never used it.

A few other boats have been fitted with Fu. G. 11 or Fu. G. 17 and each time this occurred it was rumored at the base concerned that the boats so fitted were to operate in conjunction with aircraft.

U-Boats and GAF in the Mediterranean

Source: MIS. P/W Br. G-2, B-636. 14 April 1944

It is stated that there is no cooperation in this area between German submarines and the Air Force. Data obtained by air reconnaissance were indeed constantly transmitted to the U-boats but invariably through their own HQ. One enlisted prisoner says that about ten wireless signals used to come from the BDU (Commander in Chief for U-boats) on the results of reconnaissance of the enemy at sea. They used also to get at times reports from the Interception Service and those originating with German confidential agents inside the Allied lines. These are known as "V-Men" (Vertrauersmann). The GAF in the Mediterranean is not furnished with the contact-keeping buoys which are used in the Atlantic to mark the point at which a hostile craft or convoy has been located. It here appears that all information in the Atlantic comes in the form of air recce reports or of those indicating a radar contact. Directions in the Mediterranean are apparently given by reference to map squares, even more than is the case in the Atlantic.

Chapter 12

PRINCIPLES GOVERNING THE CONDUCT OF OPERATIONS BY FLIEGERFUEHRER ATLANTIK AND AN APPRECIATION OF THE TYPES OF AIRCRAFT AVAILABLE

by Headquarters Staff Fliegerfuehrer Atlantik, 3 December 1943

I. Operational instructions from C. in C. Luftwaffe

Strategy against enemy shipping in the Atlantic in cooperation with C. in C. U–Boats and Naval Group West.

Safeguarding arrival and departure of German naval forces (both surface and submarine) against enemy attacks. Operations against enemy supply shipping in the event of enemy landings.

II. General Principles

1) Concentration of all appropriate forces in the right place at the right time in accordance with the operational demands of C. in C. U–Boats and the requirements of Fliegerfuehrer Atlantik's own operations.

2) Most economical operational use of reconnaissance forces until the commencement of operations by C. in C. U–Boats or Fliegerfuehrer Atlantik. For this purpose full advantage to be taken of technical and weather conditions.

3) Flights into areas where controlled enemy day or night fighters are operating are to be avoided. Wherever possible, operations of Fliegerfuehrer Atlantik are to be confined to areas where there is no enemy T.E. fighter defence.

III. Reconnaissance

1) Reconnaissance to be carried out mainly with ship locating radar. Reconnaissance by sectors at 1000 metres altitude. Operations not to be dependent on visibility.

2) The situation over the Atlantic will dictate the areas in which aircraft with strong defensive armament are to be used. Area of operations to be widened by exploitation of weather conditions.

3) Navigational accuracy of aircraft position up to distances of 2000 km with a margin of error of ±10 to 20 km.

4) Convoy reconnaissance. In areas requested by C. in C. U-Boats or laid down by Fliegerfuehrer Atlantik. Generally reconnaissance of area to be covered should start in the morning. On the days when operations are planned by C. in C. U-Boats or Fliegerfuehrer Atlantik, reconnaissance should be repeated in late afternoon with a view to shadowing.

   a) In the case of submarines reconnaissance to continue into the night.

   b) In the case of bomber formations reconnaissance to continue until time of attack and observation of results.

5) *Reconnaissance for Naval Group West* – Reconnaissance of sea area used by our own blockade runners, auxiliary cruisers and prize vessels arriving and leaving.

   Intention

   a) To safeguard against enemy surface vessels.

   b) Prompt recognition of ships arriving and lead them to cover. Operations to be carried out over a wide area and to the limit of range.

6) Reconnaissance to safeguard against enemy landing attempts on the Atlantic coast of France. Operations to be carried out in late afternoon. They are to cover the sea area through which the enemy can pass during the hours of darkness.

7) *Armed Reconnaissance.* Armed reconnaissance against single enemy ships off the Spanish-Portuguese coast by flights of 2 or 3 long range bombers. Action only to be taken if movement is confirmed by intelligence from secret sources. Attack at dusk or on a clear night.

IV. Shadowing with ship locating radar possible by day and night

1) *For C. in C. U-Boats*
Commence at dusk. DF signals. Use of flares for marking location of convoy. Shadowing aircraft to keep as near as possible to convoy. Shadowing to be carried on as far on into the night as possible.

2) *For bomber formations*

   a) Loose shadowing by daylight with shadowing aircraft being relieved. Schwan buoys to be dropped. (Note: A Schwan is a waterborne V.H.F. beacon).

b) As combat shadowing aircraft about one hour before bombers attack. Shadowing aircraft to be between bomber formation and target. DF signals, flares to be dropped should necessity arise.

V. Operations

1) At present in use: He-177 with "Kehl" glider-bomb control and FW-200 with "Kehl" or Lotfe bomb sight. Both types of equipment can only be used in slight, high or medium high cloud. Since convoys frequently make use of bad weather conditions as cover, it is recommended that the He-177 be fitted also with torpedoes.
2) Attacks can only hold out a promise of success when strong forces are used. Minimum strength one bomber Gruppe.
3) Attacks to be carried out during the evening, up to dusk, so that return flights can be carried out under cover of darkness.
4) When flying in cloudless weather, the bombers are to be escorted by T.E. fighters to the extent of their range.

VI. Use of T.E. fighters

1) Intentions: a) to attack enemy anti-submarine aircraft,
              b) to protect own aircraft.

2) Operations: T.E. fighters to operate only when visibility is good and there is little cloud. Possible to operate as free lance fighter patrols, escort or covering force.

VII. Anti-submarine operations

To be carried out along own coast in areas not covered by submarine chasers:
1) as a systematic search,
2) as aircraft standing by for action.

VIII. Action to be taken in the event of an enemy landing

1) So long as the base of Fliegerfuehrer Atlantik is not directly threatened, increased reconnaissance in the Bay of Biscay and Atlantic and attacks against landing forces still at sea.
2) In the event of a landing in the area of Fliegerfuehrer Atlantik then, according to the developments of the situation:
   a) reconnoitre and attack the enemy landing fleet or,

This captured Heinkel He 177A-5 Greif has underwing carriers for a pair of Hs 293A guided missiles, one of which is seen on display, inverted, in the second photograph.

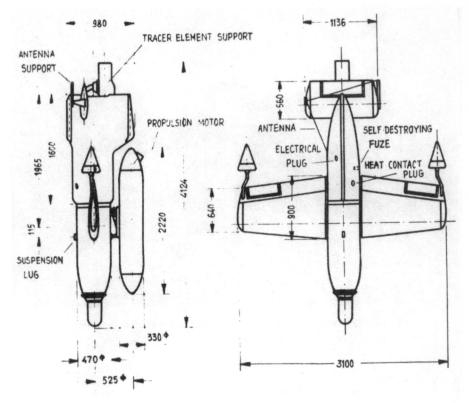

The Henschel Hs 293A-0 anti-ship guided missile, launched from He 177s, Do 217s and Fw 200s. (US Navy Technical Mission to Europe, Report on HS Series of German Guided Missiles, 16 October 1945, in US NARA RG 38 ONI NTM to Europe, Box 31)

    b) support the ground operations by attacking forces which have already landed.

3) In the event of the enemy capturing the bases of subordinate units, units will be withdrawn to prepared positions and will continue to operate as laid down in sub-para. 2.

IX. Signals

1) Complete wireless silence, to be broken only by:
    a) reports of enemy,
    b) emergency reports.
2) Restriction to a minimum of ship locating and aircraft locating radar.

Another study of an Fw 200C-8 equipped with FuG 200 radar and carriers for two Hs 293 missiles.

Although the lack of de-icing equipment limited the areas and times of year in which it could operate, the Junkers Ju 290 was deemed 'the most suitable aircraft for Atlantic reconnaissance' at the end of 1943. This is the first of eleven Ju 290A-5s, which entered production at that time and introduced heavier defensive armament, increased pilot and co-pilot protection and the ability to dump fuel.

3) Exchange of messages with own naval forces by means of signal lamps only. V.H.F. will be used only to warn ships of immediate danger.

TYPES OF AIRCRAFT AVAILABLE TO FLIEGERFUEHRER ATLANTIK

I. Reconnaissance Aircraft

1) FW-200 is at present available in three different models:
   a) Normal FW-200 with a radius of 1500 km.
   b) FW-200 fitted with auxiliary fuselage tanks (known as long range Condor) with a radius of action of 1750 km.
   c) FW-200 fitted with auxiliary fuselage tanks and two exterior tanks (known as maximum range Condor) with a radius of action of 2200 km.
   Only the long range and the maximum range Condor are suitable for the present operational commitments of Fliegerfuehrer Atlantik. Use of the maximum range Condor is limited due to the difficulties involved in taking off at night because of overloading and its use can only be recommended for major operations. In view of its inadequate armament and its lack of speed the FW-200 cannot be used in areas covered by enemy TE fighters. Recent encounters between FW-200s and enemy TE fighters when cloud cover has been insufficient have nearly always led to the destruction of the FW-200.
   Further development of the FW-200 is not recommended since:
   a) it has been exploited to the limit of its potentialities,
   b) it is being replaced by the He-177.

2) *Ju-290.* The Ju-290 meets the present requirements as far as radius of action is concerned. Thanks to its good armament and even better armament proposed, it is also suitable for operations in areas covered by enemy TE fighters. At the moment the Ju-290 is the most suitable aircraft for Atlantic reconnaissance. Its use is at present restricted to certain areas and to certain seasons of the year due to the absence of de-icing equipment.

Recommendations for further improvements

   a) Greater radius of action (Experiments are being carried out to increase it to 4000 km.)
   b) Fitting of de-icing equipment.
   c) Fitting of a special bomb rack for flares (proposed).
   d) Fitting of "Kehl" equipment for long range operations (proposed for Ju-390).

The Junkers Ju 88A-4 failed to meet operational requirements in both range and speed for Atlantic operations. This Ju 88A-4 of 8./KG6 was brought down by pilots of 29 Squadron, RAF, at Withyham, Sussex, on the night of 24/25 February 1944.

3) *Ju-88D-1 or A-4*

This aircraft does not come up to operational requirements either in range or speed. The Ju-88D-1 has to be used by Fliegerfuehrer Atlantik for sea reconnaissance in areas covered by British day and night fighters. Duties can only be carried out when weather conditions are particularly favourable.

Requests for suitable aircraft have been made to General der Aufklärungsflieger (C. in C. Reconnaissance Units).

4) *BV-222*

On account of its performance the BV-222 has been called upon to carry out roughly the same duties as the Ju-290. Its operational potentialities are only restricted because of:

a) its insufficient armament and unprotected tanks

b) its lack of speed.

Its tactical radius of action will be increased by 300 km to 2700 km when, in January 1944, delivery is taken of the new V-10 and V-11 subtypes fitted with diesel engines.

Insufficient speed and armament and unprotected fuel tanks were drawbacks of the Blohm und Voss Bv 222, which performed the same duties as the Ju 290. This is the Bv 222V8.

5) *BV-138* – In view of its lack of speed and small radius of action, this aircraft is only suitable for defensive reconnaissance along the French coast and on anti-submarine patrols. For these purposes, however, it is very suitable.

II. Bombers

He-177. With a tactical radius of action of 1500 km, this aircraft cannot, by any means, be used in all the sea areas covered by Fliegerfuehrer Atlantik's reconnaissance. Its use is thus limited to the Western Atlantic and north west Biscay. The performance of the He-177 make it suitable for use with glider bombs (Kehl) and as a torpedo bomber. The He-177 is well armed and has no cause, particularly in formation flights, to fear any type of enemy aircraft operating over the Atlantic.

267

The limited tactical radius of action of the He 177, represented here by an He 177A-3/R1 of 1./KG40, restricted its use to the Western Atlantic and northwest Biscay.

Recommendations for further development

a) Radius of action to be increased to that of reconnaissance aircraft while retaining the same bomb capacity.

b) To be adapted for quick change over from "Kehl" to torpedo bomber (according to weather conditions).

c) Increase in speed to cope with the expected appearance of faster enemy TE fighters and as a counter measure to A/A defence.

III. Fighters & TE Fighters

1) *Ju-88.* The TE fighter formations are made up of Ju-88C6 aircraft, sub-types R2, H2 to G1.

    The armament of the H2 and the G1 meets present day requirements. The expected radius of both models of 1600 to 1800 km is adequate for present needs, but the ultimate objective must be to increase the range up to that of the long range bomber.

    With regard to speed, the Ju-88 R2, H2 and G1 which are fitted with BMW 801 engines are superior in speed to most enemy aircraft used over the Atlantic with the exception of the Mosquito which is now appearing in ever increasing numbers.

2) *FW-190.* In areas other than the normal operational zones of RAF fighters, the FW-190 is the most useful of the limited number of operational aircraft in use by Fliegerfuehrer Atlantik. The most unsatis-

factory aspect of all is that, in spite of the new developments expected in the air situation over the Atlantic, the radius of action of the FW-190 (even with auxiliary tanks) is still too small. What is required is a fighter with at least the same armament as the FW-190, but a greater radius of action without auxiliary fuel tanks.

3) *Ar-196.* In armament, radius of action and performance this aircraft is obsolete. The Ar-196 can only be used for reconnaissance in coastal areas and for anti-submarine patrols and escort duties.

Chapter 13

THE ROLE OF THE GERMAN AIR FORCE IN THE BATTLE OF THE ATLANTIC

by 8th Abteilung, OKL 23 March 1944

I. Historical

By personal order of the Fuehrer, the post of Fliegerfuehrer Atlantik was created in March 1941, with the task of directing the attacks on enemy shipping in the Atlantic, in close cooperation with the C-in-C. Submarine Fleet.

The area of operations comprised the convoy routes from the Mediterranean to England, the Eastern part of the route from England to America, and the convoy routes off the East, South and West coasts of England. Our attacks on enemy shipping met with no opposition either by Flak or from aircraft, and early successes, especially in the Atlantic, were surprisingly great.

But six months later the situation had changed completely. The use of the Condor as a dive bomber, the only form of attack suited to its armament, had to be discontinued first against convoys, and later against single ships, owing to the introduction of strong defensive armament by the enemy.

The continued use of the Condor on reconnaissance missions for the submarine fleet would have been to our advantage, had systematic submarine attacks on convoys been maintained. As the convoys however, became more and more strongly escorted by destroyers and aircraft, our submarines suffered increasingly high losses, and their area of operations was therefore transferred to a point on the convoy route to America outside the range of the Condors. The plan was that by late autumn 1941, operations should be conducted exclusively in North American waters which provided both favourable fighting conditions and numerous targets.

By December 1941, practically all combined operations with the submarine fleet had to be discontinued for several months, no more submarines being available for operations in European waters. The Condor

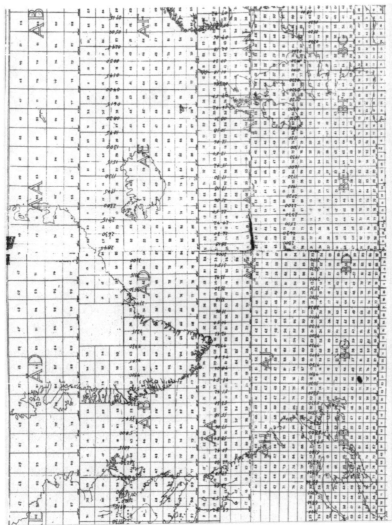

The German Navy's map grid of the North Atlantic battlefield; the grid was the key to position reporting. (US NARA RG 38 ONI Monograph files (maps))

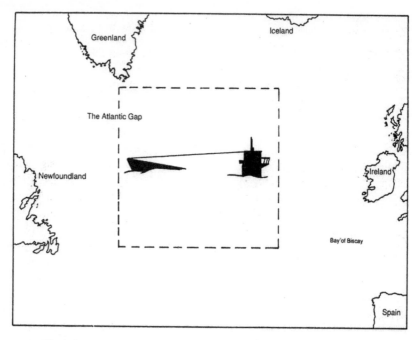

The 'Atlantic Gap', out of range of all but four-engine Consolidated
Liberators or comparable aircraft, was critical in the Battle of the Atlantic,
especially in 1942-43. (Brian McCue, U-Boats in the Bay of Biscay,
National Defense University Press, Washington D.C., 1990)

units were transferred to other theatres of war, some to reconnaissance
units to Norway, and some as transport aircraft to the Mediterranean and
Eastern fronts. Fliegerfuehrer Atlantik was then left with only one
bomber Geschwader of Ju-88s, (KG 6) consisting of a weak bomber
Gruppe, for the continuation of the Atlantic struggle. Owing to their
limited range, these forces could only be used against convoys off the
English coast.

The great possibilities of success, especially in combined torpedo and
bomber attacks, were never realised for two reasons. Firstly, because the
torpedo carrying aircraft were transferred to Norway after their first
successful operation, and secondly, because available bombers were
regularly despatched against land targets in England and were consequently greatly weakened.

In May 1942, the C-in-C. Submarine Fleet again asked for help from
Fliegerfuehrer Atlantik. His intention was not, however, to send the aircraft out on reconnaissance missions and raids against the enemy convoys,
as the Fuehrer had ordered, but primarily to protect the submarines in the
Bay of Biscay from the threatened attacks.

This task was the aim of the operations conducted during the whole of 1942 and part of 1943. The TE fighter units established by Fliegerfuehrer Atlantik succeeded in driving British anti-submarine patrols out of the Bay of Biscay into the Atlantic.

As regards reconnaissance over the Atlantic, the combined efforts of Fliegerfuehrer Atlantik and C-in-C. Submarine Fleet were directed at protecting the blockade runners. In addition, during a period of 7 weeks, with daily average of 6 aircraft patrolling the sea area between 38 and 49 degrees North and 10 to 20 degrees West, approximately 4 million tons of merchant shipping and 0.3 million tons of war ships were sighted. Individual convoys remained within range of our long-range bombers for at least 4 to 5 days, so that during the above mentioned 7 weeks, nearly one seventh of the enemy's merchant shipping lay within range of our long range bombers.

Our armed reconnaissance, however, seldom led to attacks on shipping, as such large forces were engaged on reconnaissance that aircraft were frequently not available for bombing attacks. In addition, weather conditions and low lying cloud often prevented any attacks from high altitudes.

The Summer of 1942 saw the conversion of the FW-200 to Lotfe 7 D. The successes achieved by III/KG 40 after conversion from the Spring of 1943 onwards, proved that given suitable aircraft and well trained crews, the Luftwaffe could in no theatre of War achieve such great successes with such small losses as over the Atlantic.

In the nose of this Fw 200C-3's ventral gondola is the Lotfe 7D bombsight that was installed in the type in the summer of 1942.

II. Operational Directives for Fliegerfuehrer Atlantik

In September 1943, the Reichsmarschal issued a directive to Fliegerfuehrer Atlantik containing instructions for the participation of the Luftwaffe in the attacks on enemy shipping in the Atlantic. Detailed orders were given on the following subjects:

(a) Long range reconnaissance of shipping,
(b) Defensive sorties in the Bay of Biscay,
(c) Attacks on convoys and single ships in the Atlantic, based on inter-
     pretation of aerial photographs and reconnaissance reports,
(d) Reconnaissance of enemy submarines.

It was stated that submarines and aircraft were pursuing the same aim, and Fliegerfuehrer Atlantik should therefore cooperate closely with C-in-C. Submarine Fleet. Although only limited forces were available at present, considerable successes could still be achieved.

III. Situation Report

The British are entirely dependent on the maintenance of regular sea traffic for the import of raw materials to Great Britain and the export of manufactured goods; supply routes to all theatres of war must also be kept open. Great Britain must at all costs keep the Atlantic free from any possible interference by the enemy.

The partial success of German air and naval operations over the Atlantic during 1941 and at the beginning of 1942 has led the enemy to effect a substantial concentration of defensive strength, for convoys are still Britain's principal means of conducting overseas trade, and our submarines present a very considerable menace.

The most effective weapon against submarines at sea is the aeroplane, and British sea routes are therefore planned so as to lie within the range of British aircraft. The more the British therefore succeed in establishing unchallenged air superiority over the convoy routes, thereby hampering German submarine activity, the less danger will there be for the entire supply system.

The operational capacity of our submarines is declining in proportion to the increase in enemy air activity. The enemy now has greater forces and improved equipment at his disposal, and his aircraft have now also a substantially greater range than before.

Operations against Southbound convoys have had to be almost entirely discontinued owing to the overwhelming British air supremacy, and are now only possible with considerable losses of naval craft. Convoys travelling from West to East can still be attacked by submarines in an ever decreasing sea area between America and Europe in which the enemy air force is not quite so powerful.

The fact that the enemy has since the beginning of 1942 diverted a considerable proportion of his best equipped forces from attacks on Europe to the Battle of the Atlantic is an indication of the great importance which he attaches to operations in this area.

To combat the dangers of this situation, we must intensify our fight against the enemy air force over the Atlantic, and at the same time endeavour to provide our submarines with effective support.

The attacking enemy aircraft should as far as possible be intercepted at the nearest point to their own bases at which they are outside the range of action of enemy fighters. They should be attacked on their outward route by our long range fighters.

The following forces are available at present:

1   Bomber Geschwader of 3 Gruppen equipped with He-177, FW-200 and Ju-88C6
1   Long range reconnaissance Gruppe equipped with Ju-290s
1   Long range reconnaissance Staffel equipped with Ju-88Ts
1   Short range reconnaissance Staffel equipped with Ar-196s and
1   Fighter Staffel equipped with Fw-190A5/U8's.

These forces are hopelessly insufficient for the above mentioned tasks. The aircraft used over the Atlantic must have a wide range of action over the sea, and must be equipped with every type of weapon used in naval warfare.

IV. Operational Planning

In order to continue the attacks of German submarines and aircraft against enemy shipping in the Atlantic and to provide effective support for our submarines, the following requirements must be met:

(a) A long range bomber Geschwader, consisting of at least 3 Gruppen of 36 aircraft each, must be formed and based on airfields along the Atlantic Coast. At least four airfields are necessary, two in the Southern and two in the Northern sector of the area.
(b) A new multi-purpose aircraft type with a minimum range of 2,500 km. will have to be employed. This new aircraft must be capable of carrying an additional payload of 1,000 kgs and must be equipped

with the latest technical aids to bombing and reconnaissance. An average output of 80 aircraft per month would be sufficient to enable the Geschwader to receive replacements and also to build up reserves for the subsequent formation of other units. He-177s and Ju-290s will be used temporarily, but all units will later be equipped with Ju-390s.

(c) IV KG 40 must undergo a course of training for bombing over the Atlantic and all personnel with some experience of flying over the sea will receive intensive training in tactics, navigation and armament; 40 long range bomber crews should complete their training each month.

(d) The development of the He-177 as a heavy long range fighter must be continued with a view to forming a unit to operate in conjunction with the Ju-390 against the enemy 4 engined formations.

The long range bomber forces will attack enemy convoys from the moment they leave their bases or come within our range of action until they either reach their destination or have passed out of our range. Our aim must be to disrupt the enemy defences by constantly altering our weapons and tactics.

The long range night fighter units equipped with Me-410s will operate outside the range of the enemy fighters and intercept the enemy bomber formations during their outward and return flights. They will attack the enemy 4 engined bomber formations, TE fighters operating against the German long range bombers, and TE bombers operating against our U-boats in the Bay of Biscay.

The immediate result of such a campaign will be a lessening of the enemy's air protection of his convoys due to heavy losses, and eventually its total cessation. The threat to our U-boats will be reduced, and a defensive area formed North of the Bay of Biscay which will help us to regain our air supremacy, and will serve as a protection to our forces in the area.

The He-177, which will later be used as a long range TE fighter, will be employed exclusively in defence of our submarines by means of operations against enemy bombers. This form of attack will reduce the air superiority of the enemy over the Atlantic within the range of our own air force to such an extent that our own forces will become more effective, and will also ease the position of our submarines.

Faced with this situation, the enemy may adopt any of the following counter measures:

(a) He may considerably reduce our strength by mass attacks on our bases. The enemy's air supremacy and our own insufficiently defended ground organization would make this easily practicable.

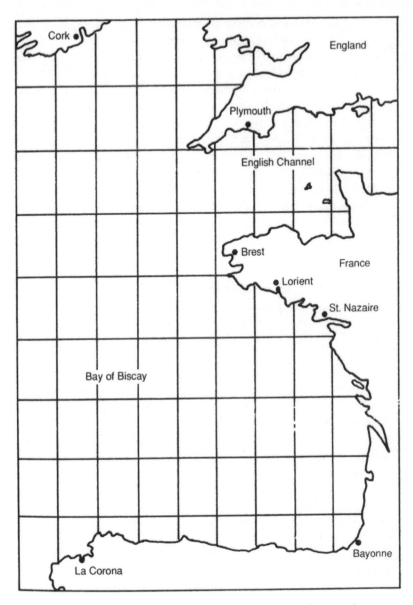

The Bay of Biscay and the southwestern approaches were the scene of many of the most significant air-sea actions of the Battle of the Atlantic. (Brian McCue, U-Boats in the Bay of Biscay, *National Defense University Press, Washington D.C., 1990)*

277

(b) He may increase the number of aircraft carriers sailing with each convoy, and thereby strengthen its defensive power.

(c) Alternatively, the enemy may occupy Spain and Portugal and establish air bases there as he has done in the Azores, with a view to providing strong air cover for convoys sailing North to South or South to North along the coast of the Iberian peninsula. In this event, our submarines and air force would be faced with a very difficult situation, and could only operate with strong day and night fighter support.

(d) Finally, and most improbable of all, the enemy may decide to use convoy routes outside the range of our aircraft. This step would however, lengthen the routes considerably, and would necessarily lead to a reduction in the size of convoys. It would also increase the chances of success of our submarines, as the range of action of the enemy's aircraft might prevent him from escorting these convoys.

The intensification of the sea war will however necessitate a complete change of strategy and the concentration of all available forces in the Western and Northern theatres of war.

To this end Major von Schroetter has evolved the following plan of organization:

1. The subordination of all forces operating against Great Britain, including those stationed in Norway, to the command of a single Luftflotte. Included in this Command will be Fliegerkorps Atlantik, for operations the open sea, including the North Atlantic, with a subordinate Command in Norway. Fliegerkorps Atlantik will comprise the following units:

   2–3 long range bomber Geschwader
   1 long range TE fighter Geschwader
   1–2 TE fighter Geschwader
   2–3 long range fighter Gruppen
   1–2 long range reconnaissance Staffeln
   2 mine detecting Staffeln
   2 airborne W/T interception Staffeln
   1 long range ASR Unit.

2. The reconstruction of our ground organization and the reallocation of operational zones between the new Luftflotte and Luftflotte 2. Under this heading will be included the extension of the ground organization on the Atlantic coast to at least 9 heavy bomber and 5-6 TE fighter airfields in the immediate vicinity of the coast.

If, by adopting a long term policy we can succeed in waging the war against Great Britain on these lines, we shall be in a position to intensify our total war effort without increasing either personnel, training or production. We can best achieve this by concentrating on the war at sea, and on increasing our fighter force, at the same time renouncing all costly bomber raids on land targets in Britain.

This strategy will strengthen the defence of the Reich by offensive and defensive fighter operations, and at the same time hit the enemy at his weakest point, namely, his overseas shipping traffic. Furthermore, the air force will then be in a position to improve the operational possibilities of our naval forces and submarine fleet, and thus enable the latter to regain much of its former efficacy.

PART V

CONCLUSION

The last word belongs to Grossadmiral Karl Doenitz, who as Commander-in-Chief U-boats throughout the war and as commander-in-chief of the German Navy in 1943–45 was in charge of fighting the Battle of the Atlantic. His views on the significance of airpower in the Battle varied. The concluding chapter shows Doenitz's views in a 1942 German propaganda statement, a 1946 response to a US Navy question (done with both his US and German lawyers), and a 1949 US Army interview (done with Konteradmiral Wagner).

These were just a few points in Doenitz's long-standing concern over his lack of control over air assets even at the height of the Battle of the Atlantic, when he had to ask the Fliegerfuehrer-level commands for sorties and was often turned down. Doenitz complained to Hitler; in his 8 June Memoranda, he stated, "Germany's war at sea is being conducted today practically without the Luftwaffe. ... The crisis in the U-boat war is thus a consequence of the command of the air over the Atlantic by the enemy". He stressed these themes in his post-war memoirs.

Chapter 14

OVERVIEW: THE ATLANTIC WAR (AND THE ROLE OF AIR COOPERATION)

By Grossadmiral Karl Doenitz and Kontreadmiral Gerhard Wagner

A. 1942

An interview with Admiral Doenitz is reported in *VB* August 4, 1942. Donetz was asked how valuable the cooperation between German submarines and the G.A.F. is. He answered "the submarines have a very limited vision while airplanes have the greatest possible range of vision. Germany has often taken advantage of cooperation between the airplane and the submarine, a cooperation which resulted in the sinking of numerous ships". The question of harmonious cooperation between these two branches is of greatest importance.

Source: V.B. August 4, 1942

Oct. 5, 1942

B. 1946

A8

907-4400
COPY:EG
sub op.
A/C Coop.
28 July 1946

1. Admiral Karl Doenitz is reported to have made a statement in substance as follows:

"Coordination between the Luftwaffe and submarines in joint operations against convoys was unsuccessful chiefly because the Luftwaffe concentrated its efforts on the large ships of the convoy. This resulted in relatively small damage to them, and left the escorts free for countermeasures against the attacking submarines. Had the Luftwaffe concentrated its efforts on the escorts, 'kept them busy', the submarines would have frequently succeeded in wiping out entire convoys."

It was mentioned by Captain A. H. Graubart, U.S.N., Commanding Officer, U.S.S. PRINZ EUGEN (IX 300), but he did not recall the details surrounding the statement.

2. It is requested that information concerning such a statement and a copy of it, if available, be forwarded to the Commander in Chief, U.S. Pacific Fleet.

D. B. DUNCAN
Chief of Staff
UNITED STATES PACIFIC FLEET AND
PACIFIC OCEAN AREAS HEADQUARTERS
OF THE COMMANDER IN CHIEF

30 September 1946

Presented by Lieutenant Commander Schrader to Grand Admiral Karl Doenitz, in the presence of his counsel, Fleet Judge Kransbuehler. He deposed as follows:

(1) As best as I can remember, I have never made the statement attributed to me.
(2) It is possible that in the War Diary of the Commander, Submarines, in the years 1941 or 1942 there is an entry which corresponds to the meaning of the statement attributed to me. At that time, a very few joint operations between submarines and bombers were carried out. The operations were directed against convoys which ran from England to Gibraltar. As soon as the submarines reported that they had made contact with such convoys, bombing squadrons of the Ju-88 type took off from the Atlantic coast. The aviators were ordered to direct their main attack against the convoy escorts. The results of these joint operations were unsatisfactory. Essentially, I see the reasons for that as follows:
   (a) As a consequence of the lack of special Naval Air Force, joint exercises of this nature were not carried out in peacetime;
   (b) The aviators directed their main attacks against the large ships, in spite of their orders, because these targets appeared to be more attractive to them.
(3) In my present situation, during the pronouncement of judgment, I do

not consider myself in the position to make more thoroughgoing observations about all the experiences of coordination between Submarines and Air Force.

Witnesses: /s/ KARL DONITZ

/s/ Kransbuehler,
Flottenrichter

/s/ A. E. Schrader, Jr.
Lt. Comdr. U.S.N.R.

C. 1949

1. *Q*: What basic plan was employed by German submarines to stop Lend-Lease and army shipments to England from 1941 to 6 Jun 44?

   A: American Lend-Lease and army shipments to England were not attacked in any special way, but in the general plan of conduct of a submarine war. The U-boats used the well-known tactics of the wolf pack, because American supplies went to England in the convoy system. The number of U-boats on hand in 1941, however, was not sufficient for this, as the German Navy had not armed for a war with England or America, and a suitable further arming was not projected until the beginning of the war. These U-boats were gradually brought into action in 1942, so that convoys going to England could be very successfully attacked in the North Atlantic. In the same way, German submarines successfully attacked American transports in American waters. These successes lasted until May 43. At that time, the wolf pack system could no longer be continued because of the superiority of the Anglo-American air forces and, more importantly, their new place-locating devices (*Ed*: probably radar).

2. *Q*: What changes were made in this plan at various times to meet our changes in Allied convoy systems, our occupation of Iceland. etc?

   A: No fundamental changes in the wolf pack system took place before May 43, as they were not necessary prior to that time. We noticed that changes in the Allied convoy systems extended only to (1) the best possible exploitation of open sea space for the dispersion of the ships of the convoy, (2) strengthening of close and long range security by means of destroyers, and (3) strengthening the air force accompanying the convoy by the use of aircraft carriers and by an increase in the number of long-range planes, whose effectiveness in patrolling the entire sea area was improved decisively by the occupation of Iceland and the Azores. This strengthening of the defense and the evasion attained by the greatest possible dispersion could be countered only by the greatest possible increase in the number of U-boats. Initially, this was successful and the greatest convoy battles were fought in Mar 43. The turning point came about through the place-finding devices mentioned above.

3. *Q*: Did you feel that the U-boat campaign was succeeding? (i.e., meeting plans and expectations?)

   A: Until Mar 43, the U-boat war, considering the few submarines available, lived up to expectations. In 1942, our successes exceeded expectations. The falling off in May 43 was a surprise in its suddenness, despite the fact that we expected it and were greatly concerned over such an eventuality. After that, U-boat successes were far behind the expectations originally entertained.

4. *Q*: Did you ever feel that the U-boats could actually prevent an adequate build-up of troops in England from the United States?

   A: Since the U-boat never knows what the ship sighted has for a cargo, it could not concentrate especially on troop transports. For this any instruction of its routes and times would be lacking. (*Ed*: The exact meaning of the preceding sentence is not known. It is assumed to mean that in order to intercept and concentrate on troop transports, the U-boat would have to be furnished with a route and a time-table and that any such instructions given would be incomplete.) The important thing was to harass the supply of men and materiel. We never assumed that we could prevent the transportation of American troops in any large measure.

5. *Q*: What was the turning point for the failure of the campaign?

   A: Already answered by answers to Questions 1, 2, and 3.

6. *Q*: In the transport of American troops into England by fast ocean liners with little protection, did you ever consider or devise a system for destroying these liners by the use of fast U-boats or other special means, or were you resigned to the inability to catch these fast ships?

   A: For the reasons named in the answer to Question 4, it was impossible to operate against the big, fast troop transports. Also, especially fast U-boats were not available for this.

SELECT BIBLIOGRAPHY

The subject matter of this book overlaps with that of a large number of volumes. However, most of the best recent work on Luftwaffe maritime operations remains in German.

Neitzel, Huemmelchen and Kurowski are probably the best single-volume accounts of the subject matter of this volume, but so far only published in German. Unit histories are scarce but include Schmidt's history of the Luftwaffe's main torpedo bomber unit and Goss' English-language history of long-range fighters. Voelker and Tessin offer German-language accounts of the Luftwaffe-Navy issues pre-war. In German, Zweng is a reference on Luftwaffe organization and personnel; Salewski on the naval operational staff. The air-sea rescue service is best covered in Born's and Kuhn's German-language accounts. Peifer describes the Naval Historical Team's post-war work. Aircraft type-specific histories (Griehl's *Do-217*, Poolman) are relatively scarce on German maritime aircraft but the standard reference sources (Green, Kay & Smith) provide performance numbers plus some operational details.

Useful for comparing what the authors in this volume claim took place and what actually happened are Rohwer's two volumes. Gundelach (in German), Mattesini and Santoni (Italian) and Mattesini (Italian) cover the Luftwaffe's role in the naval-air campaign in the Mediterranean. Among the many battle and campaign accounts that shed light on Luftwaffe operations affecting the war at sea are: Brennecke, Classen, Franks, Goulter, Howarth & Law, Nesbit, Shores & Cull, Ruegg, Terraine, and van der Vat

Aircraft-focused (largely pictorial) works include volumes in Greenhill's *Luftwaffe at War* series of paperbacks by Griehl, Smith and Phillpott.

Karl Born, *Rettung Zwischen Den Fronten. Seenotdienset Der Deutschen Luftwaffe 1939–45*, Hamburg, 1996, Mitler u.S.

Johann Brennecke, *Schlactschiffe Bismarck*, Herford, FRG, 1967 (3rd ed.) Koehlers.

Adam A. Claasen, *Hitler's Northern War. The Luftwaffe's Ill-Fated Campaign 1940–45*. Lawrence KS, 2001, University Press of Kansas.

Norman Franks, *Conflict Over the Bay*, 2002 (revision of 1986 ed.), London, William Kimber.

Chris Goss, *Bloody Biscay. The History of V.Gruppe Kampfgeschawader 40*. London, 1995, Crecy.

Christine Goulter, *A Forgotten Offensive. The RAF Coastal Command's Anti-Shipping Campaign 1940–45*. London, 1995, Frank Cass.

William Green, *Floatplanes*, London, 1962, MacDonald.

William Green, *Flying Boats*, London, 1962, MacDonald.

William Green, *Warplanes of the Third Reich*, London, 1970, MacDonald and Jane's.

Manfred Griehl, *Airwar Over the Atlantic*, London, 2003, Greenhill.

Manfred Griehl, *Dornier Do-217-317-417. An Operational History*, Washington, 1991, Smithsonian Institution Press.

Karl Gundelach, *Die Deutsche Luftwaffe im Mittelmeer 1940–45*, Frankfurt am Main, 1981. Peter D. Lang.

Gunter Hessler, *German U-Boat War in the Atlantic*, Vols. 1–2, London, 1989, HMSO.

Stephen Howarth and Derek Law, eds., *The Battle of the Atlantic 1939–45, The 50th Anniversary International Naval Conference*. Annapolis, 1994, US Naval Institute.

Georg Huemmelchen, *Der Deutsche Seeflieger 1935–45*, Munich, 1975, Wehr Wissen Schaftliche Berichte 9.

Anthony Kay and J. R. Smith, *German Military Aircraft of the Second World War*, Annapolis, 2002, US Naval Institute Press.

Volkmar Kuhn, *Der Seenotdienst der Deutschen Luftwaffe 1939–45*, Stuttgart, 1978, Motorbuch Verlag.

Franz Kurowski, *Seekrieg Aus der Luft: Die Deutsche Seeluftwaffe in Zweiten Weltkrieg*, Herford, FRG, 1979, Verlag E.S. Mittler & Sohn.

Francesco Mattesini, *L' Attivita Aerea Italo-Tedesca nel Mediterraneo – Il Contributo del X Fliegerkorps, gennaio-maggio 1941*, Roma, 1995, Ufficio Storico SMA.

Sonke Neitzel, *Der Einsatz der Deutschen Luftwaffe ueber dem Atlantik und der Nordsee 1939–45*, Koblenz, 1995, Bernard & Graefe Verlag.

Roy Nesbit, *The Battle of the Atlantic*, London, 2002, Sutton.

Kenneth Poolman, *Focke-Wulf Condor, Scourge of the Atlantic*, London, 1978, MacDonald & Jane's.

Brian Phillpott, *German Maritime Aircraft*, Cambridge, 1981, Patrick Stephens Ltd.

Dr. Douglas Peifer, "Forerunners to the West German Bundesmarine", *International Journal of Naval History*, v. 1 n. 1 April 2001.

Karl Ries, *Luftwaffe 1935–1939*, Mainz, FRG, 1974, D. Hoffman Verlag

Jurgen Rohwer and Georg Huemmelchen, *Chronology of the War at Sea*

1939–1945: The Naval History of World War Two, 2nd ed., 1992, Annapolis, US Naval Institute Press.

Bob Ruegg, *Convoys to Russia: Allied Convoys and Naval Surface Operations in Arctic Waters, 1941–45*, Bristol, 1992, World Ship Society.

Michael Salewski, *Die Deutsche Seekriegsleitung 1935–45*, vols. 1–3, Frankfurt am Main, 1970–77, Bernard & Graefe.

Alberto Santoni and Francesco Mattesini, *La Partecipazione Tedesca all Guerra Aeronavale nei Mediterraneo (1940–45)*, Roma, 1980, Edizioni dell'Ateneo & Bizzarri.

Rudi Schmidt, *Achtung – Torpedoes Los! Der Straegische und Operative Einsatz des Kampfgeschwader 26*, Koblenz, 1991, Bernard & Graefe Verlag.

Chris Shores and Brian Cull, *Fledgling Eagles, The Complete Account of Air Operations During the Phoney War and the Norwegian Campaign*, London, 1991, Grub Street.

Peter Smith, *The Sea Eagles*, London, 2002, Greenhill.

John Terraine, *Business in Great Waters: The U-Boat Wars 1939–45*, London, 1989, Leo Cooper.

Georg Tessin, *Deutsche Verbande und Truppe 1918–1939*, Osnabruck, FRG, 1974, Biblio Verlag.

Dan van der Vat, *The Atlantic Campaign: The Great Struggle at Sea 1939–45*, New York, 1988, Harper & Row.

Karl-Heinz Voelker, *Die Deutsche Luftwaffe 1933–39*, Stuttgart, FRG, 1967, Deutsche Verlagsanstalt.

Christian Zweng, *Die Dienststellen, Kommandobehorden und Truppenteile de Luftwaffe 1935–45* (Bands 1–10), Osnabruck, FRG, 1999, Biblio Verlag.